THE OLDHAM
COALFIELD

THE OLDHAM COALFIELD

JACK NADIN

TEMPUS

First published 2006

Tempus Publishing Limited
The Mill, Brimscombe Port,
Stroud, Gloucestershire, GL5 2QG
www.tempus-publishing.com

© Jack Nadin 2006

The right of Jack Nadin to be identified as the Author
of this work has been asserted in accordance with the
Copyrights, Designs and Patents Act 1988.

British Library Cataloguing in Publication Data.
A catalogue record for this book is available from the British Library.

ISBN 0 7524 2945 0

Typesetting and origination by Tempus Publishing Limited
Printed in Great Britain

CONTENTS

Acknowledgements   6

The Author   7

Foreword   9

The Collieries of the Oldham Coalfield   13

Index   191

ACKNOWLEDGEMENTS

I could not have compiled this book without help from various sources. Grateful thanks must go to Hannah Haynes, of Rochdale Library; Frances Stott, of Shaw and Crompton Library; and to the staff at Oldham Library for all their help and time, and for permission to use photographs from their collection. Thanks also to David Pollitt and Alan Davies for their time and help.

THE AUTHOR

Jack Nadin is a keen local historian and coal mining history enthusiast, and has had many local history articles published in local newspapers, as well as having written a number of books on coal mining history, including Hapton Valley Colliery: The History of an East Lancashire Coal Mine (Burnley and District Historical Society), The Coal Mines of East Lancashire, and Coal Mines Around Accrington and Blackburn (Northern Mines Research Society). Jack also worked as a supply lad for several years at the last deep coal mine in East Lancashire – Hapton Valley Pit.

No miner worth his salt would see any other man struggle at his work or task; he would instinctively go to his aid. Miners would launch themselves under roof falls and grapple at rock with bare hands if they saw a workmate injured, knowing full well the dangers to themselves. They would enter the mine immediately after an explosion, in spite of the threat of afterdamp and imminent further explosions, in order to try and save those they worked besides, or to bring to the surface those beyond help. How many trades can boast that today? Knowledge of the comradeship of working miners, and the harsh conditions endured down the pits, has had a lasting influence on Jack's views on colliery life. Particularly vivid are the memories of the Hapton Valley disaster, 22 March 1962, a dreadful day that saw nineteen men perish in an underground methane gas explosion. The Hapton Valley Colliery closed in 1982, the last deep coal mine in the once great Burnley Coalfield.

FOREWORD

Coal mining around Oldham is now an industry confined to local history books. Often the only evidence of the existence of the collieries is in old map references, or maybe the odd photograph. Yet, at one time, it was a major employer, supplying the needs of the growing towns of Oldham, Chadderton, Middleton, Bardsley, and others. One hundred and fifty-six pits are listed in the text, and, doubtless, there were many others. The area covered in this book is one that was known as the 'Oldham Coalfield', an area that stretched from Royton in the north to Bardsley in the south, taking in the towns of Middleton and Chadderton to the west. I have stepped 'over the border' into what is now Tameside, to include a few of the Ashton collieries as a matter of note. There can be little doubt that the mining of coal in these areas was an ancient occupation, and through snippets of information gleaned here and there, and eventually brought together, we can gain a little insight into this lost industry.

The History of Oldham, by Hartley Bateson, recalls that, in 1524, a sum of 10*d* was paid by Richard Wild for getting coal in Leonardine (Crompton). In 1627, 'Thomas Slater was slayne in a Cole Pitt with the fall of the roof', and was recorded in the parish records of Ashton-under-Lyne. In 1642, there is a record of 'All the cole mynes in Chadderton at Hunt Clough'. In the will of John Newton, dated 1620, it is stated that he, 'along with James Haulkerd did get coles in a certain cole myne upon Oldham Edge'. In the Ashton-under-Lyne parish records for 7 November 1681, we find recorded the burial of John Fletcher, 'killed in Duckenfeild [sic] coale pitt on the 4th Day as he was hookeing the baskett by the fall of a greate stone'. The parish records also note the burial of 'James Hardy near Bardsley coalpit' on 26 March 1711.

Coal mining on a commercial scale was begun around 1738. At this time we know that George Hall was the owner of collieries at Broadway Lane and, following the completion of the Rochdale and Ashton Canals in the 1790s, the industry really began to develop. A directory of 1814, describing Oldham, tells us that: 'The manufacture of fustian and hats form the principal business of this town, but the spinning of cotton and the extensive collieries in the neighbourhood also furnish employment to many of the inhabitants'. Baines, in *The History of Lancashire* (1824), tells that 'The coal mines in this neighbourhood open an important branch of trade, and give employment to a large number of persons. Every township in this parish (Oldham district) has its collieries, and the quantity of coals obtain for it a preference in the Manchester market. The quantity of fuel dug up yearly from the numerous beds is immense, and the supply seems inexhaustible'. One of the most successful partnerships in mining was between Joseph Jones, John Boot and James Lees of Clarksfield. This partnership was most successful and soon took over the ownership of most of the local collieries in the Oldham district. It was James Lees' family that gave the village of Lees its name. In the Ashton-under-Lyne area we have other references to coal mining. The will of Sir William Dukinfield Daniel, dated 8 December 1756, tells us 'I do give to my daughter, Henrietta after she shall have attained the age of twenty-one years also full power and authority to work my coal mines in Dukinfield, Newton and Hyde aforesaid. And I will and direct that money to be raised from the said mines and by leasing the aforesaid shall be applied in, or towards the discharge of the principal money secured on mortgages of the same premises'.

By 1834, 'Coal Masters' had become established: Barker, Evans & Co. of the Edge Lane and Dryclough Collieries; Robert Buckley of Shaw; Abraham Clegg, Highfield; John Evans of Limeside, Joseph Harrop & Co., Bardsley; Hibbert & Lees, Honeywell Lane Collieries; and Milne & Taylor of the Holebottom Colliery. Two years earlier, it was recorded that there were some thirty-seven collieries at work in the Oldham district. For some of these collieries there is very little information relating to the owner, or about when the pit was at work. Fortunately, there are other pits for which more documentation is available. I have visited scores of the former colliery sites, and noted what, if anything, remains of them in terms of industrial archaeology. Every opportunity has been taken to give accurate information about the sites, including their location. I am not a local, although dozens of visits gave me at least some knowledge of local areas. I apologise in advance for any error that more well-informed residents might be able to find.

Note too that this area has changed almost beyond recognition since the days of the old coal industry. Grid references are given where sites can be located accurately, though very often the old pits have been swallowed up as the town of Oldham has developed, and to try and give references in these cases would amount to pure guesswork. The area around Oldham Edge and Sholver Moor was peppered with uncharted shallow shafts and tunnel workings from ancient times. These occasionally led the miners into flooded workings with inevitable results.

Mining has always been a hazardous occupation, and much of the information on each colliery is taken from old newspaper reports on fatalities at that particular pit. For this reason, the book could well be termed a 'book of pit accidents'. Reports often give details of the workings and ownership of a colliery at that period in time and, more importantly, record the names of the miners who perished. Death came in many ways down the pit, and all too often. Men and boys were blasted out of existence through a firedamp explosion, crushed in haulage accidents, drowned through inundations from old workings, or buried beneath tons of rock. These are sad enough to read when adults are involved, but become even more tragic and shocking when we realise that they often involved children, sometimes as young as nine years old, who were working down the pit. These 'children of the mines' were an accepted fact of life in the mining communities of the early to the mid-1800s. Some children were actually 'adopted' from the workhouse, or imported from the streets and slums of cities, to be set to work down the pit. The Children's Employment Commission, initially set up in 1840, revealed shocking evidence, not only of child labour down the pit, but also of the employment of women underground. Happily, there appears to be little evidence of women at work in the area covered in this book. However, only through the reports in the 1840s of Commissioner Joseph Fletcher, and others like him, did the facts become widely known. In 1842, an Act of Parliament was passed that forbade the employment underground of children under the age of ten years, but, as you will read, the practice continued, as did the many young fatalities.

In the 1851 census, nearly ten years after the Act was passed, James Lees is listed as being a coal drawer living at Lower Abbots Knowl, Hollinwood, at the age of 'about seven years'. To stand on the site of a former coal pit, especially those in quiet rural surroundings, and realise the hardship and toil endured there, as well as the fact that many of those who went underground in that pit never again saw the light of day, brings home the true 'price of coal'. Only 'acts of war, and great natural catastrophes have claimed more lives than British mining', it has been said. We choose to record the names of those who perished in war, and rightly so, but then why not those who lost their lives through their employment in coal mines and associated industries? I dedicate this book to the memory of the miners, young and old, who perished in the 'Oldham Coalfield'. I trust it will be a lasting memorial to the hardship they and other miners endured during their working lives. To assist in further historical research, for the first time, entries from the Catalogue of Plans of Abandoned Mines (1926) have been included. These are purely for historical research purposes, and should not be relied upon for any legal process regarding searching for old shafts or boreholes. The information given is as follows: (a) the locality of the colliery; (b) the minerals worked, and the date of working (if known); (c) the custodian of the plans if other than the Mines Department; (d) a reference to the Ordnance Map squares, from which it is possible to locate the approximate position of an abandoned mine, using a piece of tracing paper ruled into 1.5in squares. The horizontal squares are numbered 1 to 12, and the vertical squares A to H. Using the information given in the Catalogue of Plans of Abandoned Mines, the approximate position of the workings will be shown on the plan.

★ Indicates sites mentioned in Joseph Dickisnson's Mines Inspectors' List of Mines for 1854.

THE COLLIERIES OF THE OLDHAM COALFIELD

Abram Meadows: Werneth, Oldham

An old colliery that was situated at or near the junction of Suffolk Street, at Werneth, Oldham, and worked by Abraham Fletcher, possibly during the 1830s. Abraham also kept a beerhouse near Fletcher Street, named after him. This soon acquired the name of Fletcher's Alehouse. The colliery was apparently one of the principal pits in its day, with extensive cart sales from the pit-top. Coal from the colliery was also drawn by horses to Old Lane, and then sent down a jig road to the canal. The tramway went past the eastern end of Oak Mill and through the 'Cupola Field', the name suggesting a furnace air shaft, crossed Old Lane by a wooden bridge and followed the south-side of the New Engine Pit to the 'Tippler' at 'Cut End' (see *Oldham Weekly Chronicle*, 15 June 1968). Abram Meadows Colliery is listed in the Catalogue of Plans of Abandoned Mines under 'Chamber Colliery' and it appears that the workings were connected. The colliery does not appear in a list of mines for the year 1854, and it would appear that by this date the pit had been abandoned. Also of general interest on the Oldham Coalfield is the following, from the *Manchester Guardian*, 20 May 1840:

> Statistics of accidents in Oldham. In the five years from 1830 to 1834, there were 38 persons accidentally killed in coalmines within the borough of Oldham. In the succeeding five years, 1835 to 1839, 52, total 90.

Ainsworth's and Lees: Oldham

This may be the Pit Bank Colliery (see below), as Ainsworth and Lees worked this pit in 1842. Also there is no reference to a pit of this name in the Catalogue of Plans of Abandoned Mines. The colliery at this time employed twenty-eight men and boys underground. William Mason, going on eighteen, gave evidence at the Inquiry into Child Labour in Coal Mines on 31 October 1841, and said:

Is a waggoner in the Royley Mine of Jesse Ainsworth, assisted by another younger than himself, and working to George Wright, who is a getter. Has no mother, but lives with his aunt, who washes, (for a living) his father having been killed by a stone falling on him out of the roof at the Pit Bank Colliery. Went into the pit when he was going on seven, when his father was living. This was at Royley Mine, and helped a lad to waggon. After two months at Royley got 6d. day at pit bank, now gets 7s. a-week, but is doing only four days' work a-week. Goes to work between six and seven in the morning, and comes out from six to seven, sometimes later. This is 12 or 13 hours a day of work. Gets his dinner while waiting to hook on.

Richard Barker also gave evidence:

Richard Barker is averaging about 15s. a-week in his earnings. Bad workmen are making nearly as much as good ones. Distress obliges a collier to take his own children at a young age into the pit, rather than starve them to feed an older child or some one else's.

The colliers that do think at all, want free trade, but with most of them they are pricked, and they do not know from what side. They cursen everything, and wish to be better off. Children should not be employed so young as engineers, many a man has been killed by it. There are Sunday-schools for them as wishes to send their children, but the children of many has got so low in clothing and shoes that they are not fit to go, and they don't send them. There are some that do not care about sending them. If the children are to live in hardship they had better be bought up in it, for those that were accustomed to better times are very discontented. [Signed] RICHARD BARKER. (X) mark.

The *Manchester Guardian*, 24 December 1831, reports that:

On Friday last an inquest was held at the Hare and Hounds, Higginshaw Lane, Royton on the body of a young man age 19 years named Henan, who was killed about six o'clock on Wednesday evening at Mr Lees coal-pit on Oldham Edge. It appeared that two tubs or wagons were coming together as usual, in one of which were two men, and Henan in the other. It seems the latter must have neglected fixing his tub properly on the slide rod at starting, for, on coming to the top, the tub caught the sideboard, and the force of the engine broke the chain, when the tub along with the young man was precipitated, a depth of 145 yards to the bottom. The poor fellow's head was literally split in two, his thighs shockingly mangled, and there is little doubt he was killed before reaching the bottom. Verdict of the jury: 'Accidental death'.

And, in September 1837, the newspaper states:

Ainsworth and Lees Pit at Oldham, seven men and two boys were severely burned in explosion.

There were numerous old shafts on Oldham Edge, many simply abandoned as they became worked out. Even today, the name for an old colliery is 'abandoned mine' although officially the name for a mine where access may still be made, is an 'old mine'. There are many reported cases of people falling down such shafts. The *Manchester Guardian* of 1 October 1853 reports that:

> It is supposed that the body of Stanley Fielding, who has been missing for some weeks was at the bottom of an old coal pit on Oldham Edge, into which it would be very dangerous to descend on account of the foul air. The depth of the pit is 122 yards.

The body of Fielding was eventually recovered after some effort, and advice from local mining engineers, who suggested making a cloth tube and forcing air into the pit shaft to disperse any gas. The jury at the inquest returned an open verdict. As there was no evidence to show how he had got into the pit, the general opinion was that he had committed suicide.

Alkrington: Alkrington, near Middleton
A colliery worked by the Chamber Colliery Co. in 1879 and in 1896. At the latter date the pit worked the Bent and Black Diamond Seams, with twenty-five men underground and eight on the surface. The manager at this time was W.W. Millington and the under-manager was John Bullough. The offices for the Chamber Colliery Co. were at the Canal Wharf, Hollinwood. The colliery was abandoned the year after, on 9 September 1897. The colliery is marked on a map of 1891, to the east of Higher and Lower Green Farms. A 'Brick Yard' was attached to the colliery, which is shown as having two shafts, and a reservoir. Coal was mined at depth at Alkrington from around 1700.

However, there is earlier evidence of coal mining at Alkrington; on 2 June 1172, 'men were hurt by the works falling in, owing to the negligence of some of the workmen, by which three of the poor coaliers are terrible hurt, limbs and back brouk and another so sadly bruised so that their lives are despaired of'.

The *Annals of Oldham* also reports 'A lamentable misfortune on the September 17th 1789, as Abraham Ingham and William Carr were drawing some old carbs out of a coal pit at Alkrington, the pit suddenly closed up, and taking down with it the headstocks and Richard Ramsden, the overlooker of the works, and enclosed them all in one grave. It was impossible to come at the dead bodies, as the pit was full of water, so that their bodies will never be found'.

The Catalogue of Plans of Abandoned Mines gives the following information: Alkrington (a) Middleton; (b) COAL: Black, Thick, Bent, (abandoned 9 September 1897); (d) 96 NE (1923) G5, 6, 7, 8, 9: H5, 6, 7, 8, 9, 10. 96 SE (1923) A6, 7, 8: B6, 7, 8.

Alkrington Old Colliery is also marked in the catalogue, this probably being reference to the early notes of coal mining in this area and is listed as follows:

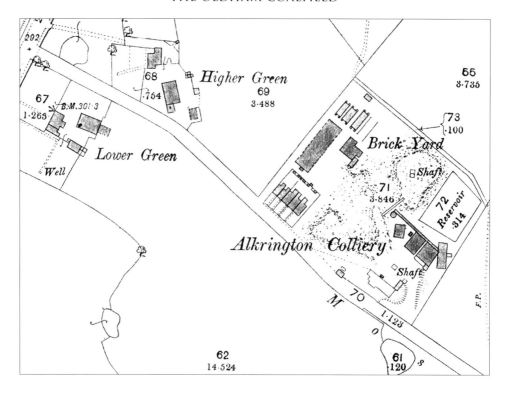

Alkrington Colliery, map of 1891.

Alkrington Old (a) Middleton; (b) COAL Higher Bent, Lower Bent, Black (1841); (c) Chamber Colliery Co. Ltd, Hollinwood, Oldham; (d) 96 NE (1923) G7, 8, 9: H5, 6, 7, 8, 9, 10. 96 SE (1923) A10.

One of the earliest collieries at Alkrington was the Black Mine, and the Old Yates Pits. The newer pits were the Bent Mines adjacent to Moss Lane. Surface tramways were used extensively at Alkrington Pits for the movement of the colliery output. A tramway from the Black Mines ran to the Rochdale Canal, and a loading bay on the canal was evident close by the old Chadderton Power Station at Slacks Valley, a coal staith for the railway was located behind the Radycliffe Arms. This continued to be used for many years after the Alkrington Colliery closed. Coal from the Bent Mine on Moss Lane was worked towards Alkrington Moss. In the Old Black Mine Seam, coal was worked towards and under Roundthorn.

Mary Birch, then aged well over eighty years recalled conditions at the Alkrington Colliery in the *Middleton Guardian* in 1888. She lived near the colliery at a place called Engine Fowt. Mary worked in the pit from the age of eight years, along with her family. She was a drawer at the pit, and descended the pit shaft by means of ladders in thirteen stages. Her job as a drawer involved hauling coal in baskets by means of a belt around her waist, the basket being attached by a chain between her legs and pulled along behind her.

From the bottom of the pit shaft, the coal was manually carried up the thirteen ladder stages by man, woman or girl. There is evidence that a system of canals were used underground at one of the Alkrington Pits. Two channels were dug from the shaft bottom to the coalface, and each was allowed to fill with water. At the coalface small boats were filled with coal and moved to shaft by means of 'legging' along the roof of the pit. Empty boats were taken back to the coalface on the other canal (see *Middleton Guardian*, 13 January 1994: article by Joe Pimlott on coal mining at Middleton).

The following extract, from the *Manchester Guardian*, 6 March 1824, not only recalls an explosion at the Alkrington Colliery, but also an alleged outrage on a young woman:

On Tuesday morning there was an explosion of firedamp at the Alkrington Colliery, near Middleton, by which a man named John Darbishire was killed and another so severely scorched that considerable apprehensions were entertained for his life. We have not heard how the accident was occasioned. We have been informed however, that a most brutal outrage was lately committed at the Alkrington Colliery, and if the circumstances have been correctly stated to us, a more shocking and disgraceful transaction never took place. It is stated that a young woman, who has the unfortune to labour under a privation of reason strayed from the house of her father at Bury, and was found early in the morning wandering on the road near Alkrington, by a carter, who put her into his cart, conveyed her to the colliery and delivered up to the colliers. By a number of these men (if that name may be applied to beings who could perpetrate such acts) we are told, she was detained several hours, and subjected to a series of indignities, infinitely too shocking to be detailed in public print, and was at length turned out in a state of complete nudity. She was taken home in a most deplorable condition, and from the treatment she has received, her life for a time was despaired of. Last week owing chiefly we believe, to the laudable interference and execrations of a gentleman who resides near Bury, warrants were procured for the apprehension of a number of colliers. On Monday last they were examined at Bolton before Colonel Fletcher (who is one of the proprietors of the colliery) when two of them were ordered to find bail to answer for the offences at the sessions. Such is the substance of what we have heard. For the credit of the neighbourhood it is to be hoped that the facts have been somewhat exaggerated. If not, the offenders deserve, and we trust they will receive, the most exemplary punishment, which the law can inflict.

Another incident is reported in the *Manchester Guardian* of 6 February 1836:

About half past five o'clock on Saturday morning last, as Charles Dawson, a lad employed in the coal pit of Messrs Thomas Livesey and Co. at Alkrington, near Middleton was sitting on one of the coal wagons at the bottom of the pit, near the furnace, waiting till his load was drawn up the pit, he noticed that immediately after John Taylor the hooker-on had attached a tub to the rope, he immediately fell down. Dawson called to Taylor, but received no answer, and he thought he had had a fit, and called for the assistance of John Hough, who worked in the same pit. Taylor, who was bleeding from a wound on the back part of his head, was carried into the furnace hole, where he died immediately. Hough found at the bottom of the shaft, a colliers pick which had evidently fallen down from the top of the pit. Just before the accident happened two men and a lad had gone up the pit, and one of them took with him four picks, and when getting out, the man whose name is Welsby discovered that one of the picks was missing. He thought it must have fallen out of the tub by a hole in the side near the bottom. An inquest was held the following day before Mr. Rutter and a respectable jury, when in addition to the above facts, it was stated that the tubs in the mine were in exceedingly bad repair. There was an underlooker, named Gott, whose duty it was to inspect the pit, which he did two or three times weekly. The coroner told the jury that if any person had been killed by coals falling out of the tubs in consequence of their bad state of repair, he was of the opinion that Gott would have been liable to be tried for manslaughter, but in this case the picks were in the care of Welsby himself, and so it would appear that this occurrence was the result of an accident. The jury returned a verdict of 'accidental death'.

A general lawlessness in the coal mining community is observed in the *Manchester Guardian,* 13 May 1840:

For two or three years past, as is tolerably well known to many of our readers, the neighbourhood of Middleton has been in an extremely lawless state, and all classes of offenders, even if but moderately numerous have set at defiance the only peace officers existing there, and who, it must be added, have taken very slight pains to enforce the law amongst them. We anticipated therefore, that the introduction of the county constabulary into the neighbourhood would lead to some collisions between the officers and the turbulent portion of the population, and this seems already to have happened. Between seven and eight o'clock on Monday evening, as six of the constables were conveying, from Middleton to another station, a collier named Jackson, whom they had apprehended for assaulting some of their body, they were met at Alkrington Brow by a number of colliers, who demanded that the prisoner be set at liberty.

The police refused to give him up, on which the colliers attacked them, striking them with their fists, and throwing stones at them. By these means they eventually succeeded in rescuing Jackson, driving the police towards Blackley. It being the hour which the factory hands were leaving work, there was speedily a very large concourse of persons on the spot. Yesterday morning, a numerous body of the county constabulary, from Heywood and other stations entered Middleton, in order to apprehend the rioters. During the forenoon, they visited Alkrington

Colliery, where the rioters were supposed to be working, but at noon they had not succeeded in discovering any of them. At that hour, a good deal of excitement appeared to prevail, and a party of police were quitting Middleton on an omnibus, in the direction of Blackley. It was supposed to obtain further reinforcements. None of the police who were attacked on Monday night were seriously injured. It is stated that several of the parties concerned in this outrage are well known to them. At all events, it will be absolutely necessary that the authorities of law should be vindicated, and that prompt and vigorous measures should be taken to ensure the apprehension of the parties concerned in this lawless rescue. When the new police was introduced into London, it had to contend with for a while difficulties similar to those that will be found to arise, and indeed that have in some two or three instances in this county already arisen, in the way of the county constabulary.

Ashes Colliery: Saddleworth, near Oldham

The only references I can find relating to this pit are from 11 December 1857, 'when at the Ashes Colliery at Saddleworth near Oldham John Mellor, a boy was crushed to death by the corves in the pit'. The pit is recorded in 1869, when worked by Leeses & Co., and the location confirmed as Saddleworth. It is not mentioned in the Catalogue of Plans of Abandoned Mines.

Ashton Moss: Audenshaw, Ashton-under-Lyne

Ashton Moss Colliery, also known as New Moss Pit and even Snipe Pit, was at Audenshaw, Manchester. The pit was sunk in 1875 and, on completion in 1881, claimed to be the deepest in the country at that time, with a shaft depth of 2,850ft. This depth considerably exceeded that assigned by the Coal Commission of 1871, as the limit possible for the exercise of human labour. The principal impediment to labour at these depths was the excessive heat, but this was overcome by the introduction of greater ventilation at the pit. The pit was situated on the eastern part of Lancashire, five miles east of Manchester, and one mile west of Ashton-under-Lyne. The two mines (seams) worked were the Saltpetre and the Black Mine, the royalty was over 2,000 acres in extent and owned by the Earl of Stamford. The Ashton Moss Colliery Co. Ltd leased these, and sunk the mine. Great difficulties were experienced during the sinking, which commenced in March 1875. In the initial stages of sinking a covering of drift extended from the surface down to a depth of nearly 50 yards. In order to cope with this mass of loose material, the shafts were started with a diameter of 24ft and lined with 9in brickwork down to the stone. Later, an inner shaft with a diameter of 17ft 6in was built within this, and the space between was filled with unmixed Portland cement, forming a barrier which was impervious to the water behind it. Below this depth the shafts were sunk, and lined with ordinary 9in brick, with a diameter of 16ft. Several springs of water were met with at further depths, and cast-iron rings intercepted these, this water was then carried down in boxes to the nearest lodge room in the shaft. These lodge rooms were situated at various levels in the shafts: 120 yards, 240 yards and 400 yards. The two shafts at the colliery were situated 60 yards apart at the centres in a north–south line. They were completed, and the drawing of the coal commenced in May 1882:

> The upcast shaft had a furnace half way down, with additional boiler fire at the bottom, and this produced the ventilation for the whole of the pit. The winding engine at this shaft was constructed by Messrs Garforth of Dukinfield, and had two horizontal cylinders 36in by 60in ordinary slide valves placed on the top of the cylinders. These, and the valve gear were worked by a 6in steam reverser. A 12in steam brake worked to a drum 15ft in diameter, 1ft 2in wide, the drum shaft was made of steel, the crank of wrought iron. The rope drum was of cast iron, and horned to admit the flat ropes; this was 15½ft in diameter at the start, and about 22ft at the end of the draw. Six tubs were raised in each cage on three decks, each holding 10-11cwt of coal. The Ormerod detaching hook was fitted to each cage, and three conductors were fitted to each of the cages. By the early 1890s, the system of work was longwall, driving levels north and south opened out the mine, with further levels driven at right angles every 100 yards. The temperature at the working face varied; in the Saltpetre seam from 70°F to 78°F, and in the Black Mine from 74°F to 82°F.
>
> The winning of the Upper Roger Seam was effected by driving a horizontal tunnel about halfway down the upcast shaft, to cut through the great fault, and undercut the Roger Seam on the upthrow or west side of the fault. The time taken to draw a load up the shaft was one minute and twenty-five seconds.

In the shaft that was sunk in 1882 at Ashton Moss Colliery, a furnace was installed halfway down the shaft for ventilation, and additional boilers were placed at the bottom of the pit. The New Moss Colliery Ltd, Audenshaw, Manchester, worked the colliery in the mid-1890s. T.H. Wordsworth was the colliery manager and John Stevenson the undermanager, with 263 men underground and 114 men on the surface. The coal seams worked were the Great and Roger Seams.

In 1938, the colliery was worked by the Chamber Colliery Co., employing 350 men underground and 110 surface men. The pit manager at this time was J.T. Hughes. The colliery in the 1950s, under the management of the National Coal Board, employed 470 men, and the manager was H.C. Gardner. The pit was merged with Bradford Colliery in September 1969 and, at this time, it mined the Colonel and Roger Seams. The site of the colliery now houses, in the main, a retail park and a breakers yard. Underground links were made between the Wood Park Colliery and the Oaks Colliery, a considerable distance away, and the system of ventilation was in common with all three pits. By all accounts the men at Ashton Moss Pit had a thriving morris dancing troupe.

A tragic incident at the site is recounted in *The Ashton Reporter*, 25 May 1901:

Disastrous fire at Ashton Moss Colliery Thousands of Pounds Damages One Man Suffocated 40 Ponies Left to Their Fate. A disastrous fire broke out in No. 1 engine-room of the Ashton New Moss Colliery about three o'clock on Sunday morning. The engineer was present at the time, but there were no available means at hand for extinguishing the fire. So far as can be gathered, the fire appears to have been caused by a short circuit having been set up in the electric cable from the dynamo under the engine-house. This would cause fusion, and as there were fine particles of coal dust about, it is supposed these have caused a small explosion, which ignited the woodwork round about and enveloped the building in flames. Unfortunately, the flames spread from the drum in the engine-house to the wire cable used for lowering and winding up the cages, and the grease and other lubricants heated the wire to such a degree that it broke, allowing the cages and a portion of the rope to fall down the shaft with a terrible crash. When this occurred, the up and down cages was stopped opposite each other in the middle of the shaft in accordance with the usual practice on Sundays when the colliery is not working. The two cages fell on to the tables, or barriers, placed at the 520 yards level, and stuck there. It is remarkable how the tables withstood the strain, and had they collapsed the cages must have been precipitated another 500 yards down the shaft, and probably into the sump holes, which were full of water. The burning cable fell into a heap at the bottom and set fire to the props and other timber work. A large store of props was in close contiguity to the shaft, and it was feared that these, too, had caught fire. At the time when the fire commenced the men ordinarily employed on a Sunday to attend to the pumping were down the pit. The men were brought to the surface by the upcast shaft, but one of them, named James BOYD, residing at Ashton Hill-lane, Droylsden, a married man with three sons and a daughter and employed as a fireman, could not be got at on account of the atmosphere having become so vitiated. It was hoped that he would have retired into the workings, so thus got out of danger. There were also 40 ponies in the stable down the pit. Smoke began to issue from the downcast shaft, and the gravest fears began to be entertained for the safety of the man BOYD, and also the ponies in the pit workings. Rescue parties were quickly organised, and the first, consisting of seven men in charge of Mr WORDSWORTH, the certificated manager of the colliery, descended the shaft early in the afternoon, but after being lowered to a depth of about 300 yards, they were driven back by the reek from the burning timbers. Another rescue party, under the direction of the assistant manager, Mr LLOYD, went down, taking with them a hosepipe with which to play on the burning timbers. They returned at 5.20, when Mr LLOYD reported that they had reached the bottom and had played on the smouldering timbers. He also stated that if they could restart the fan, which had been stopped since the morning, it might be possible to draw away the reek from the rescue party, in which case they would be able to continue their search for their missing comrade. A third party went down before six o'clock, in charge of Mr HUNTER, but also failed in their efforts to reach the imprisoned man. The fire was confined to the Roger mine; it did not touch what is known as the

Great Mine at all. Some portions of the pit were lighted by electricity, and when the current was interrupted by the short circuit being formed, the electric lights in the pit went out.

FINDING THE ENTOMBED FIREMAN The rescue parties continued their efforts until two o'clock on Monday morning before they were enabled to get into the workings. In gaining access, they found BOYD lying face down about 100 yards from No.2 shaft. He was dead, but bore the appearance of having had a struggle in his frantic efforts to save himself. The deceased was delegate to the Firemen's Union, which held its meetings at the Church Inn, Ashton. He was an experienced fireman, having been engaged in this occupation for about fifteen years altogether. He had been working at the New Moss Colliery for about two years, and prior to that he was fireman at the Astley Pit, Dukinfield, for about eight years. He had also worked as fireman for a considerable time at Messrs Reyners Limited, Albion Mills, Ashton. With respect to the entombed ponies, these could not be rescued, and they had to be left to their fate down the pit. It is probable that they would not remain alive long as the heat and the fumes were so great as to asphyxiate them. It would be practically impossible for them to escape alive, as the heat would be almost sufficient to roast them. Having found BOYD's body, only one course remained for putting out the fire which was then raging, and that was to smother it. Gangs of men were accordingly set to work to 'puddle' or seal up the two shafts and other outlets. At the time of writing, it was not known how far the fire had penetrated, or what were the dimensions, so that the amount of the damage could not be computed, but it will amount to thousands of pounds.

RESOLUTION OF ASHTON MINERS At a meeting of the miners of the New Moss Colliery, held on Monday, the following resolution was passed, on the motion of Owen BAUD, seconded by Samuel GEE: 'That this meeting of the miners of the New Moss Colliery expresses its sincere regret at the sad calamity which occurred on Sunday, and we tender our condolence and sympathy with the wife and family of James BOYD, who has unfortunately lost his life. We also wish to express our deep sympathy with the company in the loss it will sustain through damage and the enforced closing of the mine, which we trust will only be of short duration. We tender our gratitude and thanks to all who have so readily assisted in the work of rescue, and trust that the normal condition will soon be resumed.
William WARDLE, Chairman; Thomas COX, Secretary

The Catalogue of Plans of Abandoned Mines (1928) gives the following information: Ashton Moss (a) Audenshaw, Ashton-under-Lyne; (b) COAL: Saltpetre, Black (abandoned 25 March 1898); (d) 105 SW (1923) A6, 7: B6, 7; Ashton Moss Nos1-2 (a) Audenshaw, Ashton-under-Lyne; (b) COAL: Mary (abandoned 31 December 1910); (d) 105 SW (1923) A6, 7: B6, 7, 8.

Astley Deep: Dukinfield

There is some speculation that this pit and the Astley New Pit may be one and the same, or perhaps that this pit is simply a deepening of the other. Incidentally, the Deep Pit, the Victoria Pit and the Dewsnap Pit were all in close proximity to the Dewsnap Lane, Dukinfield – in fact, on some maps, the pits are named collectively as 'Dukinfield Collieries'. They are also listed collectively under 'Dukinfield Colliery', along with the Chapel Pit, in the Catalogue of Plans of Abandoned Mines. There were even earlier mines in the area of the later Dewsnap Colliery shown on Greenwood's map of Cheshire dated 1819. All these later pits were connected by a tramway, which ran over the railway separating the collieries. An earlier tramway dating from the late 1840s ran from the Dewsnap Colliery to the Peak Forest Canal. The Dewsnap Colliery was the one situated nearest to the old Dukinfield Hall and Dewsnap Bridge, known locally as 'White Bridge' as it has traditionally always been whitewashed. Dukinfield Hall was home to the Dukinfield family. By 1901 all of these pits were closed, and the map of the 1930s shows that the site of the former Dewsnap Pit had been covered over by a large building known as the London and North Eastern Carriage and Wagon Works. This was built between 1905 and 1910 at a cost of £189,000. The Wagon Works closed down in the 1960s, but the site still remains to this day, covering an area of some 30 acres, and now home to industrial units.

Astley Deep Pit was completed in 1858 (see the *Colliery Guardian*, 24 July 1858, for the history of sinking at the colliery). The *Illustrated London News*, on 21

Astley Deep Pit Explosion.

The aftermath of Astley Deep Pit Explosion.

August 1858, reported that 'the deepest coalpit in Great Britain, and probably in the world, has, after nearly twelve years labour, just been completed and opened at Dukinfield, Cheshire. The shaft of this pit is 686½ yards deep, and the sinking of it cost £100,000'. Further sinkings in 1867 took the shaft down to the Black Mine. Sinking the shaft at the Astley Deep Pit was commenced as early as 1847, but ceased at a depth of 476 yards. An underground fire at the colliery in 1849 caused considerable damage to the workings and continued to burn for a number of months. The fire finally burnt itself out, but not before it had created large unsafe voids in the roof of the pit. These had to be shored up with timbers, and backfilled with rubble. A quarter of a century later, these voids and timbered galleries were to contribute to the greatest coal mining disaster in Dukinfield's history.

At three o'clock on the morning of Tuesday 14 April 1874, the shift of 152 men arrived at the colliery. Sixty-one of these men were sent to work in a section of the mine known as the Engine Brow and the Cannel Tunnel. It was in the Cannel Tunnel that the fire had originated many years before. The pit at this time was being worked by the Astley Brothers under the title of the Dunkirk Coal Co. In 1870, the colliery was working three seams, known as the Town Lane Seam, the Black Mine and the Cannel Seam. In March 1870, there was an explosion in the Town Lane Seam which cost the lives of nine miners. After that, this seam was closed down to increase the ventilation to the other deeper seams. The Black Mine was situated at a depth of 686 yards at the bottom of the downcast shaft at the pit, and an inclined tunnel connected this with the Cannel Seam, 50 yards deeper.

From the foot of the shaft ran a tunnel in the form of a half moon, and additional tunnels off this led into the deeper workings of the pit. It was in this half moon tunnel, the Cannel Tunnel, that the fire occurred in 1849. The tunnel was filled with rubble and earth, forming an artificial roof. About seven o'clock, on the night shift, a few of the men noticed that the support couplings and bars were moving under the packed up voids, and dirt was falling from above. This was all about 30 yards distant from the shaft bottom. A number of men, including John Carr, Timothy O'Neil, George Harrison and John Swindells, were sent to repair the roof. Later, the engineer W. Hartshorn, who had left his engine to help on the repairs, joined them. All the men were working with naked lamps. This was allowed, as they were close to the bottom of the downcast shaft, where the fresher air was drawn into the workings. The men could see that their task was not going to be easy, and that there was a real danger of a heavy roof fall, so they proceeded with extreme caution. In spite of this, at around ten minutes to eight, the roof fell, bringing down the timbers and roof supports for a distance of about nine or ten yards. Above, a huge void was revealed, the consequences of the fire years before. In this void over the years, large quantities of gas had slowly been building up. This gas came into contact with the open lamps, and the gas fired. Tearing through the workings, the blast made its way around to the upcast shaft, setting fire to props and other roof supports. The fall of roof where the gas had ignited blocked the tunnel almost completely. Fortunately, none of those engaged in the repair were caught by the fall, all having leapt clear. Harrison was

The fire at Astley Pit, in the *Illustrated London News*, 9 June 1849.

separated from his workmates by the fall, and found himself in the dark, close to the shaft entrance to the tunnel. Here he found two shafts lads, David Chadwick and Henry Fielding, and a young tub hooker. They were all beginning to feel the effects of the afterdamp. Harrison got the three lads into the cage, and went up with them to the surface to give the alarm. Rescue groups were soon organised, and they made their way to the furnace to restore the ventilation, extinguishing a fire on the way which had taken hold at one of the ventilation doors.

They entered through the door to find a raging fire, and succeeded in pulling out Hartshorn, the engineer, and Carr and O'Neil, both of whom had been cut off when the roof fell. A pony lad named Bowker and the furnace man escaped by passing through the fires into a fresher part of the pit. The rescue party, having got these men away from the hottest part of the tunnel nearest the air door, were forced to retreat into the return airway in order to breathe. A second attempt was made to recover the men. The rescue team succeeded in dragging the men to a place of safety, but it was found that the engineer, Hartshorn, had died from the effects of burns and asphyxia. Near to the furnace, there was down brow running a distance of 700 yards to the top Cannel workings. Two men employed here, Matthew Robinson and Samuel Timbs, had felt the blast and the following blackdamp, but managed to escape by the return airway. Further explorations soon revealed the extent of the explosion, and the character of the catastrophe was becoming apparent. In the main down brow leading to the deeper workings, which had felt the full force of the blast, a large number of dead were found. The men in the south workings, or the 'sixteen hundred', about ninety in number, were all saved from the blast by the air doors and were able to make it to safety. By one o'clock in the morning, the rescue parties had managed to penetrate about 300 or 400 hundred yards into the workings. Here, the air stoppings had been blown down, and timbers were swept in all directions. The pony stable on a level part of the mine had been set on fire and it was feared that seven or eight ponies had died. By two o'clock the Ashton Fire Brigade had descended the pit with 500 yards of hose, and went forward to put out the raging fire near the boiler house. At ten past five, a number of the rescue parties returned to the surface and reported that they had found some men alive in the Cannel workings, but were unable to reach them.

Ten of these were thought to have survived, but they had amongst them the dead bodies of three or four of their companions. Further explorers descended, taking with them stretchers and first aid equipment. Two boys were soon found alive, a pony driver named Joseph Normanton, aged fifteen, and George Dean, aged fourteen another pony driver. The father and mother of Normanton were eagerly waiting at the pit bank, having lost two other sons in similar accidents in the past. The next of the ten in the Cannel Tunnel to be brought up was another lad, John Walker, who had been badly burned. He was the only one from that location in a serious condition. The man named Carr, together with Swindells and an un-named man, were taken to the Ashton Infirmary, but died soon after admission. The boy named Bowker was also taken to the Infirmary in a critical condition. Crowds gathered at the pit bank as news of the calamity spread but, as soon as the injured had been conveyed away, it was announced that no further information could be given until the morning. Some of the crowds dispersed, but most chose to stay on and await news just in case any was forthcoming. The day broke, and the large crowds reassembled as the first body was brought to the surface, that of twelve year-old Edwin Oliver, employed as a pony driver. He was burned in a shocking manner. The rest of the dead men and boys were brought up in quick succession, and were moved to a nearby hay shed adapted for use as a temporary morgue. Here, a number of men and women were busily engaged in the horrendous task of trying to tidy up the bodies of the deceased as best they could, a task frequently interrupted by females who recognised their husband, brother or son. As soon as the bodies were identified, and permission obtained, they were placed on carriages and removed to their former residence, followed by sorrowful and grieving crowds. A list of those who perished was soon posted at the pit bank, but it was feared that a number of others were still unaccounted for. The dead were listed as follows:

George Lindley, the youngest victim, aged 10
Edwin Oliver, 12, of Pickford Lane, Dukinfield
Robert Dugdale, 15, of Birch Lane
John Hitchen, 16, Pickford Lane
Nelson Harrison, 51, Pleasant Street, Dukinfield
William Hartshorn, 20, Astley Street, Dukinfield
Edwin Davis, a young man, age unknown, Portland Street, Ashton
Samuel Wardel, 30, Furness Street, Dukinfield
George Lindley, 17, Astley Street, Woodends, Dukinfield
Michael Connolly, 28, Whittaker's Court, Zetland Street, Dukinfield
John Roberts, 44, Peel Court, Dukinfield
Richard Fletcher, 26, Astley Street, Dukinfield
John Gartside, 19, Astley Street, Dukinfield
James Bradshaw, 40, Birch Lane, Dukinfield
James Hallam, 37, Gaskell Street, Dukinfield
John Statham, 36, Park Street, Dukinfield
Josiah Gartside, 45, father of John Gartside, Astley Street, Dukinfield
Thomas John Kein, 20, Wharf Street, Dukinfield
Walter Hibbert, 21, Astley Street, Dukinfield
Alfred Bickerdyke, Newton Wood, Dukinfield
Benjamin Williams, 29, Crescent Road, Dukinfield
William Henry Knott, 15, Hadfield's Court, Old Street, Dukinfield
James Merrick, 35, Highfield Street, Dukinfield
John Kein, 45, father of Thomas John, Wharf Street, Dukinfield
Matthew Higginbottom, aged unknown, Railway Street, Dukinfield
James Reynolds, 24, of Crescent Road, Dukinfield

Law Taylor, 30, Wharf Street, Dukinfield
William Lawton, 15, Gaskell Street, Dukinfield
John Leyland, 52, Flowery Field, Hyde,
John Shockledge, 24, Oxford Road, Dukinfield
Joseph Bickerdyke, 25, Newton Street, Dukinfield
Samuel Davis, 20, Wharf Street
William Chadwick, boy, age unknown, Wood Street, Ashton
James Carter, married, age unknown, George Street, Dukinfield
John Morgan, young man, age unknown, St Mark Street, Dukinfield
Robert Walker, 46, Leach Street, Dukinfield
John Downs (or Downpatrick), 22, Taylor Street, Dukinfield
George Wright, 40, Church Street, Ashton
Robert Thomas, 25, Wharf Street, Dukinfield
Henry Beard, 36, Leach Street
James Welsby, 28, Highfield Street, Dukinfield
Thomas Brown, 45, Zetland Street, Dukinfield
John Carr, 46, Meadow bank, Dukinfield, died at Infirmary
John Swindells, 45, residing near pit, died at Infirmary

Three persons were not identified, and five remained in the pits according to first reports – making a total of fifty-one. However, the total number of men and boys who perished at the Astley Deep Pit that day is known to have been fifty-four. Let us not forget either the number of men and boys who were injured in the explosion. Those seriously injured would have to spend the rest of their days living in poverty or on handouts. There was no accurate list, but those mentioned included:

James Butterworth, married, Hill Street, Dukinfield
Albert Bowker, 16, Astley Street, Newton Wood
Joseph Normanton, 15, Oxford Road,
George Dean, 16, Park Street
John Walker, Leach Street
William Kellett, 20, Astley Street
Thomas Hitchen, Astley Street
Matthew Lee, Leach Street
John Thomas Wood, Parkside
Allen Hulme, Oxford Road
Charles Hulme, Oxford Road
Charles Hulme, Astley Street
Squire Clayton, Kay Street

Today, a plaque located on Woodbury Crescent down Knightsbridge Drive at Dukinfield, is on the site of the former colliery, and recalls that fateful day, commemorating all those who died. Unfortunately names are not mentioned. The plaque is located over the shaft of the former colliery, and tells briefly of the disaster there. In the tragic days that followed the disaster, a sermon was suggested for those who perished in the blast by the Revd J.K. Smith, to be preached in the Flowery Field Christian Church.

Four years before this terrible tragedy, on 3 March 1870, there had been a smaller, yet still horrific, accident at the site, which caused the deaths of at least nine persons. The pit at this time was being worked by Mr B. Ashton of Woodley under a lease from the trustees of the late Mr F.D.P. Astley, and employed between 400 and 500 men and boys. The explosion occurred at an inset to a seam in the downcast shaft, and deep within the workings. Such were the extent of the workings at this time that only those caught by the actual explosion were aware of the blast, others working in the same seam were unaffected and totally unaware of what was happening. The first news of the explosion was given at six o'clock, when the underlookers, William Bailey and David Hulme, who were then on the pit bank, were alarmed by smoke coming from the shaft. They quickly arranged an exploration party. Due to the afterdamp (the poisonous gas left behind following an explosion), it was at least two hours before the first of the victims could be reached. Two men were discovered alive: Jonathan Newton (married) and Joseph Bellfield (single). Both were badly burnt. Soon, the exploration party came across those not so fortunate: eight dead bodies were soon sent to the surface. It was noon the following day before the last person was brought to the pit bank. First reports indicated that there might have been a ninth victim, that of a youth named Abraham Normanton. The belief was that his body lay beneath the fall of roof, and this seems to have been confirmed by the discovery of his cap nearby. Those known to have died were:

William Henry Hulme, Zetland Street, Dukinfield, married with one child
Henry Moreton, Oxford Street, Dukinfield, single
Joseph King, Park Street, Dukinfield, married with one child
Solomon Cambridge, White Street, Dukinfield, married with three children
William Hammond, White Street, Dukinfield, single
William Hodgson, Victoria Street, Dukinfield, married with five children
William Leigh, Church Street, Dukinfield, married with four children
Edward Cartwright, who had just come from Staffordshire, married

There were also reports of bravery on the part of the rescue workers. The air in the vicinity of the explosion had been very bad due to afterdamp, but still the rescuers moved forward, looking for their companions at great risk to themselves. A dozen or more of the rescue parties were affected in this manner. John Kelsall and Henry Whitworth actually collapsed in the foul air, and were only recovered with great difficulty. Considerable damage was also done to the mine itself through the explosion, with machinery 1,200 yards down a brow that was used to haul the tubs up being completely destroyed. A number of tubs were blown to pieces, and there was evidence of fire on the timbering in the jig brow – air stoppings had also been blown down in many places. Such are the perils of coal mining. There was a remarkable incident at the pit in September 1867, when 160 men were trapped underground when the cage rope broke, but happily there were no injuries, and the men were brought out by the Town Lane Shaft. The Astley Deep Pit was closed in 1901, after a relatively short life, and it was officially abandoned on 22 January 1902.

Astley New Pit: Dukinfield

The Dunkirk Coal Co. worked the pit in 1880, and the Dukinfield Coal & Cannel Co. Ltd, of Dukinfield, worked it in 1896, with 487 men employed underground mining the Black Mine, Cannel Mine, and the Peacock Seam. An early reference to mining at Dukinfield is in the parish records at Ashton, 23 November 1696: 'James Cropper was kyld in Duckenfeild [sic] cole pitt'. On 8 April 1857, the *Manchester Guardian* reported another tragedy:

> Fatal Accident. An inquest on the body of John Bray, who was killed at the Astley New Pit, in Dukinfield on Saturday morning was held at the Commercial Inn, yesterday before Mr. Johnson and a respectable jury, when a verdict of 'accidental death' was returned. The deceased and six other men were blasting to sink the pit to a lower mine, and had drilled three holes that morning and charged them with powder. All the three blasts were lighted at once, and two exploded. When the men discovered that one had missed, water was put into the hole. The hole in the first instance was nineteen inches deep, and after the water had been put in, the deceased drilled it afresh for fourteen inches, when he went up the pit for his 'jack bit' (lunch) The deceased returned in about three quarters of an hour, and the hole would be full of water all that time. He commenced drilling again, and in about ten minutes an explosion took place, from the effects of which he died in about an hour and a quarter. The deceased was a very experienced man, and it seems it is usual to drill a hole again when it had not exploded. The opinion of John Wielding, one of the three contractors for the works, was that a spark had been made by the drill, and he expressed his concurrence with the opinion of the coroner, that the accident might not have happened if a less drill had been used, and that it would not have happened if fresh holes had been drilled. The coroner said that there could not be a shadow of blame attached to the proprietors of the pit, but he considered that a smaller drill should have been used, or better still that fresh holes should have been drilled, and he recommended more caution.

Back o' th' Ho' Pits: Werneth, Oldham

Two pit shafts dating from around 1812, near Werneth Hall, both of which went by the name of 'Back o' th' Ho' Pit'. The coal from the Black Mine here was wound to the surface by a two-horse gin wheel. The pit shafts were located

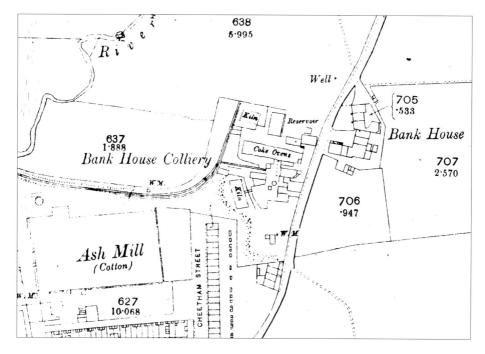

Bank House Colliery, map of 1891.

about 100 yards past Werneth Hall near Frederick Street. No other information is available on this colliery at the time of writing.

Bank House: Shaw and Crompton Oldham*, SD 945 091

This pit was at work in 1854, under the title of 'Executors of the late Charles Taylor', and was worked by Samuel Wild in 1857, and the Oldham, Middleton & Rochdale Colliery Co., Edge Lane, Oldham in 1869, 1879 and 1896. The pit was on the left-hand side of the Grains Road above Shaw Village but before the Morning Star Inn and the Nook District, taking its name from Bank House, a dwelling directly across the road. In 1896, the colliery employed 145 men underground and twenty on the surface, and worked the Mountain Mine.

John Lord was the manager. The site today of this former colliery is occupied by a leisure complex. The pit was 381ft to the Lower Mountain Mine, according to the geological survey. The colloquial name for the Bank House Colliery was 'Bunkhouse'. The colliers at Bank House had to sharpen their picks at the railway station, but had to walk up to the Bank House Pit for their wages. Most of the output at Bank House was coked on site, and the cage was so small that only three men at a time could ride up and down the shaft. The Bank House Colliery closed in 1903, and a spur line ran from the pit to the Oldham/Rochdale Line. The pit is shown on a map of the 1890s, with banks of coke ovens, and two banks of kilns. A rectangular reservoir is also shown.

Bank House Pit.

The following information is taken from the Catalogue of Plans of Abandoned Mines (1928): Bankhouse, Sholver, Holebottom (a) Crompton, Oldham, Royton; (b) COAL Mountain or Three Quarters (abandoned 1 June 1903); (d) 89 SW (1910) D12: E11, 12: F11, 12: G11, 12: H10, 11, 12. 89 SE (1910) C1: D1: E1, 2, 3: F1, 2: G1, 2: H1, 2: 97 NW (1922) A11, 12. 97 NE (1922) A1, 2: B1.

It is not known at which colliery the following fatality occurred, but it is listed under the Oldham news in the *Manchester Guardian*, 10 October 1849:

Fatal Colliery Accident. An inquest was held before Mr Dearden, coroner on Saturday the 6th inst. on the bodies of two men named Jonathan Stafford and Evan Williams. They were ascending the shaft in a tub, or bucket, and when near the top, it by some means became detached from the rope, and they were all precipitated to the bottom, about two hundred yards and were killed on the spot.

No satisfactory reason can be assigned. A verdict of 'accidental death' was returned.

Again, on 20 May 1857, the *Manchester Guardian* reported:

> Fatal Accident in a Coal Mine. On Monday morning a collier named Thomas
> Kershaw, aged 22 years, died at Nook, near Shaw, in Crompton from the effects of
> injuries he received on the 12th. inst. in the Bank House Colliery, belonging to
> Samuel Wild and Co. It appears he went to work in an old working with a naked
> candle, without orders from the foreman. An explosion took place, and he was
> severely burnt. Medical aid was of no avail.

Just one month later, the pit is in the news for yet another fatality (*Manchester
Guardian*, 19 June 1857):

> Colliery Accident. Mr Dearden, coroner, held an inquest yesterday on the body of
> a collier named Richard O'Neil who was killed on the previous day in the Bank
> House Colliery in Crompton. He was at work in the pit, when a portion of the
> roof fell upon him and he was killed on the spot. The jury returned a verdict of
> 'accidental death'.

Excess flooding occurred at the pit following the construction of reservoirs
by Oldham Corporation, which led to a court case. The *Colliery Guardian*, 29
August 1863, reports:

> Flooding of a coal mine. Wild and Others *v*. The Mayor and Corporation of
> Oldham. This action was brought against the Mayor and Aldermen of the Borough
> of Oldham by the Plaintiffs, Samuel Wild, and a number of other persons to
> recover compensation for the flooding of the plaintiffs mines by the Corporation
> Waterworks, and was tried at the South Lancashire Assizes on Friday and Saturday
> last, before Mr Justice Mellor.
>
> The declaration in the case contains two counts, the first of which alleged
> that the plaintiffs at the time of committing the grievances complained of in the
> declaration, were possessed of certain lands and subterranean excavations used as
> coal mines, that the defendants made and maintained reservoirs on the surface
> of the land, and also subterranean reservoirs, and that they so neglectfully made
> and maintained them that the plaintiffs were prevented from working the colliery
> and winning the coal. The second count alleged that the water flowed from the
> reservoir into the plaintiff's mines and caused them damages and expenses in
> additional pumping. The pleas put upon the record by the Corporation were, not
> guilty, that they did not cause the water to flow into the plaintiff's mines, that they
> committed the alleged grievance under the authority of an Act of Parliament, and
> that the lands were freehold of the defendants. The Corporation was empowered,
> by an Act of Parliament passed in 1855, to construct two compensation reservoirs
> among the other works for supplying the town of Oldham with water. These
> reservoirs were made in 1857. The plaintiffs are the proprietors of the Bank House

Pit, and stated that they had been injured by their pit having been flooded several times and had to pump the mines to a much greater extent and much greater expense, than if the reservoirs had not been constructed. The Bank House Pit is on the side of a hill upon which stands the surface reservoir. From the surface down to the coal seam, called the Mountain, or Three-Quarters Main, the depth is about 120 yards. Higher up the hill, at the Midge Hole Pit, the coal in the same mine outcrops to within ten yards of the surface. Before the reservoirs were made, seven hours pumping daily would clear the pit. Afterwards it required fourteen hours to get out the water. The first reservoir was on the surface of the land, over a brook, which formerly ran through the centre of its site. A subterranean reservoir was made in the worn out workings of the Mountain Mine. The water from this is conveyed through a tube, so as to supply a stream lower down the hill, so as to supply a gauge house where it could be stopped until it gained a certain height in the reservoir, whence it was conveyed through the tunnel containing the tube to the brook, and thence to the hands of the various proprietors for whose benefit the compensation reservoirs had been established. On the question of authorisation introduced into the pleadings, it has been ruled that those authorised by Act of Parliament to construct the works are liable for any injury occasioned by their construction. His Lordship intimidated that the proper termination to this case would be a reference. The action would only be settled as to the past, but the most material consideration was the future. Evidence was produced to show that flooding of the pits was due to the works of the Corporation. The trial was resumed on Saturday, when facts disclosed in evidence were that the workings of the Bank House Pit were themselves particularly dry. That the reservoirs were constructed in 1857, and the other, an underground reservoir in the workings of an old pit, and that the first flood at Bank House Pit was in July of the same year. The pipe, which had been inserted in to carry off from the pit water that had percolated from the reservoir, ran over at a rate, which would have filled a 22-inch pipe in addition. The water rose for five days to a height of thirteen yards in the Bank House Pit. The men were prevented working from the 11th. to the 20th of July. An examination of the surface reservoir showed that valve had been opened to let the water out of the reservoir, and it was still running through the Midgeholme Pit and thence into Bank House Colliery. On ordinary days, besides the more serious floods after the reservoirs had been constructed the pumping had been increased from seven to thirteen hours in dry weather, to ten to sixteen hours daily in wet weather. A verdict was reached after several hours in favour of the plaintiff, and damages were awarded to the sum of £150.

The Mines Inspectors Report for the year 1868 records: 'January 20th. Bank House Colliery, Shaw. Thomas Owen aged 10 years caught and killed by wagon', and also, on 9 July 1869: 'Bank House Colliery, Shaw. William Meadowcroft killed through being caught by a connecting rod'. The *Rochdale Observer*, 20 December 1873 reports:

An inquest was held on Tuesday at the Morning Star Inn, the Nook, Crompton by Mr Molesworth, coroner on the body of William Crossley who was killed on Saturday last at the Bank House Colliery. Mr Dickinson, the Government Inspector of Mines for the District watched the proceedings. Mr Evans, agent for the company was also present.

Betty Crossley, widow of the deceased, identified the body of her husband who was 32 years of age and lived at Old Bottom. James Sutcliffe said he lived at Holebottom, and was a fireman at the Bankhouse Pit, of the Oldham, Middleton and Rochdale Coal Co. He knew the deceased, William Crossley who was an underlooker and also worked the pumps in the pit. On Saturday last about twenty five minutes past six in the morning he was going with the deceased up the engine brow in a tram drawn by a rope attached to the engine. There was an old wagon in the tram behind them, and was almost six inches higher than the tram. Witness and the deceased were kneeling down, and the deceased caught against the roof. Deceased carried the only light they had with them, and when the accident occurred it went out. Witness called to the deceased and he was not answered, he then rang the bell and the tram stopped. Witness then ran up the hill and made known what had happened. From the top of the tram to the roof was about nine inches, and the old wagon would be about an inch and a half from it. When the deceased threw his hands up, as he did when he was struck, witness felt a shock. He believes the deceased was caught between the old wagon and the roof. Timber on the brow was not broken in the accident, witness saw it broken last Thursday. There were marks of blood on the roof where the deceased was caught, but witness had not examined the wagon. Deceased asked him to go down the brow with him and bring the wagon up. The roof was a little lower at the point where the accident happened than elsewhere. William Fielding, fireman at the colliery, said that on the 18th inst. he went up the engine brow and saw the deceased dead in the train. He seemed to have been kneeling down on the train, and his head was on top of the wagon, but not touching the roof. It was completely crushed. There were blood marks on the roof for about half a yard, from thirty to forty yards below where he found the deceased. Deceased was dead when witness reached him. The roof of the brow was in good order, as was the roadway. The jury returned a verdict of 'accidentally killed' the jury appeared to think however that but for the wagon referred to, the accident might not have happened.

The *Oldham Weekly Chronicle*, 9 August 1894 reports yet another accident at the site:

Colliery Explosion at Crompton. A shocking accident occurred on Wednesday at the Bankhouse Colliery, Crompton belonging to the Oldham, Middleton, and Rochdale Colliery Co. to James Henthorn who is married and has four children, and resides at Laneside, Crompton, a village about half a mile from the pit.

Henthorn is employed by the firm as a shotfirer, and on Wednesday afternoon, about five o'clock he was up one of the workings making preparations for a shot. The fuse was laid in the usual manner, and was lighted and immediately afterwards an explosion took place. A number of the workers in the mine ran to the spot, and found that an explosion of gas had resulted by the firing of the shot. Henthorn had been thrown to the ground, and was discovered in an unconscious state, but he soon revived. It was found that he had severe burns on the arms, legs, face and all over the body. PC Snowden, who lives near rendered first aid, and the man was afterwards removed to Dr Spearings in a cab, where he is progressing favourable considering the nature of his injuries.

Sadly, according to the Mines Inspectors Report, James Henthorn later died from the injuries received.

Bank Top: Bank Top/Leesbrook, Oldham, SD 951 047
This colliery was to the rear of Stanley Mill to the west of New Street, Bank Top, Oldham. Stanley Mill is now demolished and the area was declared an open space in 1995 by Oldham Council. A number of footpaths have been laid around the site, which might have destroyed any evidence of the old pit. The colliery is noted on the OS map of 1844, and was worked by Messrs Lees and Booth, and was probably worked in connection with fuel for the mills in the area. The pit worked the Royley Mine at a depth of 85 yards. The workings were apparently connected with the Greenacres Colliery, according to the Catalogue of Plans of Abandoned Mines (1928).

The *Manchester Guardian*, 6 March 1847 records a tragedy at the site:

Colliery Accident. On Tuesday last, a fatal accident occurred at the colliery of Messrs Lees and Booth, Bank Top, near Lees Brook. Two boys were working as waggoners, when one of them named Daniel Shepley, a boy of about 11 years of age, was suddenly overwhelmed by a mass of earth, about a yard thick which fell from the roof of the mine. His brother, who was at work a few yards from him, escaped without any injury, but the deceased was killed on the spot. He was the son of Lees Shepley, a banksman, or colliery workman, resident at Roxbury. It is alleged that the upper part of the mine was adequately supported by posts, but notwithstanding this, the fall of earth took place, probably owing to the giving way of a prop.

And, just over a year later, on 15 March 1848, the *Manchester Guardian* reports:

Fatal Accident at a Colliery. On Saturday morning last, a coal miner, 35 years of age, of the name Henry Ivey, resident near Lees Brook, Oldham, died in consequence of the injuries he had sustained from an explosion of firedamp, which occurred at Bank Top Colliery, Charlesfield, belonging to Messrs Lees, Booth and Co.

on Saturday fortnight. On that occasion the deceased was working alone in the mine during the night, when there was an explosion of firedamp, owing to the incautious use of a light.

Bankfield: Bardsley

This colliery is listed in the mines index for 1896, when it was being worked by the Bankfield Colliery Co., Fairbottom, Bardsley, Ashton-under-Lyne. The pit employed twenty-nine men underground and six on the surface. George Wild was the colliery manager. The seams worked, Stubbins and Fairbottom, are listed as 'abandoned', and this is confirmed below. Short term workings by all accounts, for the colliery is not listed in 1880, but abandoned in 1896! The Catalogue of Plans of Abandoned Mines (1928) gives this information: Bankfield Nos.1-2 (a) Bardsley; (b) COAL Black, or Seven Foot, White (abandoned 23 April 1896); (d) 95 SW (1910) E2, 3: F2, 3.

Bankside Colliery: Werneth, Oldham, SD 917 047

On 15 June 1968, the *Oldham Weekly Chronicle* explored the origins of this colliery:

> Around 1770, William Jones (a poor Welsh labourer) sunk a pit near Bankside (Oldham) by his own labour. Tradition states that he formed his own tools in a smithy on the pit bank. Later he drove a tunnel from Bankside to Stockbrook, where later still stood the Sun Mill. Many years later a small rude shaped anvil could be seen lying about at the Old Engine Colliery, at Hollinwood, where old Bill Jones used to sharpen the picks when he first sunk the colliery near Bankside.

There is a Bankside Close near the Oldham, Werneth Railway Station, at the above SD reference; the colliery may have been situated here. William Jones went on to own a number of collieries in the Oldham district. These included the Broadway Lane Colliery, Chadderton Colliery, New Bailey Colliery and Oaks Colliery. This William Jones was the father of Joseph Jones, who used to live at Falcon House, King Street. His son, William Jones, went on to become the first mayor of Oldham.

The *Annals of Oldham 1787-1839* record an accident at this site: 'May 7th 1790, Last night a man fell into the engine pit at Werneth and was killed on the spot. He was a collier at the pit'.

The *Manchester Guardian*, 16 June 1857, describes the funeral of William Jones:

> The remains of the late Mr William Jones, of Falcon House, were interred in the parish church, on Saturday morning. A considerable number of persons assembled in the streets through which the funeral procession passed. The boys belonging to the Blue Coat School, of which the deceased was a trustee, preceded the hearse, and lined the churchyard from the gate to the edifice. The coffin was bore by

overlookers and others in the employment of Messrs Jones was conveyed into the building. The funeral service was conducted by the Revd Mr. Lees, of St Peter's Church. The late Mr Jones was the first mayor of Oldham, having been appointed by the newly elected town council in August 1849, and the following November was re-elected for another year. He was also appointed a county magistrate on 12th February 1846, but for some time past, in consequence of ill health and advancing years, he had taken little or no part in public matters.

Bar Gap: Bar Gap, Oldham GR 927 056
A colliery worked by George Marland in 1896; he is also listed as being the manager. The pit appears to have been recently abandoned, as only three men were working underground, and the Blendfire Seam which the colliery worked is noted as 'abandoned'. The Catalogue of Plans of Abandoned Mines confirms that the colliery was indeed abandoned in October 1894. There were also two men employed on the surface in 1896. The colliery was near the Bar Gap Road, at Oldham Edge, and appears to have been short-term workings, as the pit is not mentioned in a mines list for 1880. The Catalogue of Plans of Abandoned Mines (1928) notes: Bar Gap (a) Oldham; (b) COAL Big (abandoned October 1894); (d) 97 NW (1922) F9, 10; Bar Gap (a) Oldham; (b) COAL Blendfire (abandoned 8 October 1895); (d) 97 NW (1922) E9. Bar Gap (a) Oldham; (b) COAL Blendfire (abandoned 24 December 1901); (d) 93 NE (1909) D5: E5, 6: F7.

Bardsley (Bridge): Bardsley, SD 929 014
The history of coal mining at Bardsley goes back to 1712, when it is recorded that there was a coal mine on the Bardsley Estate. Bardsley at this time was not a village, but a large house in its own grounds. The pit probably belonged to the Harrop family, and it is thought to have been the one that became 'Wild's Pit' from 1864 to 1887. It was at 'Wild's Pit' in 1858 that an explosion occurred which killed fifty-three men and boys. The colliery was worked by Joseph Harrop & Co. in 1834 and Messrs Jonah, Harrop & Co. in 1842. To this day there exists a Coal Pit Lane in Bardsley, though this is a comparatively recent change, and probably owes its name to the Wood Park Colliery. The Bardsley Colliery Co. is recorded as working the pit in 1861, and again in 1871 when George Wild was the colliery manager, hence 'Wild's Pit'. The same company was also working the mine in 1880, and the colliery appears to have been abandoned between 1884 and 1886. A lasting reminder of the coal mining days is the Black Diamond public house in Bardsley, whose inn sign depicts colliery headgear and coal tubs. The Bardsley Colliery is marked on a map of 1894, though the pit was disused at this time. The pit consisted of the 'Victoria' shaft and the 'Diamond Pit', and was between Knott Lane and the A627, the Ashton Road. The Fairbottom Branch Canal would no doubt serve to transport the colliery output. Coal winding at the Bardsley Colliery was achieved and an endless chain taken down the shaft. The following is taken from the Catalogue of Plans of Abandoned Mines (1928): Bardsley, Diamond, Victoria

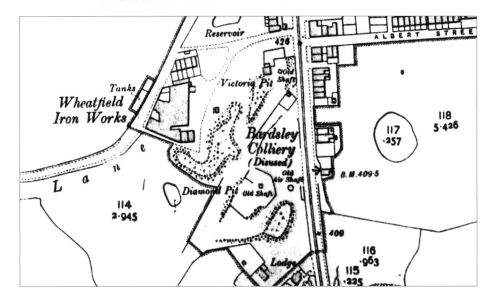

Bardsley Colliery, map of 1909.

(a) Bardsley; (b) COAL, Rowley, New (abandoned prior to 1886); (d) 97 SW (1922) H10. Bardsley, Diamond, Victoria (a) Bardsley; (b) COAL Old, Peacock, Two Feet, (abandoned 1884); (d) 97 SW (1922) G9, 10: H9, 10, 11. 105 NW (1923) A9, 10.

More information on this colliery is available from J.L. Kennedy's 'Report on Child Labour in the Coal Mines' (1841):

Samuel Kay, waggoner at Mr Harrop's Colliery, Bardsley Bridge, near Oldham — What age are you? — I shall be 17 next March. I am a parish child from the Manchester Workhouse. What did you do before you came here? — I used to break stones. Were you bound by the parish? — Yes, I was. What age were you when you were first put to work? — I was ten years old. Can you read and write? — No. Do you go to Sunday-school? — Yes, but I don't go to church. Do you get plenty to eat? — Yes, I get as much as I want, I am not stinted. What hours do you work? — I go down in the morning at half past five, and come out at half past five in the evening, sometimes it is six o'clock.

And there is a similar story from another young miner:

James Wild, waggoner at Mr Harrop's Colliery, Bardsley Bridge, near Oldham. 'What age are you? — 13 years old. How long have you been at work? — Only three months. Have you ever been in a factory? — No, they would not pass me for 13 when I went, so I went into the pit. What time do you go down in the morning? — I start from home at five o'clock in the morning, but it is generally six before I go down the pit. I live at Ashton, and come two miles to my work every morning.

What time do you come up at night? — I come up at four o'clock on Saturday, and between five and six for regular. But towards the end of the reckoning, a day or two before the pay, I used to come out at six or seven, and sometimes eight o'clock, before we were stinted. Why are you up so early today? — We are flooded out with water. The pumps were broken last night, and the wagons were swimming with water. I have not worked in my regular place today. The slutch [mud] is over the top of one's clogs at the pit-eye. Do you work at night? — No, we don't work nights here, but they do at Fairbottom. What wages do you get? — I get 8*d* per day, 4*s* a week standing wages. Have you ever been hurt? — No. Is the pit wet? — Yes, for 100 yards on the level there is water always up to the knees, but they are making a tunnel now which will keep this part of the pit dry. How far do you wagon your coals? — 240 yards, all on rails. How many times a day do you wagon this distance? — As much as 14 or 15 times a day. Do you ever get beaten? — Yes, I was once, with his hand, not much. Can you read and write? — I can read, but cannot write. Do you go to Sunday school? — Sometimes I go, my father sends me, but I do not always go. Do you go to church? — No, I don't go.

There is a memorial in Holy Trinity Churchyard at Bardsley to Henry Cudsworth, 'who lost his life by a fall of rock at Victoria Pit, Bardsley Colliery on Wednesday May 23rd 1866'. There is also, apparently, a memorial slab to the victims of one of the disasters at Bardsley, on the left of the church door, but we were unable to find it, as it was overgrown. The church is under renovation at the time of writing, and hopefully the churchyard will be tidied at some future date along with the memorial to those who perished.

Further accidents at the site are reported in a variety of publications, and include a report in the *Manchester Guardian*, 27 April 1850: 'Coal Pit Accident. On Tuesday an inquest was held at the White Hart Inn, Hollins, by Mr Dearden, on the body of Peter Pearson, aged 26, whose death was occasioned by the falling of a portion of roof, at a coal pit near Copperas House, Ashton Road. He lingered some days after the accident. Verdict 'accidental death'; 'February 2nd. Bardsley Colliery. Fifty three men and boys were killed through explosion of firedamp' (Mines Inspectors Report (1858)). A case in 1862 saw a collier from the site on trial: 'At Ashton-under-Lyne County Sessions, on Wednesday, Samuel Buckley, a collier working for the Bardsley Coal Co., Bardsley near Ashton was charged with having on the 11th inst., obstructed the free passage of air courses in the colliery, by throwing dust therein, and endangering the lives of the workmen employed in the pit'. The case was proved, and he was committed for one month, not being able to pay the 10*s* and costs. (*Colliery Guardian*, 18 January 1862). In the same year, the *Colliery Guardian* (17 May 1862) reported that: 'Edward Morris aged 68 was killed by a fall of stone at the Bardsley Colliery near Oldham'. Four years later, the Mines Inspectors Report (1866) recorded the death of a young boy working at the site: 'January 9th. Bardsley Colliery. William Jacques, aged ten years crushed to death by wagon pushed by two people'.

Bargoe: Dukinfield
This colliery was operative in 1908, when worked by T. Blackledge & Sons of Barg Lane, Dukinfield, when it employed twelve men underground and two surface workers.

Barrowshaw: Greenacres Moor, Oldham★, SD 946 066
Job Lees worked this colliery in 1854, and Lees and Mayall in 1875; John Winterbottom was the colliery agent. The trustees of John Mayall worked the pit in 1879. John Mayall, or his trustees, also worked the Count Hill Colliery, the Little Mine at Barrowshaw and the Low or Lower Moor Colliery, at various dates after 1854, when it appears that Job Lees had either given up the coal mining business or died.

The Barrowshaw Colliery worked the Gannister Mine at a depth of 140 yards in the shaft. The pit was located on the Ripponden Road (A672) at Watersheddings (a district of Oldham) on the east side just before Barrowshaw Farm, and the workings stepped over into Yorkshire. Almost across from Alva Road, on the A672, is a track between the rows of terraced properties. Immediately in front of you is a green gate giving access to the old Barrowshaw Colliery. On site, and to the left-hand side is a large mound of pit waste with evidence of fireclay spoil. On the right is the raised pit bank, and if you are able to get through the undergrowth the capped shaft is visible with its triangular marker. Two reservoirs were located at the bottom of Cornhill Street, with an additional one to the north of the pit. There was also a large bank of coke ovens here. The Catalogue of Plans of Abandoned Mines gives the following information: Barrowshaw and Paulden, Hedge Clough Lower (a) Oldham (Lancashire) Springhead (Yorkshire); (b) COAL Mountain (abandoned 22 January 1880); (d) 97 NW (1922) B12: C12: D12: 97 NE (1922) B1,2: C1, 2: D1, 2, 3, 4: F3.

The *Manchester Guardian*, 3 January 1855, reports the death of a young drawer:

> Yesterday morning, a boy named John Taylor, aged 15 years, a drawer in Barrowhead [sic] coal-pit, the property of Job Lees and Co., died from injuries he received in the pit on the 26th ult. when some firedamp ignited accidentally in the mine. The usual remedies were applied, but without any effect, for he lingered in great suffering till yesterday morning.

Only a few weeks later, the *Manchester Guardian* (21 March 1855) notes another accident:

> Fatal Colliery Accident. An inquest was held on Monday, on the body of a collier named Thomas Simpson who met his death under the following circumstances. The deceased, with three other men were being lowered in the bucket at

Mr Job Lee's Colliery, at Water Sheddings, but one of the chains becoming loose, the bucket swerved to the side, and the deceased falling out was killed on the spot. The other men, fortunately did not let go, and reached the bottom in safety. The jury returned the verdict of 'accidental death'. The deceased was 28 years of age.

The Mines Inspectors Report of 1856 tells of another death: 'May 2nd. John Crossley, 20, killed through being thrown by capstan'. *Manchester Guardian*, 28 April 1875, reports on the 'Flooded Colliery at Oldham':

> Pumping is now going on at the Barrowshaw Pit, but the water is not decreasing to any appreciable extent. All hopes of the missing men being alive is now abandoned. It appears that two other miners name Mellor and Durran were injured at the time the water broke through. In its passage it dislodged some stone in the roof where they were working. One of them is seriously injured, and it is feared that several of his ribs are broken.

In the flooding of Barrowshaw Colliery, John Buckley, aged forty-five, Thomas Jones, aged twenty-eight, and John Willy, aged fifteen, drowned. The pit was evidently de-watered for the trustees of John Mayall to be recorded as running the pit in 1879.

Barstacks: Saddleworth, near Oldham
Mr John Mills worked this colliery during the 1840s. There is no other information on this pit.

Bayley Field: Flowery Field, Hyde
I have little information on this pit, other than the fact that it was being worked in 1805 by the Ashton Brothers, and by T. J. and J. Ashton in 1880s. It appears to have been beside the Bayley Field Mills, south-west of Hyde Park. The Ashton brothers were by all accounts mill owners who worked the mines for their own use. There is one report of an accident on 23 March 1852 at the Bayley Field Colliery at Newton Moor in Cheshire, when an explosion of firedamp killed Thomas Lovett.

Bent Grange: Oldham★, SD 922 053 approx.
This pit was worked by Thomas Butterworth from around the mid-1840s, and the colliery was abandoned *c.*1869. During its short life, the Bent Grange Colliery was the scene of two major mining disasters, which claimed the lives of thirty-six men and boys, as well as several other incidents. The colliery is shown to have had just one shaft on a map of 1851, though a report below stated that a new shaft was being sunk in 1850. The Royley Mine was worked at Bent Grange at a depth of 222 yards. A boiler house was located some distance away, and close to this was a reservoir that supplied the water to the engine. A footpath gained access to the pit from Highfield House, and what appears to have been a rough

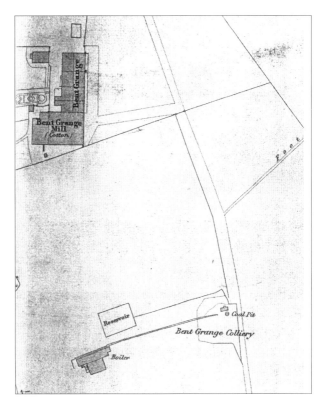

Bent Grange Colliery, map of 1848.

track was probably the colliery access road. 'On the surface there was an absence of that order and regularity which is seen in connection with larger concerns' said a report in July 1853. The Bent Grange Colliery was in the location of Grange Art Centre, Oldham, near which there is also a Grange Street. The Catalogue of Plans of Abandoned Mines gives little other information: Bent Grange (a) Oldham; (b) COAL; (d) 97 NW (1922) G7.

On 12 February 1845, the *Manchester Guardian* reports on an inquest into a 'Fatal Accident in Collieries':

On Friday last an inquest was held at the White Lion public-house, Maygate Lane, North Moor, by Mr Molesworth, deputy coroner respecting the death of a coal miner named Hamlet Steekley. It appeared that on the 3rd inst. whilst the deceased was at work in the colliery at Bent Grange, Oldham, belonging to Mr Thomas Butterworth, a large tub for conveying water out of the mine was being drawn up an inclined plane, on a sort of frame-work, with unusual violence, by the rope at the top of the shaft. The tub came in contact with the unfortunate man, throwing him down and seriously injuring his spine.

He was deprived of the use of his legs and thighs, and mortification ensued to such an extent that the poor man died on Wednesday last, at his residence, North Moor.

He was about 38 years of age, and has left a wife but no family. The engineer at the pit stated that the rope was wound more rapidly than usual, because the signal had only been rung once. He therefore supposed that something else other than water was being sent up. The jury returned a verdict of 'Died from injuries on the spine, by a carriage in a coal mine passing over him'.

On 6 March 1847, the *Manchester Guardian* relates:

On Saturday last, as a coal miner of the name John Spurr, was at work in the colliery at Bent Grange, belonging to Mr Thomas Butterworth, he accidentally got in to a passage which was so narrow, that a wagon, in passing him, thrust him with great violence against the side of the mine. The poor fellow was extremely crushed that he died about five o'clock on Sunday morning, at his residence at Highlands, near Royton. The deceased was about 32 years of age, and has left a wife and family'.

In a more fortunate case, the *Manchester Guardian*, 19 May 1849 notes:

Narrow Escape. About half past three o'clock, on Wednesday morning, the policeman on duty at the bottom of Bent, was attracted by a light in a coal pit cabin, when he entered and found a man asleep by the fire, and his clothes almost entirely consumed, but strange to say, his body was not seriously burnt.

He was brought before the magistrates, and presented a strange spectacle. He said he was drunk when he went into the cabin. He was committed as a vagrant for 14 days.

A major pit disaster is recorded at the Bent Grange Colliery in October 1850. Ventilation at the Bent Grange Pit at this time was implemented by partitioning the shaft into two sections with timbers and brattice cloth. The winding engine turned a fan of 3ft diameter, which forced air into the workings, but only when winding was in operation. At other times water raised from the workings was turned back down the mineshaft to cause ventilation current. However the men at Bent Grange all felt that the ventilation circuit was adequate. In 1849 the shaft was sunk further to a depth of 221 yards to make contact with the Riley Mine. The pit workings were then opened out in a north and south direction on either side of the shaft. By October 1850, the south level was about 140 yards from the shaft and the north level around 60 yards from the shaft. The workings were of the 'pillar and stall' method whereby 3ft pillars were left to support the roof, the coal between (the 'stall') was taken to a width of 8 or 9ft, and around 5ft high.

A new shaft was in the process of being sunk as a downcast shaft and was around 40 yards deep. A new fan for this shaft of 9ft in diameter had been ordered. On Wednesday 9 October 1850 a tremendous thunderstorm beat down on the Manchester and Oldham Districts accompanied by lightning and heavy downpours of rain. Around a quarter past one that day, Thomas Newton, of Edge Lane, Royton, a collier at the pit, was walking away from the pit shaft having finished his work for the day, when he heard a 'rush of wind up the pit'. His instant reaction was that the pit had fired, and he and others with him ran back to the pit mouth. Over 600ft below ground, the shaft was a scene of chaos and destruction. The cloth and timber partition had been blown down by the blast deep within the bowels of the earth, and yet there was no loud report as would be expected from a colliery explosion. Smoke, soot and a sulphurous yellow cloud now drifted up from the silent hell in the workings far below. Forty-two men and boys had entered the workings at Bent Grange Colliery that morning, and as a number had made their way out of the pit prior to the explosion, the management had little idea who was still down the pit. Thomas Butterworth, the colliery owner, was in the town, a mere 500 or 600 yards from the pit when he heard of the disaster, and was on the scene within minutes.

His first priority was saving the lives of those underground, or at least getting those less fortunate creatures to the surface. The foreman, William Lane, along with another person descended the smoke-filled shaft in a makeshift hopper. Slowly, the hopper was lowered into the depths until, at 80 yards below ground, the signal was given to raise them back to the surface. The foulness of the air in the shaft prevented any further exploration for around an hour, when another attempt was made. The basket was lowered to within seven or eight yards of the pit-shaft bottom, when they were compelled to leave it and make their way through a mass of tangled timber and brattice cloth that blocked further progression. With difficulty they wormed their way through the blockage, and with means of a rope completed their hazardous journey. Near the mouth of the shaft they found John Jones, John Lane, Daniel Dunkerley, and several others, all burnt, bruised and in shock. The rescuers sent these men up the pit, before searching for others. At the top of a small tunnel some five or six yards from the shaft they came across six dead bodies.

The air in this part of the mine, although only yards from the shaft, was too thick and un-breathable to carry on. The two rescuers retreated and were drawn to the surface. The foreman, William Lane, was so exhausted on arrival at the surface that he collapsed and had to be removed to his home, where he remained ill for some time. The scene on the surface of the colliery must have presented a pitiful sight, as hundreds of mourners gathered in the downpour awaiting news of their loved ones. Seeing the effects of the foul air on the rescuers, the men on the surface were disinclined to follow the rescue attempts in the underground holocaust. Mr Butterworth offered a bonus to the gathering of miners, yet still refused to go himself. Samuel Scholes and a man named Nathan presented themselves, and within a short time succeeded in sending up William Greenhalgh, alive but a little injured, with burns on his back and legs. The rescuers were again forced to retreat from the workings due to foul air. Around 4 o'clock, William Mason and a man named Geary made yet another attempt into the pit workings and managed to succeed in getting Daniel Dunkerley, still alive, to the part of the shaft blocked by debris. Daniel was a bulky, tall man, and unable to get through the small aperture in the timbers through to the hopper. William Mason returned to the surface and returned down the pit with a ladder, but by the time they had got back down to Dunkerley he was dead. Leaving Daniel where he lay, the pair made renewed efforts to find anyone who was still alive. Geary found the body of his brother, Edward, who had died, some seven or eight yards from the bottom of the pit shaft. Other would-be rescuers had now plucked up courage, and more hastened attempts were made to find any of those still alive. Two or three men were found alive and sent out of the pit, but beyond a few yards from the shaft the air was totally un-breathable. Rescue was again halted. Between ten and eleven o'clock at night, William Mason again descended into the workings, and was able to find George Clough alive near the mouth of the shaft, and he was brought up the pit.

Intermittent explorations between then and five o'clock in the morning by William Mason, Thomas Mason, Benjamin Roberts and William Beswick recovered a further nine dead bodies, many within yards of the shaft bottom. Rescuers descended into the sump hole where the mine water collects at the shaft bottom, and found the dead bodies of three boys: Jonas Fox, Bartholomew Bambling and James Parkin. During the course of the following twenty-four hours, several more dead men and boys were recovered. At five o'clock that evening, on examination of a list of men employed, only one man was missing. Edmund Butterworth, married and about forty years of age was to be the last victim of the Bent Grange Colliery Disaster to remain underground.

The dead men already recovered were removed through the grieving crowds to the White Hart public house, Low Moor; the injured were conveyed home for treatment. More pitiful scenes surrounded the White Hart, where fourteen bodies were laid out in an upper room as friends became anxious to see and identify those who had suffered. The room presented a spectacle not easily described. Upon tables and trestles and barrels and planks, disfigured and burnt bodies of the unfortunate men and boys littered the room. Some defied identification, while others had little if any marks upon their bodies, almost as if they were asleep. One little fellow (Bartholomew Bambling) aged just twelve years had lost his left eye, probably as a consequence of being hurled against the side of the workings by the force of the blast. A public subscription was set up for the relief of the widows and orphans; Joseph Saxon pledged an immediate 20 guineas to the fund. When the explosion occurred several men and boys were at the bottom of the shaft, getting into the cage, and these escaped uninjured.

One boy was said to have seized hold of the cage as it was going up, but after clinging for about seven or eight yards, he fell, and was killed. The total death toll of the Bent Grange Colliery Disaster was put at sixteen:

Bartholomew Bambling, 12, a drawer

Thomas Bramwell, 21 or 22, a drawer

Edmund Butterworth, 40, left a wife and five children

James Butterworth, 21, married (probably brother of the owner of the pit)

Daniel Dunkerley, 31, left a wife and child

Robert Fidiham, 25, wife and two children

Benjamin Fox, 34, married, no children

Jonas Fox (brother of Benjamin), 17, a drawer

Edward Geary, 32, wife and three children

James Jackson, 54, married, no children

William Lees, 32, wife and two children

Ralph Mytton, from Wigan, only in Oldham about one month

George Newton, 19, drawer

John Newton, 19, drawer

John Parkin, 13, drawer

John Stott, 47, wife and six children

A number of men and boys survived the disaster, though suffered minor burns. John Lane, a married man aged forty, was slightly burned. Robert Lane, his son, and a drawer at the colliery, was slightly injured, as was George Clough, a twenty-five year-old drawer, married, but with no children. William Greenhalgh, aged twenty-five, had slight burns on the chest and arms. James Halkyard, a twenty-two year-old drawer, married, but no children, was injured, and so was John Jones. It is sad to say but, as far as I am aware, there is no memorial to those who perished in this or the other Bent Grange Colliery disaster in the town. In fact, the Oldham and Ashton Districts have little to commemorate these terrible events, and surely this should now be rectified.

The *Manchester Guardian* reports a less serious accident, 21 December 1850:

On Thursday morning about 11 o'clock while a number of men were employed putting on a new rope (at Bent Grange Colliery) a piece of rail got entangled and was thrown down the pit. Its fall was fortunately broken, but nevertheless it struck a man named John Newton, who was at the bottom and cut his flesh severely. A rumour instantly flew through the town that a portion of roof had fallen, and that several people were injured. Messrs Fletcher, Kershaw, Dunkerley and Earnshaw were immediately on the spot, but beyond dressing Newton's leg there was no need for their services.

Another incident that thankfully passed without injury is noted in the *Manchester Guardian,* 18 January 1851:

Accident in a coal pit. On Tuesday morning last, a slight accident occurred at the Bent Grange Coal Pit, while a wagon of coal was being wound up. When only a few yards from the bottom, the wagon met with some obstruction, and the engine which is a powerful one, continued to work at its usual speed causing the headstocks and all the top gearing to give way, and it fell with a tremendous crash. A rumour instantly ran through the town that another serious accident had occurred at the pit, and a great number of people were soon on the spot. We are happy to say not a single individual was hurt by this accident.

Exactly five months later, a tragic incident is recorded in the *Manchester Guardian*, 18 June 1851:

Supposed suicide in a coal pit. On Monday morning, as the workmen descended the Bent Grange coal-pit, they discovered by the broken cross-trees that some heavy body had fallen down the shaft. On further examination, a man's body, shockingly injured was found in the well hole, and proved to be that of Thomas Tristham, aged 26, a clogger of West Street. The deceased had last been seen on Saturday night, and it appears that he had lived unhappily with his family.

Thomas Butterworth found himself called before the Inspector of Coal Mines, as reported in the *Manchester Guardian*, 28 October 1856:

Violation of the Colliery Regulation. At the petty sessions, yesterday, Mr Thomas Butterworth, proprietor of the Bent Grange Colliery, was summoned by Joseph Dickinson, Inspector of Coal Mines for the Manchester District for neglecting to employ a fireman as required by the rules of the colliery. Mr Dickinson stated that by the Act 18 and 19 passed last session of Parliament, and which came into operation last January, each colliery owner was required to draw up a set of special rule for the manager of his mines, and those rules had to receive the sanction of the Home Secretary. One of these rules required that in every colliery where firedamp prevailed a fireman should be appointed to go down and examine the workings every morning before the men commenced their work. The colliery in question was notoriously known as a fiery one, twenty persons having been killed by one explosion a few years ago, and another explosion having previously occurred by which several lives were lost.

He [the inspector] visited the colliery on the 6th inst. and found a place in the down brow giving off firedamp in such quantities that if anything occurred to obstruct the ventilation, such as accidentally leaving a door open, a fall in the roof, or a defect in the bratticing, a dangerous accumulation of firedamp might readily be occasioned, and owning to the want of a fireman it might not have been detected, until it had exploded, probably causing the loss of many lives. From the warnings the proprietor had previously had of the destructive effects of firedamp, and the necessity of taking proper precautions, this breach of the rules was, in his [Mr Dickinson's] opinion, wholly inexcusable, and he asked for the infliction of the highest penalty, namely £5. He then gave Mr Butterworth notice in accordance with the provisions of the Act, requiring the proprietor to appoint a fireman, and added that he was liable to a penalty of £1 per day, as long as he continued without one. Mr William Blackburn, viewer of the pit, stated that there was no fireman employed at the mine, and in cross examination, he said that the mine was one of the best ventilated in the district. Mr Ponsonby, for the defendant, contended that no fireman was required, as Mr. Butterworth had made great alterations to improve the ventilation of the pit, which was now in a better condition than any other in the district. The Magistrate inflicted a penalty of £2 and costs.

Three separate incidents are recorded in the Mines Inspectors Reports for the next few years: 'October 22nd. Bent Grange Colliery. James Williamson, aged 30, crushed against roof while riding tram up engine brow' (1859); 'Bent Grange Colliery, February 27th. Daniel Mills, aged 18 killed through fall of roof in wagon road' (1863); 'January 1st. Bent Grange Colliery. James Lord burned while blasting. Died 29th January' (1864).

The *Colliery Guardian*, 19 March 1864, sees Thomas Butterworth charged under employment laws: 'Thomas Butterworth, the owner of the Bent Grange Colliery at Oldham, Lancashire was charged with employing below ground a boy named James Edwin Cook between the age of ten and twelve years without a certificate to say that he could read and write, or that he attended school for three hours a day'.

Fifteen years later, a letter to the *Oldham Chronicle*, 15 March 1879, asks for information about the site, which is 'now filled up':

Bent Grange Coalpit. Can any reader of the 'Notes and Queries' give me an account of the Bent Grange Coalpit, now filled up? I see there is a large mass of brickwork cemented together in Mr J. Green's brickyard, which seems to be part of the chimney bed of the late pit, but now unfortunately, little good only for unpaved roads. An attempt has been made to separate the cement from the bricks, but it has proved a failure, as the former article has gone as hard as rock. Near to where this coalpit now stands a stump about two feet six inches high, whether to mark anything or not I cannot say, but desire to be informed, if any kind person would so oblige. Almost opposite the West End Mill Company's reeling rooms, in the open space of land there are large flags laid flat on the earth, which cover either an old pit shaft or air-hole. Can any reader say what year this was erected, and its real use?

A correspondent in the same newspaper, dated 29 March 1879, was able to supply some details to his query:

In answer to 'S.C.' I have to say that this pit was sunk after the first explosion in 1850, when 16 lives were lost. It was called the 'New Pit' the old pit having been worked out many years. They got the Neddy Mine at the old pit, and at the new pit they got the Royley Mine, in which an explosion occurred on the 1st of July, 1853 when twenty lives were lost. On October 9th, 1850, 16 lives were lost at the old pit. They were filled up about the year 1869. The block of brickwork in

W. Green's brickyard is the bottom of the chimney, and the stump about 2ft 6in out of the ground is one of three that formed a stile over the footpath at one time called the Pingate. The large flags opposite West End Mill are to cover an old coalpit called Highfield Colliery, which was sunk in 1848/49 but abandoned in a few years as worthless. The flags have been over the pit about twenty years, though it has not been worked for 30 years or thereabouts. It once belonged to the father of the writer of this note, and three other working miners.

Besom Hill 1: between Shaw and Sholver, near Oldham
Besom Hill Colliery was worked by William Higginbotham in the 1840s, and, in 1854, worked by James Wilson. This pit was at the sharp bend in the A672, the Ripponden Road, at Besom Hill, Oldham.

Below the extensive old quarry is an enclosed fenced off area, inside of which is a large mound. This is the old shaft of the Besom Hill Colliery. The locals around here no doubt gathered the twigs to make the Besom brooms in times past. There was also a Besom Hill Fireclay Mine at work in 1879, by W.H. Bentley. The Besom Hill Collieries and Fireclay Works are all under one heading in the Catalogue of Plans of Abandoned Mines (1928), suggesting that the workings were all interconnected: Besom Hill Nos 1, 2, 3 (a) Oldham; (b) COAL and FIRECLAY: Mountain (abandoned 3 October 1914); (d) 89 SE (1910) H4,5.

Besom Hill 2: between Shaw and Sholver, near Oldham★, SD 952 083
A colliery at work in 1854, and worked by James Taylor. The colliery is marked on the OS map of 1891. This pit may have had connections with the above

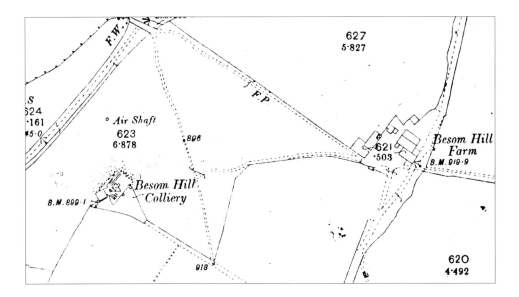

Besom Hill Colliery, map of 1891.

pit, it being a short distance away. At the bottom of Wells Road off the A672, a lane continues to the Besom Hill Farm. At the start of this lane, a footpath goes through two fields to a fence enclosed area containing a number of trees. This is the site of the other Besom Hill Colliery, and extensive colliery waste litters the area. From here can be seen the A672 and colliery spoil from the Besom Hill Colliery No.1. An air shaft is shown on a map of 1891 to the north of the colliery. One of the Besom Hill Collieries was abandoned in 1914, but I do not know which one this was. On abandonment the pit employed just two underground men, and was worked by William Dransfield & Sons.

Black Ridings: Chadderton, SD 906 046 approx.
A colliery marked on the OS map of 1844, appears to have been located near Ramsey Street, Nibble Nook, Chadderton, and was worked by the Chamber Colliery Co. Two coal pits are also shown to the south-west of this colliery. The Black Ridings Colliery worked the Bent Mine at a depth of 160 yards. Further information, albeit sparse, can be gleaned from the Catalogue of Plans of Abandoned Mines (1928): Black Ridings (a) Oldham; (b) COAL Higher Bent, Lower Bent or Peacock (1843); (c) Chamber Colliery Co. Ltd, Hollinwood, Oldham; (d) 97 SW (1922) A5.

Boarshaw (Clough): Middleton
Boarshaw is, literally, Boar's Wood: the wood where the wild boar could be found. The first pit at Boarshaw was one named the 'Old Pit', situated on land that is now the Boarshaw Playing Fields, between the canal and the cemetery. This colliery shows up on the 1844 Ordnance Survey map. The Boarshaw Pit referred to below was what was known as the new pit of the mid-1850s. This was located on the spare land behind the houses on Green Lane and Valley Road. The slag heaps are still evident here, and the place was a popular spot for coal picking during the many coal disputes. The pit was worked by Messrs Hague (or perhaps Haigh) & Co., although the Oldham, Middleton & Rochdale Colliery Co. worked the pit by 1869. The seam worked was the Arley Mine, and extraction took place towards the Rochdale Canal in one direction and as far as Barrowfells in the other. Much of the output from Boarshaw went by the Rochdale Canal, and a loading bay belonging to the colliery can still be seen on the right-hand side of Boarshaw Bridge looking towards Chadderton. The colliery was abandoned in 1874. Catalogue of Plans of Abandoned Mines (1928) Boarshaw (a) Chadderton/Middleton; (b) COAL Royley (abandoned 1874); (d) 96 NE (1923) B8, 9: C8, 9, 10, 11: D8, 9, 10, 11.

An indication of when the pit was being sunk may be found in a brief and sad account in the Mines Inspectors Report for the year 1854: 'October 1st. Boarshaw Colliery, worked by Thomas Roscow and Co. Robert Heap fell down sinking pit while trying to land a water barrel'.

Another accident, this time an explosion, is reported in the *Manchester Guardian*, 22 March 1857:

Colliery Explosion, Two Men Killed. On Friday morning, a colliery accident occurred at the Boarshaw Clough Colliery, by which two persons named William Wolstenholme [it appears that this person is named Joseph in the Mines Inspectors Report], and James Underwood lost their lives. Wolstenholme, a young man of 18, worked as a banksman, Underwood, aged 50, was the underlooker. The mine is a new one and belongs to Messrs Hague [sic] and Co. Much water has been accumulating in the pit, and stopped the works.

Means have been adopted to diminish it, and the two men descended on Friday morning, between six and seven o'clock to ascertain whether the water had increased or decreased. Underwood, although the day before they had been cautioned against using naked lights, took with him a common oil lamp, with naked flame. As soon as they had got down a tremendous explosion took place, and killed them both, besides doing other damage to the property. Wolstenholme was taken out in a short time, but on Saturday Underwood had not been found, and he is supposed to be in the water. An inquest will be held tomorrow, Tuesday.

Booth Hill: Royton
I have little information on this colliery other than what is recorded in the Catalogue of Plans of Abandoned Mines (1928): Booth Hill (a) Royton; (b) COAL Blendfire, Little (abandoned 2 March 1889); (d) 97 NW (1922) D8, 9: The map reference should give its location, for those interested in further research.

Boothstead: Denton
Mainly a fireclay mine, but coal was mined here. Listed under 'Leadbeaters Ltd, Grotton Brickworks, Oldham Lancashire' in the *Guide to the Coalfields* (1948).

Bower: Hollinwood, near Oldham, SD 903 026
Details of owners of colliery are: Messrs Marland, 1869, with J.W.R. Marland and Co., 1879, William and R. Marland, Hollinwood, Oldham, 1896. The coal seams worked were the Colonel, Foxholes, Great and Major, and the colliery employed 186 underground and 29 on the surface in 1896. The under-manager at this time was James Goddard. The pit was off Bower Lane behind the railway station at Hollinwood. A tramway ran from the colliery in a south-western direction to the Rochdale Canal, which was used for some of the output of the colliery.

Two accounts in the *Annals of Oldham 1787-1830* record tragic deaths near the site: 'March 14th 1803, James Tetlow, a hatter of Hollinwood in a fit of despair drowned himself in a pit near that place'. And, later: '14th September, 1803, Rebecca Taylor, of Old Can, Northmoor drowned herself in a pit at Bower, near Hollinwood. She had quarrelled with her sweetheart the night before, she was aged 19 years'.

The Catalogue of Plans of Abandoned Mines tells us the following: Bower (a) Chadderton Failsworth; (b) COAL Moston (abandoned 1891); (d) 97 SW E3, 4: F3:; Bower (a) Chadderton Failsworth; (b) COAL Big (abandoned March 1919)

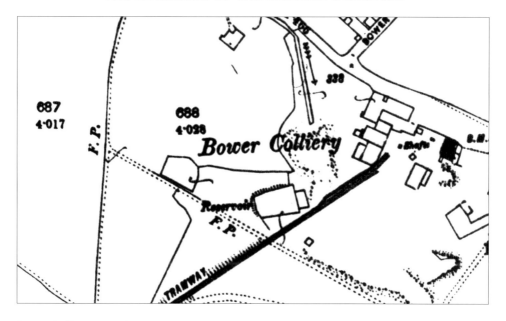

Bower Colliery, map of 1891.

Foxholes (abandoned July 1908); (d) 96 SE (1923) C11, 12: D11, 12: F12: 97 SW (1922) D1, 2, 3: E1, 2, 3, 4: F1, 2, 3: G1, 2.

An accident is recorded in the Mines Inspectors Report for the year 1861: 'December 30th. Bower Colliery. James Coley killed through explosion of firedamp. Died 7th January 1862'.

The colliery owners were charged under safety laws, as recorded in the *Colliery Guardian*, 25 January 1862: 'Marsland, Bailey and Booth owners of the Bower Colliery at Hollinwood were charged under the Collieries Act, for not providing sufficient ventilation, that safety lamps were not locked, that there had been neglect to send in notice of an explosion that caused the death of a collier, and that they had employed a boy aged under 12 years'. In addition to this, Mines Inspectors Reports for the years 1866–1868 record three fatal accidents: 'January 8th. Bower Colliery. William Beswick killed through fall of roof while setting props' (1866); 'November 6th. Bower Colliery. Henry Collett killed through wagon running against him' (1867); 'April 16th. Bower Colliery. John Whitaker killed through stone falling from roof of mine' (1868). The *Colliery Guardian*, 2 December 1921, records more casualties in another accident: 'One man was killed and two others injured at the Bower Colliery Hollinwood, Oldham through a large fall of roof'.

In the *Oldham Newspaper* of 21 February 1953, we find some interesting information on the history of the site:

> I have been very interested in the recent article concerning the Marlands and Bower
> Colliery, and as the grandson of Robert Marland, who was for a time a partner in

Bower Colliery, Chadderton's last pit, closed *c.*1920.

the colliery undertaking in Bower Lane, perhaps my contribution may be of interest. It is true that the Marlands came from Hurst originally, and that they were colliers, but I cannot say whether or not they actually sunk the Bower Pit. However, my grandfather, Robert Marland was born on December 20th 1835 to James and Ruth Marland, the father being described on the birth certificate as a collier residing at Hurst. There were three sons of this marriage, William, Robert and James.

At the time of my grandfather's marriage on May 1st 1860 to Betty Siddall, his father, James Marland is described on the marriage certificate, as a coal proprietor residing at Hurst Nook, Hurst. It is probable that James Marland was even at this time connected with the Bower Colliery, for when my father, who was the third son was born on August 15th 1868, Robert and Betty Marland were residing in Bower Lane, my grandfather being described on the birth certificate as a colliery proprietor. There were seven children of this marriage, five of whom (four boys and a girl) all survived, twins dying in early life.

Bowling Green: Windsor Road, Werneth, Oldham
A colliery of this name was worked by Greenwoods, Baron & Tattersall in 1854, though there is an earlier reference to coal pits at Coppice Nook. The first account of an accident is in the *Annals of Oldham 1787-1839*: 'February 6th 1806, two young men going down a coal-pit to their work near Coppice Nook, the rope broke and they fell to the bottom and were most shockingly bruised. One having both his legs, one thigh and an arm broken, but hopes are still entertained

of both their recovery'. Another tragic death is reported in the *Manchester Guardian*, 2 December 1843:

On Saturday last as Thomas Taylor, a boy of 13 years was at work in the Bowling Green Pit, Coppice Nook, Oldham, a large amount of coal rock about six foot long, eighteen inches broad and fourteen inches thick fell accidentally upon him from the roof of the mine. His back appeared to be broken, and he was otherwise dreadfully injured. He was taken out of the pit alive, but died shortly after reaching the dwelling of his father, James Taylor, toll keeper, Hollinwood. The inquest returned a verdict of 'accidental death'.

Broad Oak: Hurst, Ashton-under-Lyne

A colliery worked by Broad Oak Colliery Co., of Ashton-under-Lyne, with ninety-seven men underground at the Broad Oak 'Nook' and twelve underground at the Broad Oak No.2 in 1896. The colliery manager at this time was Arthur Miller, and the pit was mining the Great Seam. Evidence of an earlier colliery named Broad Oak is recorded in a directory of 1828, when it was being worked by Lees, Jones & Booth.

The *Manchester Guardian*, 4 February 1846, clarifies the details of an accident, and calms worries that a major disaster had occurred:

Coal Pit Accident. On Monday a report was very prevalent in this town (Ashton-under-Lyne) that a most serious accident had taken place at the Broad Oak Colliery, attended by the loss of many lives. We are happy to say however, that the accident, although serious, was much exaggerated. It appears that for some days past, the coal behind the boiler, and engine-house wall at the bottom of one of the pits belonging to Lees, Jones, Booth, and Co. has been on fire. The miners have been engaged ever since this was known to be the case, and in endeavouring to put it out. But the task has been extremely difficult, in consequence of the great heat arising from the burning mass, which is about 50 yards in extent. The men have for some days been unable to get near, so as to throw water onto it. A drift way has been cut in order that they might continue to direct the water by means of a fire engine, which has been taken down the pit for the purpose. The steam having got in to the roof, on Monday morning, just as the men were changing shifts, when nearly one hundred tons of rock and dirt from above fell with a tremendous crash. Fortunately the men had not commenced work, otherwise there would have been no less than twenty of the poor fellows crushed to death. The persons seriously injured were, John Fletcher, the engineer, who was examining the joints of a pipe near the boiler, when a portion of the roof struck him, and broke his collar bone, put out his right shoulder, nearly cut off his left thumb, and injured him on the head and other parts of the body. A miner named John Garside, was buried in the mass near the boilers. A piece of rock struck him on the head, making a most dreadful gash. This poor fellow was forced against the nearly red hot bricks in the fire-hole, and when extricated his back was found to be almost burned to a cinder. A boy named Henry Marland, received slight injuries to the leg. No others were hurt. The men gave great praise to a miner named Marland, father of the boy who was hurt, for the exertions he used in extricating those who were partly buried in the ruins. The sufferers are doing as well as can be expected. The fire is not out.

Another accident that could have been much worse if there had not been such a quick response is recorded in the *Colliery Guardian*, 6 July 1861:

> About eight o'clock on Monday morning, as John Sidebottom aged about 18, the son of Joseph Sidebottom, West Street, Harrison Houses, Ridgehill Lane Staleybridge, was at work in the Old Pit at the Broadoak Colliery, on the Oldham and Ashton Road, belonging to Messrs Lees and Booth (The Fairbottom Colliery Company, Oldham) a large stone and a considerable quantity of earth fell upon him from the roof. Fortunately a boy saw the accident, and an alarm being given, the father of the young man and two other men assisted by a lad, were immediately at work trying to extricate him from his perilous position. In about a quarter of an hour they succeeded, and the injured young man was taken home in a cart, and attended to by Mr Hopwood, surgeon of Staleybridge. Sidebottom was much crushed about his abdomen, and it will be some time before he is well.

The death of John Gartside is reported in the *Colliery Guardian*, 16 August 1862, and is made even more tragic by the news that he was planning to leave the pit the following day:

> An inquest was held at the Wellington Inn, Bardsley, near Oldham on the body of John Gartside aged 16, son of John Gartside, colliery manager. The deceased up to the day of his death worked at the Broadoak Colliery. On the Tuesday night previous he had just had his supper in the pit, and had just got up, when without any warning a stone fell from the roof. He was rescued as soon as possible, but he was so fearfully injured that he died a short time afterwards. We understand the youth was about to leave the pit the next morning to find other work. 'Accidental death' was recorded.

About a decade later, the site came under criticism from the Inspector of Mines, as reported in the *Colliery Guardian*, 23 May 1873:

> At the Ashton County Sessions on Wednesday, Mr Dickinson, Inspector of Mines summoned Sampson Maiden, one of the members of the Broad Oak Colliery for having a pit-shaft unfenced. The shaft was near a public footpath, last March a woman threw herself into the pit, which was nearly full of water, and she drowned. At that time the company had only been in possession of the pit sixteen days, and afterwards they fenced it off. The former owners had several times built

fences around the shaft, but these had been demolished by persons unknown. The company was fined 20s.

Broadbent: Royton Moss, Oldham

Sometimes called Moss Colliery, this pit was at work during the early 1840s under a partnership of Milne, Travis and Milne. An accident occurred in 1845, and was recorded in the *Manchester Guardian,* 27 August 1845:

> Accident at a Colliery. On Tuesday an inquest was held by Mr Dearden, coroner at the Wagon and Horses, Higginshaw Lane, Royton, on the body of a collier named John Lees. He died on Sunday in consequence of the injuries he received by a piece of wood called a 'cut' falling upon him whilst at work in the colliery of Messrs Milne and Travis, Royton Moss, on the Tuesday previous. The cut or plank fell from the top of the pit, a distance of one hundred and forty yards, and most dreadfully injured the poor fellow. The deceased was 40 years of age. Verdict: 'Accidental death'.

A safety issue was taken up by the Inspector of Mines, and John Mayall was summoned (*Colliery Guardian,* 11 September 1858):

> Mr Dickinson, Inspector of Mines put two charges for the magistrates against Mr John Mayall owner of the Broadbent Colliery, Barrowshaw, Oldham. The first charge was for neglecting to provide a break [sic] for the engine used for raising and lowering the men, the second was for not providing an indicator to point out the position of the cage in its ascent and descent. Mr Dickinson visited the colliery on August 11th and found the break and indicator wanting. A boy named Charles Wrigley aged between 15 and 16 had the entire charge of the engine. The defence was that there was a pump connected with the engine, and that was a sufficient break, and a piece of hemp was tied to the rope to act as an indicator. These, Mr Dickinson said, were not in accordance with the requirements of the Act, which had been approved of by Mr Mayall when submitted to him and other colliery owners. He considered the use of a pump as a break highly inappropriate. A fine of £5 and costs was imposed in both cases.

Broadcarr: Higher Hartshead

This colliery was located to the left of the aptly named Colliers Arms, and a large area of colliery spoil marks the spot, a capped air shaft can be seen on the left-hand side of the track that runs past the old pit. The pit is marked on a tithe map of 1861, although there is no reference to it in a list of mines for 1868, nor in any other. I am afraid I have no other details of the pit, not even the name of the colliery owner.

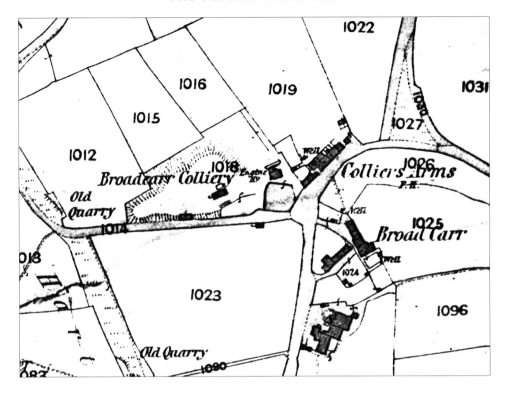

Broadcarr Colliery, map of 1861.

Broadway Lane: Oldham

Must have been in the Broadway/Haggate Holden Fold area of Oldham. The pit is mentioned in the Report on Child Labour, in 1842, when Stanley and Schofield were working the colliery. At this time it employed fifty-two men and youths aged eighteen years and over, twenty-four aged thirteen to eighteen years, and twenty aged less than thirteen years. Evidence given in the report includes:

> Benjamin Stanley, going on 12. November 4th 1841. Does not know how old he is, works in Broadway-lane Pit, wagons, his butty (older waggoner) is 'Jack'. It's not hard work, likes it. Cannot read or write; two and two are four; two more make five, is son of Edmund Stanley. [Signed] BENJAMIN STANLEY.

And another example:

> Arthur Gordon, going on 9. November 4th 1841. Is going on nine, gets into pit about six, his butty (older waggoner) is William Gordon, his brother; does not know how much he earns, his father takes his wages. Has been to school since four years old, can scarce go through the alphabet. Is son of John Gordon. [Signed] ARTHUR (X) GORDON, mark.

As well as:

> William Gordon, going on 14. November 4th 1841. Is a waggoner in the same pit with his father; does not know how far it is to the further end, has been there 30 times to day. 'All his life since he started' has been going to Sunday school, has been going to night school six or eight months, has been working in the pit ever since he was eight years old. 'Can read, but not so weel [sic]; can read a bit in Testament; canna write, canna count much'. [Signed] WILLIAM (X) GORDON, mark.

Joseph Byrom, bookkeeper to Messrs Stanley and Schofield, Broadway Lane Colliery, speaks about the employment of youths, on 3 November 1841:

> The engine employed at these works is high pressure, and is managed by an adult. He is upwards of 30, it is not because the engine is high pressure that an adult is employed, but because of the danger, in employing young children, that they may wind over the coals and the men. This applies equally to low pressure as to high. A person under 16 or 18 years of age ought not to be at such an occupation at all. Judges from his own feelings. The men themselves think little about this or any subject until an accident happens. But they will sometimes turn out against an engineer or banksman who they think does not do his duty. The engineer has 18s a week, and his predecessor had 24s. These wages are paid entirely for safety, in preference to employing young children or persons, as in the case of other employers. These, if they are to save the cost of safety in wages, ought, at all events before they employ very young engineers, to be required to provide some mechanical means of saving from destruction such persons as may be overwound as a consequence. [Signed] JOSEPH BYROM.

Brook: Crompton Fold
These pits, probably drift workings, are shown on a tithe map of 1847, and appear to have been an extension of the Old Brook Colliery. Both these pits worked the sides of Old Brook (stream) that runs through the Brushes Clough area.

Browns: Crompton Fold, near Oldham
This colliery was worked in 1854 by John and Thomas Mills, who are listed as having also worked the Brushes Colliery in 1842. The pit was located north of Browns Barn, now a ruin, below Slences to the north of Brushes Clough, Crompton Fold. The pit was 63 yards to the Gannister Mine, according to the geological survey. The Catalogue of Plans of Abandoned Mines gives little information other than the location of the entrance. Browns (a) Crompton (b) COAL (d) 89 SE (1910) B3.

The coal owners thought nothing of employing young boys, and even females, to boost their profit, and John and Thomas Mills, on at least one occasion, were taken to court for breaking the rules, as reported in the *Manchester Guardian*:

'Employment of females in Mines. Owing to an intimidation of legal action which were about to be taken on this subject by the County Police Sergeant Scott, the practice of employing females in the coal-mines at Crompton, near Oldham has been entirely discontinued' (17 February 1844); 'The Employment of Young Boys in Collieries. At the Oldham Sessions, Messrs Joseph and John Mills, colliery owners of Crompton were summoned for employing two boys named Squire Dearden and James Heathorn to be in their mines, they having been under the age of ten years. They were convicted under a penalty of £5 and costs' (29 March 1844).

Brushes Clough: Crompton Fold SD 949 101
James Milne worked this colliery in 1828, employing just five men, and T&J Milnes in 1837, with eight men employed at this time. The Platt Brothers & Co., the Oldham machine manufacturers, were working the pit in 1879. The upcast and downcast shafts at the colliery can be seen by following a vague footpath on the right of the continuation of the reservoir spillway to the left of the road going to Brushes Clough Recreation Area, off the Buckstones Road (B6197).

Within a short distance the two capped shafts, marked with the familiar triangular concrete markers on a raised pit bank can be seen behind some stables/garages. The shafts are remarkably close together, maybe 10-12ft apart, and are recorded as being 12ft in diameter. The shafts were sunk 208ft to the Bassy Mine. The colliery had a tramway running down to Top o' th' Green, and then to Brushes Clough Works, a stone-crushing plant. There was another Brushes Clough Colliery at Crompton Fold worked by John and Thomas Mills in 1842, this is probably one of many coal pits, or small ventures, that worked this area of Brushes Clough. By 1896, J.R. Buckley was working the colliery, mining the coal from the Little Mine.

Seven men were employed underground, with three men on the surface. Edmund Buckley, no doubt some relation, was the colliery manager in 1896. The Brushes Clough area is littered with small spoil heaps and other indications of coal mining activities, in addition to the many stone quarries. The Catalogue of Plans gives a bit more information, with no less than three entries: Brushes Clough (a) Crompton; (b) COAL Half Yard, Foot, Yard (abandoned prior to 1886); (d) 89 SE (1910) B3: C3, 4: D3, 4; Brushes Clough (a) Crompton; (b) COAL Yard (abandoned January 1906); (d) 89 SE (1910) B5: C4, 5; Brushes Clough (a) Crompton; (b) FIRECLAY (abandoned June 1906); (d) 89 SE C3, 4: D3.

Bull's Head: Moorside
Little is known about this pit, which was listed in a mines index of 1869, when Thomas Mellowdew & Co. was working the colliery, as confirmed below. However, there is a Bull's Head public house on the Ripponden Road, at Moorside, to this day. The colliery may have been in this area. Based on evidence, the pit appears to have worked from a shaft.

One of the few sources of information is the Mines Inspectors Report, for the year 1869: 'April 29th. Bull's Head Colliery, Oldham worked by Thomas Mellowdew. George Haigh, aged 13 years jerked out of tub while descending, and killed'.

Burnedge: Shaw and Crompton
This colliery was advertised for sale in the *Manchester Guardian* of 30 June 1827 as follows:

> Valuable freehold estate and colliery situated in the township of Castleton in the Parish of Rochdale and Crompton in the Parish of Prestwich cum Oldham by order of the acting trustees and executor under the will of John Milnes and Charles Milnes, late of Marygate in the township of Castleton aforesaid, by Mr Richard Sellers at the house of George Trewhill of the Wellington Hotel, Rochdale in the county of Lancashire on Thursday 12th day of June 1827 at the hour of three in the afternoon, subject to such conditions of sale as will be produced…

There followed details of the coal works, which had a steam engine, and was subject to a surcharge of *6d* for every twenty-eight baskets, or fourteen horse loads raised. Apparently, 'in 1832, the pit at New Burnedge was using a 24hp steam engine' (see *Historical Sketches of Oldham* by E. Butterworth (1832)). The colliery was worked by Taylor Milne & Co. in 1842, with employment provided for thirty-two men and boys, and Taylor, Lord & Co. in 1846, and in 1851. A Burnedge Colliery shows up on a tithe map dated *c.*1848, near Stockfield, but is not listed in the Catalogue of Plans of Abandoned Mines published in 1928! An accident at the site is recorded in the *Manchester Guardian,* 24 April 1844:

> Colliery Accident at Crompton. On Friday last whilst a coal miner named James Greenwood was at work in the colliery near Burn Edge, [sic] Crompton, cutting through one of the pillars which supported the roof, a large mass of the overhanging earth fell upon him, instantly killing him. His back was broken, and his shoulders dreadfully injured. A similar occurrence happened to him only on the previous Wednesday, when he escaped without injury. The deceased was 31 years of age, and has left a wife and one child. He was noted as a race runner, and was generally known by the name 'Spanker'. On Saturday, Mr Dearden held an inquest on the body, at the Bull's Head, Threadmill, Crompton, when a verdict of 'accidental death' was recorded.

Two years later, the death of a young man is reported in the same newspaper, 4 February 1846:

> Shocking Accident. On Friday last, Mr. Dearden, coroner held an inquest at the Collier's Arms public house, near Castleton, on the body of a young man named

Thomas Greenwood. It appeared from the evidence that on the day previous, the unfortunate man was ascending one of the coal pits at Burnage [sic] Colliery belonging to Messrs Taylor, Lord and Co. and when within a few yards of the top of the pit, a nut flew off, the tub or cage was upset, and the young man fell to the bottom of the pit, a distance of about 80 yards, and was killed on the spot. He was 19 years of age. A verdict of 'Accidental death' was recorded.

In the summer of 1846, the *Manchester Guardian* recorded a similar accident, 11 July:

> Accident at a Colliery. On Wednesday last a man named Isaac Buckley, a joiner, the son of Mr John Buckley, farmer of Marl Field was descending a colliery at Burn Edge to go to his work, when the tub fell to the bottom of the pit in consequence of the rope slipping off the drum. The unfortunate man was dreadfully injured, one of his arms is broken, a leg severely injured and his head bruised. He still remains in a perilous position.

Chadderton: Chadderton
A colliery worked by William Jones & Co. during 1854, the pit does not appear to have worked for long.

A controversy regarding Sunday working at the site is reported in the *Manchester Guardian*, 24 April 1852:

> At the petty sessions on Thursday, eight persons were summoned by superintendent Jervis, for working on Sunday last, at a colliery at Chadderton. The pit belonging to Messrs Jones and Co. Mr Booth, the agent for the company, attended and stated, that the work was one of necessity, as it was to get out water, and lay certain workings dry. For a fortnight the men had been working day and night to prevent the accumulation of water, which would not only have caused a great loss to the proprietors, but would have also thrown about forty men out of employment. The work has now been completed, and there would be no further work necessary. The bench, after maturely considering the case, dismissed the defendant on payment of costs.

There is a record of a death in the Mines Inspectors Report for the year 1852: 'August 18th. Chadderton Colliery, worked by William Jones & Co. Thomas Wood, run over and killed by a wagon'.

Chamber (Lane): Chamber Lane, Oldham, 922 039
The pit was located off what is today Chamber Road, and was between Gainsborough Street and Kennedy Street. Little now remains of the colliery, except for a patch of colliery waste at the left-hand corner of Coppice Infant School. Notice too, *'Th'owd Pit House 1836'* at 129 Chamber Road. The shafts at Chamber Colliery are recorded as being 192 yards to the Lower Bent Mine on a

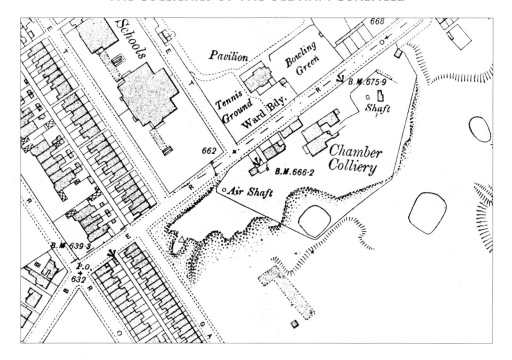

Chamber Colliery, map of 1906.

geological survey, considerably shallower than those at Chamberdam Colliery, which worked the same seam a short distance away, an indication of the steepness of the seam. Chamber Colliery, or Chamber Lane as it was then, all take their name from Chamber Hall, which dates from 1648. The pit dates from at least 1838 (see below) and, in 1842, was worked by Joseph Jones junior. William Jones & Co. worked the colliery in 1854; the Chamber Colliery Co. in 1869 and 1879; Hopwood, Heron & Others in 1896; Hopwood Collieries Ltd in 1929. The seam worked was Royley Seam, the local name for the Arley Mine in 1896, and the colliery employed fifty-three underground and eleven on the surface in 1896 when William Needham was the manager. Under Hopwood Collieries in 1918, just after the First World War, the pit employed 147 underground workers and twenty-eight surface men. There were two shafts, and an airshaft located to the south-west of the pit. Chamber Colliery closed in 1951, according to most sources, but it is not mentioned in the *Guide to the Coalfields* (1948). The old stables that once housed the horses that drew the carts to the canal wharf at Hollinwood were demolished to make way for the car park of the South Chadderton Conservative Club in the 1970s.

A shocking and tragic accident occurred in the pit, as reported in the *Blackburn Gazette*, 28 November 1838:

On Thursday week about half past three o'clock, William Wild, a young man, Edwin Rowson and John Mattocks, two boys were ascending from their work in one of the coal pits at Chamber Colliery in a tub when the engine tenter, a boy of only eleven years of the name James Chadderton instead of attending to the engine to stop it was engaged in placing nails in a wall of the engine house, in a moment of thoughtlessness, as is usual for a boy. In consequence the tub was wound over, and the unfortunate miners thrown out. The eldest Wild, a resident of Priory Ground was dreadfully shattered and instantly killed.

Mattocks whose limbs were shockingly broke died within a few moments, he lived at Lord Street, Oldham. Rowson whose person was much maimed expired while being carried to his home at Hollins…

The following report in the *Manchester Guardian*, 21 June 1843, may be a reference to an incident involving a miner who worked at the Chamber Pit:

Suicide by Drowning. On Monday last, Thomas Evans, an elderly man, resident at top of Hollinwood, Oldham, who whilst employed at a colliery in the neighbourhood began whilst at work to quarrel with his brother respecting some property belonging to the family. The brother came to high words, and it is said blows. In a short time afterwards, Thomas went off, and drowned himself in a fit of desperation in the Oldham Canal, near Hollinwood.

The *Manchester Guardian* reports a roof fall at the site, 14 September 1844:

Colliery Accident. On Wednesday last, shortly after noon, a boy of 14 years of age named Thomas Hearne, was accidentally killed in Chamber Lane Colliery, Oldham by a fall of roof in the mine. A large quantity of stony material or coaly rock fell upon him, and killed him instantly. It is rumoured, but whether correct or not it is difficult to ascertain, that the fall of earth was owing in some degree to the want of adequate supports to the roof. Another boy at work near the deceased narrowly escaped being killed in the same incident. The deceased was the son of Thomas Hearne, coal miner of Little Town, Hollinwood. The coroner's inquest was held on Thursday evening at the Wagon and Horses, Hollinwood; verdict 'accidental death'.

A tragic accident in which the colliery manager was killed is recorded in the *Manchester Guardian,* 25 January 1845:

Appalling Accident; On Tuesday afternoon last, a number of workmen were engaged in taking down a dilapidated cottage at Knowl Hollins, Hollinwood. Whilst they were thus employed, Mr Cornelius Backhouse, colliery manager in the services of Messrs Joseph Jones junior and Co. was standing in the lower storey, giving some directions to the men as to how they should proceed, when the floor of the story suddenly gave way, and Mr Backhouse was overwhelmed by the ruins. Two of the workmen were also injured, but only to a slight degree by the fallen materials.

Mr Backhouse was speedily extricated from the rubbish, and every assistance rendered as promptly as possible, but he died in about ten minutes after being taken out. Mr Backhouse was about fifty years of age and was extensively known, not only for his intelligence as a colliery manager, but also for his attainments in geology. He was a married man, and has left a family. He formerly kept the Rope and Anchor Inn, Oldham.

The *Manchester Guardian* of 6 August 1845 reports on the controversy surrounding a brawl between two coal miners:

Assault by a turn-out coal miner. At the petty sessions, on Monday last, a turn-out coal miner, named James Hewitt, was brought up under warrant, charged with having committed a serious assault on Samuel Taylor, a coal miner in the employ of Messrs Joseph Jones and Co. Chamber Lane Colliery. Mr. Ascroft, solicitor appeared for the complainant, stated that the assault in question had occurred so long ago as the 12th of April last, but the case could not have come earlier, as the defendant had been out of the way almost ever since. The complainant stated that on the evening of Saturday, the 12th of April last, he and the defendant, and others were drinking at the Dog and Partridge public-house, George Street, Oldham. Hewitt and his son, who were also present began to use abusive language to Taylor without any provocation, and among other things called him a 'knobstick' Taylor then told Hewitt, that if that were so, both he and his father had been knobsticks too, for they had worked for a company when there had been a turn-out. The defendant then threw a glass of ale at the complainant's face, on which the complainant said, if he was a strong a man as Hewitt, he would stop him from doing that another time. The defendant then attempted to strike him, but a female by the name of Matty Bennett, the wife of a coal miner, who was present, went between them to prevent any fighting. Taylor then lifted up one arm to prevent Hewitt striking him on the head, on which the latter reached over the shoulder of Bennett's wife and dealt such a blow on Taylor's arm, that shortly afterwards it was discovered to be broken. The complainant has been disabled from work for five weeks, owing to the injuries received.

The evidence of the complainant was confirmed by that of John and Matty Bennett, who were present at the time. The defendant alleged that he said nothing whatever to Taylor until that person charged him and his father with having been 'knobsticks' when they began to work at Chamber Lane Colliery. He had only thrown some beer in Taylor's face, as to striking him on the arm, he had no recollection. John Blackburn, a sawyer, who had once lodged at Hewitt's, stated that Taylor had commenced the dispute by calling Hewitt most disgraceful names, and that all the defendant had done in return was to throw a glass of ale in complainants face. There had been no striking, although Bennetts' wife had got between them. Margaret Blackburn, wife of the last witness, gave similar evidence as her husband.

She said that Hewitt's son had began to use irritating words, and that Taylor had uttered disgusting language to Hewitt, on which the latter threw the glass of ale, and that was all that was done. Mr. John Earnshaw, surgeon, deposed that several small bones in Taylor's arm had been broken. He had been under his care three weeks. It would take him three weeks or a month to become well again. The defendant was convicted in a penalty of £5, or in default of payment, to be committed to prison for two month.

The *Manchester Guardian* reports a roof fall at the site, 9 January 1850:

Fatal Accident at a Coal Pit. On Saturday the 5th inst. a fatal accident occurred at the Chamber Lane Colliery. A man named Samuel Brooks, aged about 33 years was engaged in drawing posts, when suddenly a portion of the roof fell upon him and was killed. He has left a wife and four children.

An explosion, killing one miner, is recorded in the *Manchester Guardian*, 11 December 1850:

An inquest was held at the White Hart Inn, Hollins on Saturday before Mr Dearden on the body of John Elliott, aged 56, who had died as a consequence of an explosion at Chamber Colliery about a fortnight ago. No blame was attached to anyone, and a verdict of 'accidental death' was recorded.

A small rock-fall unfortunately resulted in the death of a young miner, as reported in the *Manchester Guardian,* 5 August 1854: 'On Thursday a man named Joshua Street, off Broadway Lane, aged 23 was killed in the Chamber Coal Pit by a stone falling on him whilst at his work'. And two separate Mines Inspectors Reports record very similar accidents: 'Chamber Colliery. John Saville aged 10, crushed by wagon at bottom of brow' (1856); 'May 26th. Chamber Colliery. Thomas Seal aged 22, crushed by tram wagon at top of jig brow. The bottom wagon had not been attached' (1858).

Falling stone caused a tragic death here in 1884, as the *Oldham Evening Chronicle,* of 16 September, reports:

Fearful Colliery Accident at Chamber Pit. This morning a fearful colliery accident occurred at Chamber Pit, Hollins. A miner named John Meredith, resident at Primrose Bank, Oldham, was about nine o'clock engaged with three other miners, named John Howarth of Edge Lane and William Wild of Bardsley in propping the roof. Four props had been raised, and the deceased was employed in raising the fifth when a mass of stone weighing nearly a ton fell upon him, doubled him up and killed him instantly. Wild and Howarth escaped without injury. The deceased was 54 years of age, and leaves a widow and a grown up family.

Chamberdam: Chamber Lane, Oldham, SD 920 038

This colliery was located to the south of Chamber Colliery and to the east of the ancient Chamber Hall, and is shown on a map of 1891. Two shafts are marked here, and a reservoir along with a disused tramway that ran up to the Chamber Colliery. The colliery does not appear to have been working at this time, though the depth of the shaft is recorded elsewhere as being 'about 260 yards deep to the Lower Bent Mine'. The map on page 63 is the one of 1906.

Chapel: Dukinfield

A colliery operative in 1896, when worked by the Dukinfield Coal & Cannel Co. Ltd. The manager at this time was R. Clay, the undermanager W. Hyde, and the pit employed twenty-six men below ground and six surface men mining from the Sod Mine.

Clarksfield: near Oldham

Worked by Mr James Lees in the 1840s, the colliery may have been off the present day Clarksfield Road, that runs up to the Greenacres Cemetery, Oldham. The pit is not listed in the Catalogue of Plans of Abandoned Mines for the year 1928. However, there is a report in the *Manchester Guardian*, 20 January 1849, regarding an accident in which a young miner was killed:

> Death in a coal pit. Mr Dearden, on Tuesday last held an inquest at the Robin Hood, Oldham, on George Kenworthy, a boy of 14 years, who worked as a collier. On Friday last, at half past eight o'clock, the deceased was ascending from the bottom of a colliery of Messrs Lees, of Clarkesfield, while Edward Radcliffe was lowering down a pair of rails, tied to the rope with string. The tubs clashed together, and the rails fell upon Kenworthy fracturing his skull. Mr Knott came to the cottage where deceased was taken, and dressed his wounds, and ordered Radcliffe to take him home, where he died on Saturday morning, about half past ten o'clock. The jury returned a verdict of 'accidental death'.

Clough: Shaw and Crompton, SD 947 088

This must be the 'coal pit' marked on the 1844-48 maps to the east of Clough House, Mark Lane, Crompton. The colliery is noted in the Catalogue of Plans of Abandoned Mines (1928) as follows: Clough (a) Crompton; (b) COAL; (d) 89 SE (1910) C3, 4. In the *Manchester Guardian*, 1 June 1844, there is a report on a roof fall accident: 'Colliery Accident. On Friday last whilst a young man named William Booth was at work in the Clough Colliery, Crompton, the roof of the mine gave way, apparently from want of sufficient supports, and a large amount of earth fell in on the poor fellow's back, and he was dreadfully injured'.

Coppice Nook: Oldham

A colliery situated near the bottom of Manchester Street, Oldham, at Coppice. A disaster at the mine is reported in the *Manchester Guardian*, 1 October 1836:

> On Thursday morning last a dreadful explosion of gas took place in a pit nearly opposite Coppice Nook, near Oldham, by which four young persons were killed on the spot, and another so much injured that his life is despaired of.
>
> It appears that a little before six in the morning, three men and two boys descended to work in one of the bays in the pit, which was well ventilated and considered to be perfectly safe, and the oldest of the men, Robert Blount, was a very skilful miner and thoroughly acquainted with the nature of inflammable gas found in coal mines. They were known to be unprovided with safety lamps, and must of course have worked by candlelight. Shortly after they went down the pit, a terrific explosion occurred which was heard through out the whole neighbourhood, and two boys and two of the men were killed on the spot, and their bodies dreadfully mangled by the force of the explosion. The third man, William Chambers, was dreadfully hurt, and although still alive, is considered to be in a hopeless state. The persons killed are: Robert Blount, aged 30, his son Thomas, aged 10, William Lees, 20, and Thomas Rowen, 17. The elder Blount, left a wife and three young children.

The pit appears to have closed around 1849, as confirmed in the *Rochdale Observer*, 3 December 1859:

> Falling in of an old coal-pit shaft at Oldham. Near the bottom of Manchester Street, Oldham at Coppice Nook a coal-pit shaft was filled up in 1849, and recently a house has been built over it. The front wall of the house crossing directly over the spot where formerly was the mine mouth. The house belonged to Mr Barnes, and was occupied by Mr Matthew Ormrod, who has a wife and six children. About one o'clock on Wednesday morning, Mr Tempest Whitehead, landlord of the Plough Inn, Manchester Street, was awakened by a sound, as he says 'Like an earthquake'. He went to his back door, where he discovered a large hole, just where the shaft used to be. He awoke the Ormrod's, and they got through one of the windows, and were safely taken to the Plough Inn. Large masses of earth continued to fall during the night, and when the morning dawned, it was seen that the wall of the house had given way in several places, and the lower portion bent down in the opening several inches. The gulf was plumbed with a cord and weight, and was found to be 67 yards deep. When the shaft was first sunk, coal was found at a depth of 60 yards, and this seam when worked was called the Black Mine. The shaft was sunk 64 yards further, and another seam of coal was got. When the mine was exhausted, the shelf was filled up from the scaffolding, but the 64 yards below remained unfilled. The scaffolding has now given way.

Copster Hill: Copster Hill, Oldham

This colliery is mentioned during the coal strike of 1831, when Lees, Jones & Co. was working the pit. The colliery in the Catalogue of Plans of Abandoned Mines is listed under 'Chamber' with which it must have had underground connections. The *Manchester Guardian*, on 9 July 1831, reports on an industrial dispute at the colliery:

Ever since the last turn out of colliers, and the advance of wages consequent thereupon, the proprietors of coal works in the neighbourhood of Oldham more especially, have found the management of their concerns entirely taken out of their hands, or those of their agents, and transferred to the committee of the collier's union which sits every day at the sign of the 'Horse Shoe' at Bardsley, and is by the workmen styled their 'board'. If at any time extra quantities of coal have been required for the fulfilment of orders, or other cause, the men when appraised of it have replied that they would 'inform the board' or 'hear what the board has to say about it' and if 'the board' signified its assent, the coal was supplied, if not, it was withheld. Messrs Barker, Evans and Co. of Edge Lane have not been particularly incommoded with this sort of practice, the men having refused to work more than three quarters of a shift (a shift is a day of about eight hours) and frequently they have given over at half a shift, or four hours. In consequence of which, numbers of persons who would have taken coal from the concern, or have not been supplied have gone elsewhere. By the last turn out 'the board' fixed the rate of wages, or nearly so. Since then 'the board' has directed what quantity of coal should be got. 'The board' has discharged old servants, and appointed others in their place, whether the owners approved of them or not. 'The board' has in fact been the master, while those who should have been exercising authority over the works have been released from all care and responsibility, save that of finding the monies, and making good their losses. The state of things, as may naturally be supposed, could not long continue, and last week all the masters in the vicinity of Oldham, with one or two exceptions came to a determination to abolish a dictation which was harmful to both parties. The resolutions were served to the men on Saturday last. 'That unless they gave up their union within fourteen days from that date, their services would no longer be required. If any of them do wish to continue work, they might do so upon signing a written agreement to renounce and give up their connection with the union'. Since this notice was issued, the collier's belonging to Messrs Barker, Evans and Co. have worked only half time. Those at Hole Bottom Colliery, belonging to Messrs Lees, Jones and Co. begun the same system, but on Wednesday morning, they were informed by the manager, that unless they either worked three quarters or a whole shift, they would not be suffered to work at all, on hearing which they quitted the ground. Of the three pits belonging to Lees, Jones and Co. at Copster Hill, one is working full time, and two three quarter's time. At Low Side, the men gave over working on Wednesday, and at Werneth, the property of Edward Lees, no notice respecting the union has been, or will be given to the men. The works at Hunt Lane continues in full operation, an abundance of hands have offered themselves who could not be employed. At present about thirty colliers are at work, and the remainder of the work is performed by weavers. Until Thursday week the union kept a guard on this place, which since that day, has been discontinued, and new hands now pass without experiencing molestation. This is perhaps because of the consequence, which took place before the magistrates at Oldham, when two of the colliers were sentenced to imprisonment in the New Bailey.

And the *Manchester Guardian* provides an update on the situation, on 16 July 1831:

With the exception of the colliers at Werneth, and those at one pit at Copster Hill, all the hands in Oldham and its neighbourhood have struck work, and their places are daily taken by weavers and regular miner's from Yorkshire, and the northern part of the county. On Thursday morning eight colliers from the neighbourhood of Leeds were set to work at a pit near Spa, but some of the Oldham colliers got among them, and either terrified or persuaded two of them to quit, the other six remained in work. At Hunt lane, and Old lane, nineteen colliers went to work on Wednesday, and the other pits will shortly be filled with hands. These measures have been precipitated by the workmen themselves, who on receiving notice to quit, began to work only half stint, and on being informed that they must either work full time or not at all, chose the latter and turned out to a man.

The *Manchester Guardian* of 23 July 1831 observes the dispute becoming increasingly violent, and reaching its peak:

It was stated just last week in the Guardian, that in consequence of the turn out of colliers at Oldham, and its neighbourhood, the master's were supplying their pits with old hands from other parts of the country, and with weavers. About a dozen of the latter reside in Denton lane, and are employed at Messrs Lees, Jones and Co. in their pits at Copster Hill, and in going to and returning from their work morning and evening have to pass the old hands at Old lane and Hollinwood. On these occasion great crowds have been collected, and the men have been subjected to much insult and considerable danger, particularly from crowds of women and boys, whilst the men stood looking on at a distance. Early on the morning of yesterday week, Denton lane was crowded with colliers evidently come in expectation of being able to intimidated the new hands from going to work, but a party of men connected with the firm Lees, Jones and Co. arriving on horseback with several constables, the men were conducted to the pit without injury, through a crowd of women, who kept up a continual volley of reproach, mingles with the sounding of cans and frying pans. In consequence of this occurrence, the men are now lodged and boarded at the pit, and will only return home at the weekends. Among the men now employed at Hunt lane, are about a dozen old colliers from the Rocher works, who are not connected with the colliers union. In order to secure these men from intimidation or violence, it has been found necessary to covey them every Sunday evening to their work in a coach, guarded by their employers, and superior servants, and re-conduct them to their families in the same manner every Saturday evening. Last Sunday they were taken up as usual at Ashton, and conveyed through Oldham, by the way of King Street and Bent Green, which is the direct road to the works. It had been previously observed at Bent Green, and the causeway passing through it were strewed with a greater number of stones that were usually there, but it does not appear that the circumstances was made known to the police, or that any means were taken for their removal.

At this place there was a crowd of many hundreds of colliers, and, as might have been expected, the escort here was attacked by showers of stones, and most of the persons forming it were struck, some of them many times, but though some of them were bruised, none received any serious injury. The crown of Mr James Marland's hat was cut by a stone with a sharp edge, and about a pound in weight, but he escaped uninjured. Several of the police, who arrived to assist the escort were also pelted, and in the confusion and violence it was necessary to order the coach through thick and thin, while the escort held back the crowd in the best manner they could. In the performance of his duty, one or two persons were injured by the horse's feet, but the manoeuvre succeeded, and the coach passed into Hunt lane.

During the riot, Mr Holmes, the magistrate arrived, and ordered out a party of the second dragoon guards, stationed at Oldham, and some fresh hands from Padiham having been intercepted by the old ones at Middleton, the magistrate proceeded hither with the military and conducted the men to their destination. From Middleton to Hunt lane, crowds followed the escort, but no violence took place. The same evening, Mr Ogden, who is connected with the firm Lees, Jones and Co. was pelted with stones when conducting two men from the works at Hunt lane by a circuitous road. A number of colliers intercepted him and the men, and one of them being forced into a public house, he told them he was only going to draw his wage, after which he would leave, they wanted him to sign a paper for them to draw his wages, but he refused, and at length got away. Mr Ogden was struck violently on the back part of his head by a stone, which had it struck a little lower, would have knocked him down, and might probably have seriously injured him. On Monday John Stafford was charged with being drunk and disorderly in the public streets of Oldham contrary to the provision of the police act.

Mr Ogden stated that there was a great crowd in Bent street, that there was many stones thrown, one of which struck Mr James Marsland, and that the person who threw it said 'D— thee, I'll kill thee' that he saw Stafford run towards Mr Marsland with his hands uplifted, but whether he threw or not he could not tell. He was however, in his dirty shirt, and apparently in liquor.

Mr Holme said he was called out, and found a great crowd, he thought it quite necessary that such proceeding should be put to a stop, and he therefore convicted the defendant in the sum of 20 shillings, and the expenses. The defendant declared he could not pay it, and he was taken and locked up. In consequence of the disturbed state of the district, the magistrate have issued a notice, stating that workmen have, in several instances, assembled together, and paraded from one place to another in great numbers, and have conducted themselves in such a manner, as to intimidate those workmen who are still in employ, and all other peaceable inhabitants of the district, and that such proceedings are clearly illegal, and tend to create alarm.

Among other places where the workmen received notice to quit the union, or give up their employ, were the works at Tonge, near Middleton. The time expired yesterday, when the men were called into the counting house, and the question was put to them, and with the exception of one, who remained silent, they all declared they would abandon the union. They were doubtless aware that if they turned out, their places would at once be taken and filled by the weavers.

There is an accident, killing one, reported in the *Blackburn Gazette,* 9 January 1833: 'On Thursday night a youth in the coal pit at Copsterhill, near Oldham lost his life by falling beneath a quantity of rubbish which had suddenly gave way. The inquest was held at the Waggon and Horses, Hollinwood, where a verdict of "accidental death" was recorded'.

An explosion, caused by a candle, is reported in the *Manchester Guardian,* 8 March 1837:

On Thursday seven coal miners while at work in the No.4 pit at Copster Hill, near Oldham were seriously burnt by an explosion of firedamp, owing to one of them named Thomas Birks incautiously lifting his candle too high. Birks was burnt to a shocking degree, and died on Monday morning. His son, John was dreadfully injured and is in an extremely precarious state. Five others were more or less injured. The utmost precaution is stated to be observed in these mines, to prevent as far as possible the occurrence of accidents of this nature, yet frequent casualties have taken place at this colliery.

Count Hill: Oldham★, SD 954 072
The pit dates at least from 1829, when a colliery of this name is shown on Dunns Map for that year. From around the early to mid-1840s, the colliery owner is noted as being a Mr Dunkerley. The pit is listed in the Catalogue of Plans of Abandoned Mines as follows: Count Hill (Higher and Lower) Haven, Highfield (a) Oldham; (b) COAL Foot (abandoned 22 January 1880); (d) 97 NE (1922) B8: C2,3: D8.

It is not unknown for colliery proprietors, or the colliers, to 'adopt' children from the local workhouse, on the pretence of offering to bring them up, educate and provide for them. In reality, many of these children were put to work down the mine, supplementing the wages of the collier who 'adopted' them, or working as child labour for the pit owner. A case below highlights the danger these and other children were subjected to. Mr Dunkerley appears to have given up his interest in the colliery by 1848, when Job Lees is recorded as working the pit. This colliery is also mentioned in the list of collieries at work in 1854, compiled by Joseph Dickinson, Inspector of Mines, when the colliery was then worked by Job Lees. By 1879, the pit was worked by the Trustees of John Mayall. The colliery was located at Count Hill to the south-east of Moorside at the above reference. A footpath off Turf Pit Lane on the right leads past the football ground, through a stile made up of old scaffolding, the colliery is not the one on the right at an area of noticeable colliery spoil, this is Sunfield Colliery. The Count Hill Pit is found on a continuation of the footpath and is on the left-hand side of the track. The shallow quarry-like depression first passed along the track below the football ground may be the remains of the 'Turf Pits', which gave Turf Pit Lane its name.

Reported in the *Manchester Guardian,* 7 August 1847, is an instance of the tragedy that could occur as a consequence of the practice of taking children from workhouses to work in the collieries:

> Boy killed at a colliery. On Wednesday last, Mr Dearden, coroner held an inquest at Watersheddings, on the body of a boy aged ten years, named James Hadfield, who was accidentally killed in the colliery of Mr Dunkerley, at Count Hill. Whilst the deceased was at work in the mine, on Saturday last, engaged in drawing coal wagons, a considerable quantity of earth fell upon him from the roof of the mine, and killed him on the spot. The quantity of earth, which fell, was extremely large, and took a considerable time to remove. The deceased who was an orphan, was formerly an inmate of Oldham workhouse. The jury returned a verdict to the effect that 'the deceased died from injuries received from the roof of the mine falling upon him'.

Mr George Hallas was charged over the taking of coal from Mr Lees, as reported in the *Manchester Guardian*, 12 July 1848:

> Charge of Felony against a coal proprietor. On Thursday last, Mr George Hallas, proprietor of a coal-pit, on Count Hill Estate, Oldham, was brought up before the magistrates under a warrant, charged with feloniously taking coal from the ground of Mr Job Lees, on the same estate...

This is followed by some lengthy proceedings, claims and counter-claims. The magistrates decided in the end, that the felonious intention was not proved, and that therefore they had no jurisdiction in the case. George Hallas apparently went on to work one of the collieries on Sholver Moor, by the year 1854.

A death at the site is recorded in the Mines Inspectors Report for the year 1859: 'July 28th. Count Hill Colliery worked by John Smith. John Whitehead a 12 year old drawer killed by breaking of a chain dropping a balance weight down a hand turn pit. The chain had been borrowed and was not fit for use'.

Cowlishaw: Royton, SD 934 082

A colliery situated close by the Cowlishaw Lane off Shaw Road, between Shaw and Royton. The colliery worked the Arley Mine at a depth of 135ft. The pit is marked on the OS map of 1844, the site today, is probably that taken by the electricity sub-station at the start of Charlbury Way. Although a number of new housing has been built in this area, the local authorities are often aware of old mine workings, and steer clear of potential dangers – thus the sub-station rather than housing occupies the spot. The Catalogue of Plans gives little information other than the location of the shaft: Cowlishaw (a) Royton; (b) COAL; (d) 89 SW (1910) H10. The colliery was worked by Evans & Co. during the early 1840s and probably also mined the Royley Mine that outcrops to the north of the pit. The following, in the *Manchester Guardian*, 18 October 1823 is a reference to a colliery worked by Evans; it may or may not be the Cowlishaw Colliery:

> On the night of the 7th or early in the morning of the 8th, a quantity of metal ladders were stolen from the colliery of Mr F. Evans at Longsight, near Oldham. The loss of which was not perceived by the men when descending to their work, caused the rope to slip and three of them were dashed to the bottom of the pit. They now lie in a very dangerous state with little hope of their recovery.

Crow Knowl: Crompton Fold, near Oldham, SD 956 102

The Crow Knowl Colliery was a very old pit, with at least three shafts 300 yards apart. It is recorded that 'in 1766, a lease for newly enclosed land near Crow Knowl included all mines [and] veins of coal and stone, with liberty to sink and mine' (Lancashire Records Office, DDX 520/31). The Crow Knowl Farm was built in 1741, but the colliery was working long before this. In 1828, a Mr Milne is recorded as working the pit at Crow Knowl, and in 1837 T&J Milne worked the mine. Edmund Butterworth & Co. is recorded as working the colliery in 1861, and also in 1869 (see report on accident there that year). Two of the shafts are reputed to have been worked by horse whim, but the main shaft was worked by water wheel. To supply this wheel a reservoir was constructed at the top end of Brushes Clough, 1,150ft above sea level, and the water ran through a stone drain a distance of 800 yards to another reservoir at the pit. In later years this reservoir was used by a later Crow Knowl Colliery worked by the Buckley Brothers, who are recorded as working a colliery here in 1938, when they employed eight men underground and one on the surface, and again in 1940. The colliery is listed under Buckley Bros, Oldham, Lancashire in a mines index for 1951 and 1956. The pit employed seven men underground and one on the surface. The coal mined was the Yard Mine. In an index for 1959, the pit is worked by A.H. and F. Buckley, mining the Mountain Mine, with eight underground and two on the surface. The Buckleys are reported to have come across various items in the old workings at Crow Knowl Pit. Picks, spades, wedges, rails, a candle, belt and chains used by small boys to pull the tubs, and the soles of old clogs. At one time near the shaft bottom they came across a broken basin with some bones inside... the remains of a meal. Other items included a bottle, strangely shaped with a curved base so that it cannot stand up, long and narrow with the words 'E. Duckworth, Oldham' worked into the glass. An old clay pipe with a sailing ship and an anchor in its design, and an iron-rimmed wooden wheel about 6in in diameter. The workings at the old Crow Knowl Colliery were abandoned in 1864, although Edmund Butterworth is known to have opened another Crow Knowl Colliery nearby (see *Oldham Newspaper*, 16 October 1957).

The Crow Knowl Collieries are listed in the Catalogue of Plans of Abandoned Mines (1928) as follows: Crow Knowl (a) Crompton; (b) COAL Mountain, Half Yard (abandoned prior to 1879); (d) 89 SE (1910) C45; Crow Knowl Nos 1 & 2 (a) Crompton; (b) COAL Yard, Delph (abandoned 1890); (d) 89 SE (1910) A5: B5.

A curious report is to be found in the *Manchester Guardian*, 2 October 1844: 'Trespassing on a Colliery Railway. At the petty sessions on Monday, an elderly man of respectable appearance named John Wild was charged by James Buckley with having trespassed on a colliery railway belonging to Mr Harry Bentley, situated between Shaw and Sholver. Ordered to pay costs'.

A Mines Inspectors Report for the year 1861 records a tragic fall: 'January 11th. Crow Knowl Colliery worked by Edmund Butterworth and Co., J. Wolfenden aged nine years, fell down shaft and killed'.

Cupola Pits: Old Lane, Hollinwood
These pits were located between Shooting Butts Colliery and New Engine Pit, Old Lane. Nothing much is known about them, except that one Joseph Marland, who was once a member of the Society of Friends in Oldham, drove a horse gin here for a halfpenny an hour when he was a lad. A cupola pit was a bye pit, or ventilation shaft generally situated at the highest point of the workings where the naturally warm air in the mine would rise to the surface, drawing fresh air down other shafts. These shafts were sometimes artificially aided with a ventilation furnace situated at the bottom.

Deanshutt: Bardsley
This colliery is mentioned in the Catalogue of Plans of Abandoned Mines as follows: Deanshutt and Tanner Fold, Furnace, Hill (a) Bardsley; (b) COAL Foxholes (1888); (c) Chamber Colliery Co. Hollinwood, Oldham; (d) 97 SW (1922) D11, 12: E11, 12: F11. Nothing else known. A boiler explosion in February 1877 injured four men.

Denton Lane: Chadderton
Colliery had underground connections with the Fernyfield and Stockfield Collieries. Worked by the Chamber Colliery Co. in 1869 and 1879. The

following is from the Catalogue of Plans of Abandoned Mines 1928: Denton Lane, Stockfield, (a) Chadderton; (b) COAL Black (abandoned June 1886) Lower Bent (abandoned June 1894); (d) 97 NW (1923) G1, 2, 3, 4,: H1, 2, 3, 4; 97 SW (1919) A1, 2, 3, 4: B3, 4.

Mines Inspectors Reports record two deaths: 'April 1st. Denton Lane Colliery. Henry Dingsdale, aged 29, killed through chain breaking while riding down incline (1864); 'June 20th. Denton Lane Colliery. Thomas Eckersley killed through stone falling' (1868).

Diamond Pit: Bardsley, near Oldham
The pit worked the Peacock Mine at a depth of 490 yards, part of Bardsley Bridge Colliery, along with the Victoria Pit.

The *Colliery Guardian*, 12 July 1862, records a very unpleasant death:

An inquest was held at the Ashton-under-Lyne District Infirmary on Friday week on the body of Samuel Jones, collier, employed at the Diamond Pit, Bardsley, on the Oldham and Ashton Road. It seemed that the deceased and three other men had just entered the tub at six o'clock, on Tuesday morning week, to descend the pit. As soon as the tub began to move, the deceased was in the act of throwing his coat in the tub, when his head caught against the sheet iron at the mouth of the pit, which was used as a landing plate, and got received a fearful wound from which he bled profusely. He was taken to the infirmary, but notwithstanding treatment died on Thursday week.

A recent report, 28 September 1982, in the *Oldham Newspaper*, tells of a reclamation of the mining land:

The National Coal Board has earmarked land at Bardsley for future mining, and prospecting for the coal will begin early next year. Mr Les Coop, Borough Planning Officer, said that he expected to be served notice of the proposed explorations within the next six weeks. The authority will then have another six weeks to comment on the proposals. Mr Coop said that initially the NCB was interested in two sites at Oldham, one at Glodwick Lows, and another at Bardsley off Coal Pit Lane. Now they are prospecting the Bardsley site only, which covers a large area from Hathershaw School playing fields and stretching across Werneth Golf Club, and Oldham Rugby Union Club. After the inspections have been completed, the NCB will report back on the findings to Oldham Council, and if they intend to work the site, the Secretary of State would have to approve. All this could take twelve months, and it could be into the 1990s before the site was opened for mining. Mr Coop is to prepare a special report for councillors at a future meeting of the Development Committee on this matter. A spokesman for the Coal Board confirmed that prospecting is to begin on the site of the old Wood Park Colliery site at Bardsley in about three months time. He said the

Board's interest in the site was sparked off after Greater Manchester Council said they intended to reclaim it. Mining experts will explore the area at Bardsley for open cast reserves, or for coal, which is close to the surface, and which, can be excavated without the use of shafts. This is done by a small drilling rig on the site, which would remove samples to be analysed. After the workings have finished, if they do start at all, the reclamation of the whole site would be carried out by the NCB.

Dingle: Shaw and Crompton, Oldham, SD 948 084

This colliery is marked on a map of 1863, and is shown with a tramway running down to the Moss Hey Cotton Mills, and the gas works at Crompton. The mineral rights at Dingle Colliery, however, were negotiated in 1771, as part of a lease between Abel Crompton, of Crompton, linen weaver, and James Wilde of Crompton, woollen clothier, to John and James Butterworth of Crompton, woollen clothiers (*Oldham Local Studies*, Misc.1/13). The site of the colliery is reached down Knowl Road off Mark Lane, Shaw past Lilac Cottage and a derelict building on the left. A footpath leads off to the left, skirting a small stream and field to a stile. Over to the right is an area of disturbed ground with colliery spoil, part of the tramway from the pit. Make your way diagonally to another stile, and turn right up the hill to join Fullwood Lane. Turn left here up the lane, and where the track turns sharp right, go straight on through another stile. In the hollow below on the left-hand side is the remains of a former sandstone quarry. The Dingle Colliery was on the other side of the old quarry. A raised banking appears also to have been part of the colliery tramway mentioned below, having no other obvious use. Pit shales and pieces of coal are evident in this area. If you continue up the track from the hollow, at the top is the ruin of Dingle Farm from which the pit took its name.

The *Manchester Guardian*, 13 July 1844, reports on an accident on the colliery railway:

> Fatal Accident on a Colliery Railway. On Monday last, Mr Dearden held an inquest at the Royal Oak, Cowlishaw, Crompton on the body of Joseph Shaw, a coal miner, aged thirty years. From the evidence it appears, that on Saturday last as the deceased was riding on some coal carriages on the railway from Dingle Colliery to Moss Hey, the wagons accidentally ran off the rails, when on an embankment, and he was precipitated into a hollow 14 feet below. The deceased was shockingly injured by the fall, and was immediately taken to the Duke of York Inn, Shaw, but died within twenty minutes. Reports were in circulation that the accident had been caused by carelessness of persons connected with the colliery, but no evidence was shown to prove this. The deceased left a wife and one child. A verdict of 'accidental death' was returned.

Dirtcar: Oldham

This pit shows up on Dunn's map of 1829, to the north of Dirtcar Road, Oldham. Few records exist relating to this early colliery, although it is mentioned in the Catalogue of Plans of Abandoned Mines (1928): Dirtcar (a) Oldham; (b) COAL; (d) 97 NW (1922) E12. The latter is the location of the mine entrance only.

Doghill: Crompton, near Oldham★, SD 953 093

The colliery is mentioned in Joseph Dickinson's 'Statistics of Collieries in Lancashire, Cheshire and North Wales', a paper read on 7 March 1854. The pit at this time was worked by Joseph Cook and John Marland. The colliery was located off what is now the B6197, the Buckstones Road to the east of Shaw near Oldham, near its junction with the Grains Road. There were numerous pits on Dog Hill, one being known as 'Top Dog Hill', and employing two men in 1837. This pit was worked by John Scholes. Opposite Chapel Farm, the building on the right going up the Buckstones Road, but before the Black Ladd Pub, is a track besides a cottage. Up here, a number of raised mounds in the field indicate former coal workings. At least one of these is formed of dressed stone and rubble, which is perhaps part of a former pithead structure. The pits worked the Foot Mine. The Chapel Farm, incidentally, was formerly the Dog Hill Methodist Chapel, originally built in 1823, and re-built in 1992.

A sad death is recorded in the *Manchester Guardian,* 17 January 1846: 'On Wednesday last, Mr Dearden, coroner held an inquest at Shaw on the body of a young man named William Dawson, the son of the manager of the gas works at Shaw. It appeared that on Thursday the 8th inst. the deceased who was twenty years of age attempted to slide down the rope into the Doghill coal-pit, when he lost his hold and fell to the bottom. He died on Monday last. Verdict:"Accidental death"'.

The following may be a reference to another Dog Hill Pit, one probably worked by Wild and Smith. The lad killed was only nine years old, and should not have been down the pit, as this was in breach of the Coal Mines Act (1842). Poor Benjamin was the son of one of the owners of the colliery, a needless death that the father would have to live with for the rest of his life. The incident is reported in the *Manchester Guardian,* 22 May 1847:

Fatal Accident at a Colliery. On Wednesday afternoon last, whilst a boy of about nine years of age, named Benjamin Wild, was at work in the colliery of Messrs Wild and Smith, at Doghill, Crompton, a large quantity of earth from the roof of the mine fell upon him, and instantly deprived him of life. Another individual narrowly escaped being killed at the same time, but a tub interrupted the fall of the earth in the direction where he was. The deceased was the son of one of the owners of the mine.

Two years after he read the statistics paper, Joseph Dickinson again mentions the pit in 1856, in his capacity as Inspector of Mines for the Manchester District, when he took the owner of the pit to court, as reported in the *Manchester Guardian*, 28 October 1856:

> Mr Joseph Crook, owner of the Doghill Colliery, at Crompton was charged under the Coal Mines Act, with neglecting to provide an adequate amount of ventilation in his pit. Mr Dickinson inspected the pit on the 17th instance, and found that the air was so noxious that a candle would scarcely burn, so that it was not only detrimental to health, but also almost dangerous to life. Indeed, the mine was in such a state that a person was actually suffocated in it on the 4th inst. from the bad air. The defendant, who said that he had been the owner of the pit for five years, but that he never went into it, leaving its workings to other people, whom he paid well for attending to it. He was fined £2 10s and costs.

The person said to have suffocated is Josiah Hardy, a 'boy' recorded as having been killed at Doghill Pit in the Mines Inspectors Report for 1856.

Dog Lane: Dukinfield
There are few references to this pit, which by all accounts was near St Marks Church at Dukinfield. It may have been confused with the Dunkirk Colliery which was to the south of St Marks Church.

Dry Clough: Edge Lane, Oldham★, SD 922 070
We can list the owners of this colliery, from the 1840s through to 1879, when it appears to have been abandoned: E. Evans, 1842; Evans, Barker & Co., 1854; Oldham, Middleton and Rochdale Coal Co., 1879.

Dry Clough Colliery appears to have been another name for the Edge Lane Colliery, or a shaft connected with Edge Lane Pit, although Evans, Barker & Co. are listed as working both Dry Clough and Edge Lane Collieries in 1834. There does not appear to be any reference to the Dry Clough Colliery as such in any accidents, in the period 1850-1920; all reports on these refer to Edge Lane Colliery. Indeed, the Catalogue of Plans of Abandoned Mines also says 'see Edge Lane'. This is the entry for Dry Clough and Edge Lane Collieries from the Catalogue of Plans of Abandoned Mines for 1928: Edge Lane, and Dry Clough, Higginshaw Lane (a) Royton; (b) COAL Black, Bent (1850); (c) Winstanley and Ashworth, 42, Deansgate, Manchester; (d) 97 NW (1922) A7, 8, 9: B7, 8, 9, 10. C7, 8, 9, 10: D9.

The Dry Clough Colliery is shown on a map of 1851, located at Edge Lane, south of Royton. One of the earliest references to coal mining at Edge Lane is in the *Annals of Oldham 1787-1830*, when it is recorded that 'Thomas Heap, collier was much bruzed [sic] in a coalpit at Edge Lane, 28th August 1788'.

The *Manchester Guardian*, 7 September 1833, reports an accident at the site:

> On Saturday last James Mallalleu, a coal miner, employed at Edge Lane Colliery, near Oldham, was accidentally killed by falling into one of the coal pits there. In his descent he seized hold of the conducting rods, and whilst clinging to them, a person named Pierce attempted to save him, at the peril of his own life, but in vain. The deceased was an unmarried man.

There were three more notable accidents at the colliery, the first reported in the *Manchester Guardian*, 9 December 1843:

> Fatal Accident in a Colliery. On Tuesday last as James Marshall, a coal miner, was at work in the Dry Clough or Edge Lane Colliery, Royton belonging to Messrs Barker, Evans and Co. a large mass of coaly rock, about four yards square fell upon him from the roof of the mine, and instantly killed him. Two other miners were near, but they both escaped. The deceased was about thirty-seven years of age, and was married but had no children. He resided near North Moor Toll Bar.

The second report is also in the *Manchester Guardian,* on 13 January 1847:

> Explosion at a Colliery. On Saturday last, an accidental explosion of firedamp took place in the colliery of Messrs Evans, Barber and Co. at Edge Lane, Royton. A miner named Joseph Bottomley, resident at Royton, sustained injury. He was severely scorched by the explosion, particularly about the head and neck.
>
> Bottomley is a married man, with a family, but they are all, or nearly all, adults. The explosion is said to have occurred in consequence of some carelessness on the part of the miners.

The Mines Inspectors Report records the third accident, in 1854: 'January 13th. Edge Lane and Dry Clough Colliery, worked by Barker and Evans. G. Beswick killed by a fall of roof'.

Dukinfield: Dukinfield
A colliery worked by Swires and Lees during the early 1840s, and John Hall & Son in 1880. Extensive details are available on the conditions of work at the colliery in J.L. Kennedy's Report on Child Labour in the Coal Mines, April 1841. Joseph Andrews, a collier at Messrs Swire and Lees Colliery, responded to questions:

> At whose mine do you work? — I work at Messrs Swire and Lees. How long have you been a collier? — I have been a collier for 17 years. What is your work? — We are not coal getting, we are driving a new road just now. Is it wet work? — No, it is quite dry. How many shifts are you working just now? — We are working three shifts just now. Have you ever known children go out of the pits in to the mills?

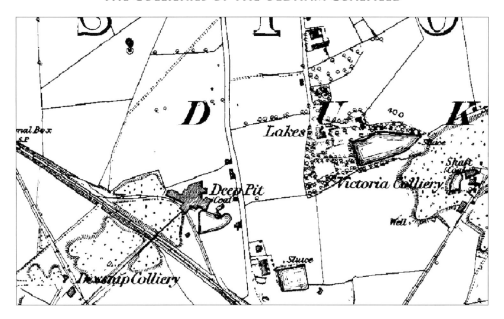

Dukinfield Collieries, map of 1882.

— I have never known any children go out of the pits into the mills, but I have known them go out of the mills and into the pits.

Similarly, Jeremiah Partington, a collier, aged fifty-five, at Messrs Swire and Lees Colliery took part:

How long have you been a collier? — Since I was seven or eight years old. Have you ever been hurt in the pits? —Yes, I have broken almost every bone in my body, but not at this mine. I have had my wrists broken, my ankle broken in two places, my collarbone broken, three ribs slipped, and my thigh broken. The chain on the gig broke once, and the wagon hurt me, and my ankle was broken by two wagons coming together and catching me. Which do you consider the most dangerous part of a collier's work? — Drawing posts, sometimes the posts will not stir, and then the next stroke will knock them out, and the roof will be on you before you are aware of it.

Cooper, a strapper at Messrs Swire and Lees Colliery, gave some curious answers:

Have you ever been hurt? — No, I have never been hurt in the pit, but I have had several bones broken. How did that happen, out of the pit? — With fighting. Do you fight naked? — Yes, up-and-down, with clogs on. How much beer do you drink on a Saturday night? — Sometimes half a barrel!

John Wright, underlooker at Swire and Lees Colliery, provided a revealing insight into working conditions and practices:

How long have you been a collier? — I have been a collier since I was a child of six years old. Were your parents colliers? — Yes, my mother used to get coals, but there are very few women who ever become coal-getters. The men like them as drawers full, as well as boys or men, they do the work cheaper. Does it make any difference to the master whether women or men are employed? — It makes no difference to the master, they pay the same way, the colliers find their own drawers. Do you approve of women being in the pits? — No, we never have women, I don't like to see women down the pit. To what cause do you ascribe the greatest number of accidents? — The greatest number of accidents arise from the roof falling in when the posts are drawn, and from firedamp. There are some cases from bad machines and ropes, but not many. Are there any ghosts seen in these pits? — We have some men who are very superstitious. Three years ago we thought we should have to give up the Flowry [Flowery] Field Mine at Hyde, the men would hardly go into them, there were so many ghosts and boggarts. There was one man I knew who declared he heard something supernatural come and take away his picks in a wagon and go up. He heard the tread of his feet, and the noise of the wagon going along, and the clatter of picks in the wagon, but he never saw it. He was working at night, and nobody had been down the pit but himself. He was a good scholar and could read and write well. We have seen today a man who believes firmly in boggarts, the strapper, his proper name is Cooper. His brother-in-law was killed, and he saw boggarts, and believes in them at the present time. He is one of the roughest men in the pit, a great fighter, he keeps a fighting dog, and is given to cock-fighting.

The answers of John Wilde, at Messrs Swire and Lees Colliery, show just how young some miners were when they first started work:

What age are you? — I am 14 years old. At what age did you begin to work? — I began to work in the pit when I was six years old, I worked for Mr Howard first. What wages do you get? — I get 2s a day as a waggoner, when I am at work, but I don't work more than eight days a fortnight. We have turned out for seven weeks [on strike] but I expect I shall go in again tonight, a man has just been to my father. Has your father any other waggoner? — No, I can wagon all the coal my father can get, he is reckoned to get 5s a day. There are not so many as can get quite so much as that. Have you ever been hurt? — I have never been hurt much, I have been lucky for that. My brother was killed in Newton Hall Pit, he had his head laid open by a winch that worked a 'down-brow'. He lived 11 hours after it happened. Have you ever seen any ghosts? — No, I have never seen any ghosts. I have worked where the men said they were, and I have blown out my candle on purpose to see them, but I never could see ought. After my brother was killed, my father used to stop his work, and he thought he saw him standing at his back.

Did your brother work for your father at the time he was killed? — No, he did not work for him when he was alive, he worked in another pit. How many cases of accidents do you recollect? — I have known 11 or 12 men and lads killed since I began. Do you ever fight? — Yes, many a time we fight, a big lad munna prate (must fight) or the little uns will thrash him. What wages did you get when you first went into the pit? — I got 6d a day, when I first went into the pit, some gets a shilling, but they are older'.

William Kay, aged seventeen, at Messrs Swire and Lees Colliery moved from a mill to the pit:

Have you always worked in a coal-pit? — No, I worked three years in a mill before I came into the pit. What made you leave the mills? — I was badly off when I was in the mill, I only got 1s a day, now I get 2s a day. Have you ever been hurt in the pit? — Never to signify, I have never been off my work but a day in my life.

The answers of George Wilde, aged seventeen, at Messrs Swire and Lees Colliery, suggest that regulations are not always strictly adhered to:

What wages can you earn a day as a drawer? — I get 3s a day, a man's wage. Can you read? — Not much, I have forgotten how, when I was 12 years old I could read, but since then I have been my own master, and I have never done much in that way. Do the boys who come out of the factories into the pits make good colliers? — No, not one in a hundred ever gets to be a pickman. I suppose you have always been able to get enough to eat? — Oh yes, sometimes I have had more, and sometimes I have had less, but I have always been able to get a bellyful. Do you ever work at night? — Yes, when it is my week to work the night shift. Have you ever worked one day and a night together? — Yes, I have once, but it is not once in a thousand times that it is ever done. Do you stop at a regular time? — Yes, we stop half an hour sometimes, sometimes we cannot stop at all, and sometimes we stop an hour. Is it usual for the colliers to pawn their clothes? — No, I don't think there is much of that. I never pawned anything except a handkerchief once at Whit-Sunday, and that handkerchief is there yet for anything I know, for I never got it out of pledge.

William Wilde at Messrs Swire and Lees Colliery, aged eighteen, reveals the shocking abuse young miners sometimes endured, both in fights, and even from relatives:

What age were you when you first went down the pit? — I went into the pit when I was six years old. What wages do you get? — I get 1s 8d a day when I am in work, but I have not been in the pit for seven weeks and two days. What time do you come to work in the morning? — We come at six in the morning, and go away at five in the afternoon, sometimes later. Have you ever been hurt? — No, I have never been hurt. Do you sometimes fight? — Yes, we have many a fight. Do you ever get thrashed, and how? — When my father begins a-thrashing me, he takes a pick or anything.

The workings at Dukinfield went on to become extensive, as shown by the listings in the Catalogue of Plans of Abandoned Mines: Dukinfield, Astley, Chapel, Dewsnap (a) Ashton-under-Lyne, Audenshaw, Denton (Lancashire) Dukinfield, Newton (Cheshire); (b) COAL Great, Roger, Black, Cannel (1889); (c) J. and P. Higson, 18 Booth Street, Manchester; (d) 105 NW (1923) H11, 12: 105 SW (1923) A11, 12: B10, 11, 12: C9, 10, 11, 12: D9, 10, 11, 12: E9, 10, 11, 12: F9, 10, 11, 12: G12. 105 SE (19123) C1: D1; Dukinfield, Astley, Chapel, Dewsnap, Victoria (a) Denton, Audenshaw (Lancashire) Dukinfield, Newton, Hyde (Cheshire); (b) COAL Peacock, Cannel, Black, Little Black, Town Lane, Great, Roger, Sod, Three Sheds (abandoned 22 January 1902); (d) 105 NW (1923) H11, 12: 105 NE (1923) H1: 105 SW (1923) A10, 11, 12: B9, 10, 11, 12: C9, 10, 11, 12: E9, 10, 11, 12: F9, 10, 11, 12: G9, 10, 11, 12: 105 SE (1923) A1: B1, 2: C1, 2: D1, 2: E1, 2: F1: G1.

There were at least two serious explosions at collieries in and around Dukinfield, with great loss of life, on 14 June 1866, with a further explosion on 4 June 1867. Other accidents include, on 31 January 1851, Edward Bailey and R. Ridings were killed by an explosion at the Dukinfield Colliery at Dukinfield, Cheshire, worked by the Dukinfield Coal Co.

Dunkirk: Dukinfield

Two collieries of the same name, one worked by Newton and Taylor, and one worked by Thomas Ashton, both during the early 1840s. The pits appear to have been around Dunkirk Wood and Dunkirk Lane, to the west of Flowery Field. There were numerous accidents at the pit, which dated from at least the 1850s.

In December 1850, a boy died at the Dunkirk Colliery at Dukinfield in Cheshire, worked by the Dunkirk Coal Co., through being struck by a handle. Six months later, the head engineer was killed through the scaffold plank giving way while he was repairing the pumps at the Dunkirk Colliery. The *Manchester Guardian* reported on 8 January 1852 on the inquest into an accident by which four youths lost their lives at the Dewsnap Pit of the Dunkirk Colliery, the property of the Dukinfield Coal Co. at Dukinfield. The deceased were: Ellis Jones aged seventeen; Henry Harris, aged sixteen; Fredrick Jones, brother of Ellis, aged sixteen; and William Crosby, aged eighteen.

The *Manchester Guardian*, on 22 September 1856 reported:

Fatal Accident in a mine. An inquest was held yesterday afternoon before Mr Rutter, county coroner at the Albion Inn, Katherine Street on the body of a youth, named William Henry Kay, aged 16 years employed at the Dunkirk Colliery, Dukinfield, and resided with his father, a miner at Ashton-under-Lyne. The deceased was engaged at the bottom of an incline in the above colliery to receive tubs filled with coal sent down by a waggoner named Jonathan Braiththwaite, and to hook on the empties at the other end of the chain, which went up the incline, and acted as a counterbalance to the tubs coming down. On Monday morning last, about seven o'clock, John Seddon, who was working about ten yards off the bottom of the incline heard a cry, and running to the place he found the deceased much injured, he having been struck by a full tub coming down the incline and knocked against the side of the mine. He was picked up and carried towards home, but though he spoke several times, he died in the market place at Ashton. Mr Rose surgeon to the mines in the district was in immediate attendance, but his services were of no avail. The accident was the result of careless and reckless conduct, and disobedience of orders. The deceased had neglected to hook on his tub, and had also disobeyed a strict order coming within the sphere of danger, of which he was aware. Another youth had been discharged from the works the previous Saturday. The coroner enquired whether a bell could be used, and on it being shown it could not, and that there was no danger if the rules of the mine were obeyed, an unanimous verdict of 'accidental death' was returned, with an expression that it had resulted from carelessness of orders.

Edge Lane: Oldham★
See Dry Clough Colliery.

Fairbottom: Bardsley, SD 941 019
The pit was up Alt Lane at Bardsley, and a map of 1909 shows numerous 'old coal shafts' in this area.

The antiquity of the trade of the collier is illustrated in the parish records of Ashton, when a burial is recorded on 18 February 1673: 'Elisha Knott killed in a coale pitt att Fairebotham'. This was a pit worked by the Fairbottom & Werneth Colliery Co. during the 1840s, and Lees & Booth in 1854. A beam engine here gave the name 'Fairbottom Bobs' to the locality due to the bobbing motion of the engine. The engine at Fairbottom was made by Thomas Newcomen, of Dartmouth, and was one of the few examples of the Newcomen atmospheric engines to have survived. The engine consisted of a cylinder open at the top, as in all engines of this class, and about 28in in diameter. It worked a stroke of about 6ft, and the steam entered the cylinder at the bottom, the condensation being effected by injection into the cylinder. There was no condenser. The beam was made of wood braced with iron; the piston rods and pumps were attached by chains. A writer in the *Manchester City News*, in November 1850, stated that steam was supplied in a 'wagon' boiler which was then standing alongside, and that the coal was wheeled from the pit at the other side of the river. The piston was packed by pouring upon it a bucket of horse dung and water. The engine also performed the novel duty of bird-scarer. A cord was tied to the elevated centre of the beam that communicated with a 'ricker' in the cornfields beyond. Its habit of bobbing its

Fairbottom Bobs. (Oldham Library)

head when about its daily work caused the place to be called 'Fairbottom Bobs'. Henry Ford, the American car manufacturer, purchased the engine in 1929. The colliery appears to have been abandoned around 1862, when the last fatal accident occurred, according to the Mines Inspectors Reports.

Emanuel Morris Edwards, forty-two years of age, underlooker for the Fairbottom Co. at two of their pits on the Ashton Road gave the following evidence at the Inquiry into Child Labour in Coal Mines on 29 October 1841:

His father and his father's father were lead-miners in Wales, and his father came from the lead-mining to colliery work at Marple, Cheshire. Began work himself at Marple, where his father was steward, as a door-tenter, at 6d a-day, being then about seven years old. Has been at work for Messrs Lees from 19 years of age, and has been an underlooker under them for three years; having now two pits under him, those of Wood Park Rise Pit and Wood Park Deep Pit. Has two children in the pit, both commenced at seven years old, one was first driving the gin. He was then jigging, and then he left jigging to be a waggoner. Has a third boy going on seven yet at school. Sent them all to school for a year or two before they went into the pit, teaches them at night himself, and they all go to the Fairbottom Sunday-school at Alt Hill, towards the building of which he gave 5s himself, as did many other colliers, while some at lower wages, gave 2s 6d.

Another view of Fairbottom Bobs.
(Oldham Library)

It is a Wesleyan Methodist Sunday-school, in which he was himself a teacher, but his oldest son, now going on 17, is teacher in his place. The land and some assistance were given by Messrs Jones and Booth, and the colliers and others in the neighbourhood subscribed to build it. The children may be generally eight years of age or so before they go into the pits. They generally begin with air-door tenting; they then go to jigging, next to taking-off at the bottom of the incline, and lastly to waggoning, from which they generally go to getting.

The Fairbottom Company have air-door tenters in various parts of the mines paid by the employers themselves, there are at this moment preparations in the pits under his care for the employment of trappers after Christmas. The jiggers let the waggons down the 'broos' or inclines, being stationed for that purpose at the jig or winch, which lets the loaded waggon down and draws an empty one up. The takers-off are boys of 12 or 13, who take the waggons off the jig gear ready for the horse-driver (where horses and takers-off are employed) to harness his horse to it. One horse takes four and sometimes five waggons, but in some pits, and especially those newly commenced, the waggoners waggon all the way to the shaft.

A single waggon load is 4cwt of coal, but double waggons also are used, containing properly 8cwt. In the thin-seam mines single waggons are used, which a boy can manage, but these are thin seams. From the depression in the coal-trade, are nearly abandoned for present working, and only the 'Black Mine coal', which is the best in quality in the district, and one of the thickest, is now mainly worked. This 'mine' is about four feet thick, and, in working it, two-load waggons are used, carrying properly 8cwt, and carrying actually nearly that. It takes nearly a man's strength to manage a double-load wagon, it will take a youth of 16 or 17 years of age. His eldest son is working now as a getter, but the younger one, who is in his 13th year, is working with another, going on 14, at double-load waggons. This is easy work for the two, but its easiness makes them thrive. It is common for two to work together in this way, and then they share between them according to their strength. These two boys earn 3 to 5s a-day, and divide it equally.

They put the waggons on iron rails, on which they run on wheels. This is the case in the company's pits throughout. The belt and chain used formerly to be in universal use to draw the loads, with rails for only part of the distance. This is still used in the small Mountain Mines, and in various of the others, such as Mr Wrigley's at Low Side, but it is entirely abandoned in the larger and deeper mines (at least in those of the Fair-bottom Company) for the more extensive use of horses, rails, and machinery. There are not in this country pits equal to those of the Fairbottom Company for ventilation. Work from eight to nine hours a-day; but for lads the time is nearly eleven hours, from about seven to six, to get out the coal hewn by the men. [Signed] EMANUEL EDWARDS.

The site is mentioned several times in the Mines Inspectors Report: 'February 19th. Fairbottom Colliery worked by Lees and Booth, Thomas Lester killed by fall of roof' (1853); 'Fairbottom Colliery, James Brierley, killed through premature firing of a blast' (1853); 'September 2nd. Fairbottom Colliery, E. Brooks (boy) crushed by jigging machine in the Moss Pit' (1856); 'October 23rd. Fairbottom Colliery Joseph Needham killed through fall of roof in Dock Pit' (1856); 'November 23rd. Fairbottom Colliery. Reuben Crossley, aged 15, killed through chain breaking in the Moss Pit' (1856).

The following information is given in the Catalogue of Plans of Abandoned Mines (1928): Fairbottom (a) Bardsley; (b) COAL Black; (c) Chamber Colliery Co. Ltd, Hollinwood, Oldham; (d) 97 SW (1922) C10, 11: D10, 11, 12: E11, 12: F11, 12.

Fenny Hill: Glodwick, Oldham district, SD 939 039
This colliery, marked 'disused' on the OS map of 1891, was on the Abbey Hills Road (B6194) near its junction with Skipton Street and Warren Lane, Netherhey. Lowside Colliery was a short distance away to the north west, and its workings may have connected with those of Fenny Hill. The colliery was probably on the land now occupied by the garages on Warren Lane, close to the junction with Abbey Hills Road.

Two deaths are recorded in the Mines Inspectors Report, 1867: 'September 19th. Fenny Hill Colliery. John Lunn and William Taylor killed through explosion in the Upper Bent Mine'.

Catalogue of Plans of Abandoned Mines (1928): Fenny Hill (a) Oldham; (b) COAL Black, Great, Little, Higher Bent, Lower Bent (1857); (c) R. and E. Buckley, Lowside Colliery, Oldham; (d) 97 SW (1922) A11, 12: B11, 12: C12: D12: 97 SE (1922) B1: C1: D1. Another entry for Fenny Hill says 'see Lowside', and the fact that Buckley's had the abandonment plans must confirm the workings of both pits were connected.

Ferney Field: Chadderton
A colliery worked by the Chamber Colliery Co. in 1869 and 1879. The Chamber Colliery Co. Ltd, Hollinwood, Oldham, worked the colliery in 1896, when Mr W.W. Millington, was the colliery manager. The colliery at Ferney Field was at the end of Ferney Field Road off the Middleton Road West, Chadderton. A small branch cutting off the Rochdale canal served the colliery. The *Colliery Guardian* described the pit in 1856:

> Fernyfield Colliery Oldham, the single shaft here was ten feet in diameter. During the sinking of this shaft, which began about 1852, considerable difficulties were experienced before its completion. The material sunk through from the top of the shaft down to around 46 yards depth consisted of quicksands and other drifts. To

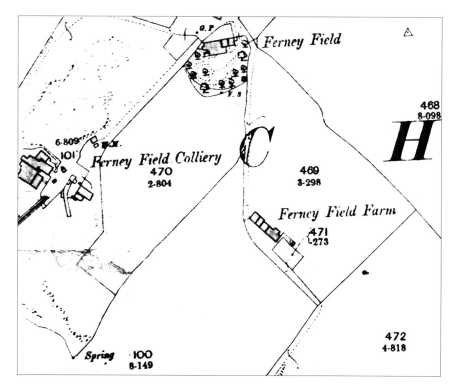

Ferney Field Colliery, map of 1891.

overcome this obstacle, cast iron cylinders with a cutting edge at the lower end were brought into use, other cylinders were added to the one with the cutting edge as it descended, aided with weights at the top end. The first length of cylinder was 18 feet in diameter, the second 15 feet, and the third 10 feet in diameter. The first two cylinders failed to penetrate the quicksand, though the third was successful making the diameter of the shaft ten foot. The winding engine had one horizontal cylinder 30in by 60in plain drum. Two tubs were raised in each cage, one above the other, and each tub carried 7cwt of coal. The conductors in the shaft were of pitch pine and two to each cage. Two seams were worked, the Black Mine, at a depth of 130 yards, by the early 1890s this seam was practically exhausted, and the other seam was the Bent Seam. At a depth of 200 yards in the shaft, a level tunnel was driven to intercept the Bent Seam after 30 yards, here a dip tunnel was driven into it for a distance of 230 yards in a south west direction. Much water issued from the roof of the two seams as soon as it was broken.

Notwithstanding the limited circumference of the shaft, room was found in it to accommodate the two cages and seven sets of pumps at the sides. Two horizontal pumping engines were placed at the shaft top on opposite sides, and could raise as much as 500 gallons of water per minute day and night if required. The No.1 pumping engine had two horizontal cylinders 20in by 36in with two horizontal rods and two L legs placed over the shaft. This raised the water from a depth of 205 yards to a lodge room at 70 yards from the surface. The No.2 engine was of similar construction, and raised the water to the surface from the 70 foot lodgement. A considerable amount of this water issued from a coal seam which was located at the bottom of the shaft tubbing.

Information from the Catalogue of Plans of Abandoned Mines (1928): Ferney Field (a) Chadderton; (b) COAL Black, Higher Bent, Lower bent (abandoned 13 September 1897); (d) 96 NE (1923) F12: G12: H12: 97 NW (1922) F1, 2: G1, 2: H1, 2, 3.

A Mines Inspectors Report for the year 1869 records a death at the colliery: 'April 20th. Ferney Field Colliery. Thomas Latham aged 24, killed through roof fall'. Two men were charged with incautious use of their lamps, as reported in the *Colliery Guardian*, 10 January 1873: 'On Wednesday at the Royton petty courts, Samuel Taylor and Robert Jackson, day men employed at the Ferney Field Colliery at Chadderton near Oldham were charged with being in the mine on the 13th with their lamp tops off'.

Flowery Field: Flowery Field, near Hyde
A pit of some antiquity, probably dating from the mid-1790s. It is recorded that, on 8 April 1842, at the Flowery Field Colliery near Hyde, Cheshire, in the Black Mine Pit, seventeen were killed and eight others seriously injured. All the miners were provided with safety lamps, but chose to use candles instead. The Black Mine, at 4ft 8in in height, was famed in the area for its excellent quality. The pit

was formerly worked by Bateman and Sherratt, for upwards of sixty years before this disaster, but had passed into the hands of the late Francis Dukinfield Astley Esq., and its executors, who leased the pit to Sawyer and Lees of Ashton for a period of twenty-one years. At the time of this accident there remained about eight years on the lease. The reports left little to the imagination when describing the injuries to those who perished and were burnt that day:

James Brookshaw alias Lees, of Colliers Row, Flowery Field, a boy aged 12 years. He was the son of Henry Brookshaw, a collier who was also in the pit, and at first was not expected to recover. The deceased appears to have been killed by the explosion, and his body, limbs and face was much burned. Although so young, James was the eldest of six children. The father who is now so ill from the effects of the chokedamp will not be able to resume work for some days.

Robert Downing, of Colliers Row, Flowery Field. Elizabeth Downing, stated that the deceased was her son, and that he was 16 years and 11 months of age, and that he was the eldest but one of five children. Her husband, Emanuel worked at the same pit, and got hurt at the lifting engine. He was sent to the Manchester Infirmary, where he died about twenty-two week ago. This poor boy was much burnt about the face and body, and appeared to have perished through the effects of the explosion.

James Oldfield, of Thomas Street, Flowery Field. Selina Oldfield, wife of Henry Oldfield, shoemaker stated that the deceased was her son, he was 13 years of age, the eldest of three children. With the exception of two or three small specks on the face, fragments of coal having been driven against it by the explosion, there were no external marks of injury on his body. The body was swollen, one of the characteristics of cases where death has resulted from suffocation – in this instance by the blackdamp. Which, when the explosion occurred had thrown the poor sufferer upon his face on the ground, and would instantly commence its deleterious action, to which the sufferer must have been exposed for several hours. This gas, after the explosion would have covered a greater part of the pit, so that all who fell would be subject to its influence.

Robert Unwin, of Thomas Street, Flowery Field. Betty Unwin, wife of Joseph Unwin, collier stated that the deceased was her son, and that he was 19 years of age, the eldest but one of six children. His face was much swollen and discoloured, but there was no abrasion of the skin or scorching, and in all probability this young man perished from suffocation from the blackdamp.

Samuel Derbyshire of Newton Hall, formerly an old residence, then a farm, and now occupied in four tenements by as many families. George Derbyshire, head banksman at the pit, stated that the deceased was his son, and was 16 years and

8 months old. He was one of eight children, six boys and two girls. His mother died when he was nine days old. The only visible marks of injury were on the left cheek bone, which was grazed, as if by a fall on some hard substance. The back appeared to be a little scorched, but the cause of death was the suffocating effects of the afterdamp.

John Wild, of Newton Hall. Ann Wild stated that she was the deceased's widow, he was 42 years of age, and had worked in the pit doing odd jobs, shoeing mules etc. It was supposed that he was in the stable when the explosion occurred, and that the blast had brought down a portion of roof which had fallen upon him fracturing his skull. He was much bruised, and his face was perforated with the coal and rock. He left a daughter 20 years of age.

William Ragg, of Throstle Bank, Flowery Field. This poor lad, we believe to be an illegitimate child who lived with his grand-parents, Adam and Ann Ragg. The latter stated that her husband had of late worked at a forge, but was a cutler by trade. The deceased was their grandson and was 16 years and 8 months of age and was a collier. He had a sister living aged 21 years, his mother was also living, but he had been brought up by the grand-parents. The poor lad had fine regular features, long hair and eyelashes, and the face resembled that of a girl. It was a good deal pitted with small particles of coal, and both the face and lips were discoloured, but there was no mark of scorching. The deceased had probably died from the effects of the afterdamp.

William Bowker, of Spring Gardens, Flowery Field. Mary Bowker, widow of John Bowker also killed by this accident, stated that the deceased was her son. He was 17 years of age, the eldest of nine children. His face was much discoloured, in parts almost black, but he did not appear to have been burnt at all. He appears to have lost his life through the afterdamp—the body was in the same bed as his deceased father.

John Bowker, of Spring Gardens, Flowery Field. The widow stated that the deceased was a collier, and was 47 years of age. He was not at all burned or wounded or disfigured, and the appearance of the corpse with the placid and natural expression gave the impression that he was in a sound slumber rather than the 'deep sleep of the grave' He has left a widow and eight surviving children.

Adam Gill, of Haigh Houses, Hyde. Ellen Gill, widow of the deceased said, that the deceased was a collier, and 41 years of age. He appeared to have lost his life from the severe injuries inflicted by the explosion, when he was probably driven with great violence against some wall or other obstacle. The back of the head as fractured and much crushed, his legs were broken, and his thighs were driven upwards into his body. His face was pitted with the coal as thickly as if he had the smallpox. He left a widow and four children, the eldest of whom was eleven years of age on that fateful day, and the youngest is about 18 months old.

William Williams, who lived near the Crown Inn, Hyde Lane. Betty Williams, wife of William Williams, collier, stated that the deceased and his brother Thomas, both of whose bodies were laid out on the same bed were her sons. William was sixteen years old and nine months. He was not much marked externally, and appears to have been overtaken by the afterdamp.

Thomas Williams, brother of the last named, and who lived in the same house, near the Crown Inn, Hyde. The weeping mother stated, that this poor lad was 14 years of age, and she had, besides the two instantly snatched away, four children all younger than the deceased—the youngest not more than two years of age. Except for a mark on the forehead, there was no external bruising, and these two lads had died from the effects of the afterdamp.

John Hardy, of John Street, Hyde. This seemed in all respects the most distressing of cases. The widow, Alice Hardy, stated that her deceased husband was just turned 33, and that he was a collier. We were assured by all who knew the family that the unfortunate man had left that morning with no better breakfast than a crust of dry bread and a little mint tea, without sugar or milk. The poor man had no wounds, except for a little scouring on the chin, but his hands were much discoloured. Death appears to have arose from the effects of the afterdamp. The deceased left three children, the eldest nine years old, the youngest a year and seven months, and as the poor widow said 'I may be confined any day'.

John Aspinall, of Shaw Hall, Newton. The bodies of the deceased and his son were laid upon the same bed. The head was much discoloured at the back, but the face bore little mark of suffering, and was remarkably fresh, calm and life-like. James Aspinall stated, that the deceased was his brother, he was a collier aged 44 years of age. The deceased had left a widow, and two surviving children, of the ages of six years and two years, and the widow is nearing confinement. It appears that the deceased died from suffocation.

John Aspinall junior, of Shaw Hall, Newton, son of the last named. His uncle, James Aspinall, stated that the deceased was in his 15th year and a collier. His back, arms, legs and thighs, were much bruised. The face of the corpse was placid in expression, and free from any wound – he too appeared to have died from suffocation.

William Grimshaw, alias Stokes, of Newton hall, whose body was laid out on the same bed as that of John Wild. Josiah Grimshaw, stated that the deceased was his only brother, he was 52 years of age, a widower with one child, about eight years of age living at Dukinfield. He was the last of the sufferers found, and was sought for several hours. He was found about two o'clock on Saturday morning up a jig brow, having ran up there for safety from a shunt, where he was last seen by his comrades. There was a discoloured swelling on his right cheek, but in all other respects there was little external injuries. Death was due to the chokedamp.

James Lees, of Denton. This was a boy of 11 years and 10 months. Betty Lees, the mother identified the body, which it was stated was bruised at the back of the head and loins. The nose, left eye, and right cheek were also bruised and injured. It was supposed that he died from the afterdamp.

This accounts for 17 of the 25 men in the pit at the time of the explosion who were killed. The other eight were Joseph Mosley, of Colliers Row, Flowery Field, who was brought out almost suffocated, being quite insensible. His right forearm was broken from being forced against the side of the pit by the blast. Henry Brookshaw, alias Lees, of Colliers Row. He continued to be in great danger, but began to recover on the following Sunday. Robert Merrick, a boy living at Haughton Green, was for some time insensible, but later gave signs of recovery. Thomas Merrick, brother of the last named, was not much hurt. John Merrick, father of the last two, was able to walk when taken out, and afterwards walked home. James Dunk, an aged man was able to walk and make his way home. Samuel Rogers, of Colliers Row, soon recovered on being brought to daylight, and William Hurst, a boy, was at first much affected, but came round soon afterwards.

It would appear that no lessons were learned here, for another man was killed here through working with a naked light on 20 March 1844, less than two years after the above disaster.

Friar Ground
A colliery evidently worked by Thomas Broadoak in the early 1840s, mentioned in the evidence given at the Report on Child Labour by John Buckley, aged forty-nine, on 4 November 1841:

Is assistant banksman at Thomas Broadoak's pit, at Friar Ground, being now unfit for underground work, which has given him, as he supposes, the oppression in his breathing, which now never leaves him. Went into the narrow mountain-mine pits when going on six. Worked naked, as the last witness has described worked with his father; went on to be a collier working in those pits, but listed for a soldier at 18, and was in the army for seven years. It is now seven years since he worked in any of the mountain-pits. When last he did work there the plan was what the last witness describes. It is bad to take children into the mines so young.

If they kept them out till 10 or 12 years or age they would get some learning; but they 'would na break down to it half so well as if they go at eight', that is in the thin mine; in the thicker mines 12 years old would be soon enough. Now gets only 5*s* a-week himself; he is not fit for strong work, and has a wife and boy to keep. Had one boy killed in drawing props in the pit, and a half-brother and a brother-in-law killed by being jerked down the pit on the rope partly slipping from the whimsey, [Signed] JOHN (X) BUCKLEY, mark.

Glodwick: Glodwick, Oldham★

This colliery was situated in the Glodwick area of Oldham during the 1840s, when James Collinge & Co., employing seventy-five men and boys underground, five of which were aged thirteen and under, to work the pit. James Collinge & Co. were still working the mine in 1861, although by 1876 the pit was being worked by John Wild & Co., John Wild being a former manager at the colliery. The colliery consisted of four shafts, the No.1 Pit, the Sackry Lane Pit, the Brown Cow Pit, and the No.4 Pit. The pit worked the Bent Mine at a depth of 164 yards.

This information can be gleaned from the Catalogue of Plans of Abandoned Mines (1928): Glodwick (a) Oldham; (b) COAL Higher Bent, Lower Bent (1867); (c) B&E Buckley, Lowside Colliery, Oldham; (d) 97 SW (1922) B11, 12: C11, 12. Although this gives the date of abandonment as 1867, there is a report below of a miner being burnt in an explosion in March 1868. It would appear that the Glodwick Colliery was notoriously fiery, and there were many firedamp-related deaths and injuries, as well as several other accidents due to different causes. The *Manchester Guardian,* 11 February 1846, reports:

> Fatal Accident at a Colliery. On Friday last, whilst a coal miner named Benjamin Dunkerley, was at work in the colliery of Mr Collinge, at Glodwick, a large quantity of earth fell upon him, in one of the branch shafts from the giving away of a portion of the roof of the mine. The unfortunate man was rescued as soon as possible by the other colliers at work in the pit, and conveyed to his residence near Cannon Street Oldham, where he died on Saturday, the following day. The deceased, who was 42 years of age, was a quiet inoffensive man, and has left a wife and several children.

The *Manchester Guardian,* 18 April 1846, provides an example of the dangerous volatility of the site:

> On Wednesday last, Mr Dearden held an inquest at the Ordnance Arms, Glodwick respecting the death of Henry Roxby, coal miner aged 46 years. Whilst the deceased was at work on the 31st of March last in the colliery belonging to Mr Collinge, Glodwick he was severely burnt by an accidental explosion of firedamp. The poor man died on Tuesday last leaving a wife and four children.

A tragic death due to a roof fall is reported in the *Manchester Guardian,* 23 January 1847:

Fatal Accident at a Colliery. On Monday evening last, whilst a coal miner named Jonathan Hilton was at work in the colliery belonging to Mr Collinge, at Glodwick, a large quantity of earth fell from the roof of the mine, and immediately covered the poor fellow, killing him instantaneously. The quantity of earth that fell upon him was so large, that it took several men half an hour to get at the body. The deceased was an unmarried man, 26 years of age and a native of Middleton.

An almost identical accident is recorded in the *Manchester Guardian* on 3 November, later that year:

On Saturday last, Mr Dearden, coroner held an inquest at the Ordnance Arms public-house, Glodwick, on the body of James Street, a coal miner. On Thursday last whilst the deceased was at work at the colliery of Mr Collinge, Glodwick, a large quantity of earth accidentally fell from the roof of the mine and overwhelmed the unfortunate man, who was immediately killed. The deceased was 35 years of age, and has left a large family of young children. Verdict: 'Accidentally Killed'.

A few years later, the same newspaper reported another fatal accident, 7 April 1852: 'On Saturday an inquest was held by Mr Dearden, at the Ordnance Arms, Glodwick, on the body of John Beswick, a coal miner aged 21, who was suffocated by black damp, in a pit belonging to Mr Collinge, on the 30th inst. A verdict with the facts was returned'.

The Mines Inspectors Report, for the year 1853, recorded: 'September 27th. Glodwick Colliery worked by James Collinge, John Higham aged 17 years, run over by tram in engine brow in pit and killed'. This could be argued to be the same incident reported in the *Manchester Guardian* on 15 October 1853, though the names and ages are different: 'On Wednesday an inquest was held by Mr Dearden, coroner, on the body of John Kershaw, a youth aged 16 years, who was killed by a wagon passing over him, while he was working in a "down brow" at Mr Collinge's colliery, Glodwick. A verdict of "accidental death" was returned'.

Another large explosion, highlighting the firedamp problem, is reported in the *Manchester Guardian,* 2 June 1856:

On Saturday afternoon between one and two o'clock an explosion of firedamp occurred in one of Mr James Collinge's Coal Pits at Glodwick, by which two men were severely burnt. Two getters, named Horatio Hilton and Thomas Hilton had been directed to clear out a 'run' or road at the bottom of the pit. Their orders were to use only their picks, and not to use any powder. Contrary to these instructions and with recklessness often manifested by colliers, they procured some powder and made use of it to procure their labours. One of them incautiously took the top off his lamp for the purpose of lighting the straw (to use as a fuse) and immediately on doing so the firedamp that had accumulated ignited with a loud explosion. The two men at once took to their heels, but not before they had been severely burnt.

They mistook the way, and instead of running towards the shaft went further into the pit and were overtaken by afterdamp, suffering severely from its effects. Another man Abraham Kershaw, who is employed as a waggoner for his father, and who at the time of the explosion had been taking wagons of coal to the shaft bottom was also seriously injured by the afterdamp overtaking him. He was dashed against the wall and rendered insensible.

When the accident occurred, a young man named Wild, son of John Wild, the underlooker was in a passage between the shaft and the run which the Hiltons were employed, and observing from the flame of his lamp that something was wrong, ran to the shaft and escaped without accident. On hearing the explosion he communicated with his father who was on the top of the pit, and by his orders a large quantity of water was forced down the old run by the engine. After this Mr Wild went down and risked his own life and rescued the sufferers from their dangerous position.

Further research in the Mines Inspectors Report shows that Abraham Kershaw died from the results of this accident on 3 June.

Also in a Mines Inspectors Report, for the year 1859, is a record of another fatality: 'January 14th. Glodwick Colliery. George Dronsfield, 13 years of age, killed by roof fall, not propped'.

A tragic and dramatic accident is reported in the *Colliery Guardian*, 13 July 1861:

On Friday morning about a quarter past six o'clock, an accident of fatal character occurred at the Glodwick Colliery, belonging to Messrs Collinge and Lancashire. The pit is one, which has not been in use for some time, and the shaft is at present being widened. At the time of the accident four of the workmen were standing on a scaffold fixed to the sides of the shaft by means of chains. A large stone fell from the side of the shaft and broke one of the chains, and consequently one end of the scaffold gave way, and two of the men, Thomas Oakes and John Martin were precipitated down the shaft. The scaffold was about 16 yards from the bottom of the pit, but there was water to a depth of eleven yards. It appears that the chains extended as far as the water and Oakes had the presence of mind to grab one, by means of which he raised himself to the surface, and was thence extricated by his fellow workmen. Martin however, did not offer to rise again, so the men commenced grappling for him, and in a short time he was brought up lifeless. There was no violent bruises on his body, but a mark was discovered around his neck, and it is supposed that he got strangled by the chain as he was falling. The unfortunate man was taken to his residence at Roundthorn, where he leaves a wife and three children with an aged mother. The deceased was thirty-one years of age.

Another Mines Inspectors Report, for the year 1868, again underlines the prevalence of firedamp at the site: 'March 19th. Glodwick Colliery. Thomas Mills burned by explosion of firedamp, died 8th April'.

Greenacres: Oldham*

Eighty-seven men and boys were employed at this colliery during the early 1840s, when it was worked by Messrs Lees, Jones and Booth. Obviously in the Greenacres district of Oldham, the exact location is unknown at the time of writing. Lees & Co. worked the pit in 1869, according to a mines list for that year. Catalogue of Plans of Abandoned Mines (1928): Greenacres, Bank Top (a) Oldham; (b) COAL Royley, Neddy (1857); (c) Engineers Office LMS Railway Co. Ltd Crewe; (d) 97 NW (1922) H1, 2: 97 SE (1922) A2.

Two Mines Inspectors Reports provide details of accidents here: 'June 25th. Greenacres Colliery. Wright Brierley killed by roof fall between slips' (1863); 'March 17th. Greenacres Colliery. John Lees killed through being caught by underground cogs' (1869).

Greenacres Hill

This, an apparently different colliery from the one above, is listed in the Catalogue of Plans of Abandoned Mines (1928): Greenacres Hill (a) Oldham; (b) COAL Royley (about 1869); (c) Chamber Colliery Co. Ltd Hollinwood, Oldham; (d) 97 NW (1922) D12: E12: F12: 97 NE (1922) F1. Nothing else is known of the colliery.

Hanging Bank: Oldham

Listed in the Catalogue of Plans of Abandoned Mines (1928): Hanging Bank (a) Oldham; (b) COAL Royley (abandoned May 1883); (d) 97 NE (1922) G2, 3: H3. Nothing else known, not listed in a mines index for 1880.

Hanging Chadder: Thornham, Royton, SD 915 093

This colliery was worked by Robert Holt in 1848, James Stott, Milne & Co. in 1854, the Oldham, Middleton & Rochdale Colliery Co. in 1869 and 1879, and the Middleton & Rochdale Coal Co. Ltd, Edge Lane, Oldham, in 1896. In 1896, the pit is listed as a 'Pumping Pit'. The pit was officially abandoned in January 1900. There appears to have been just one shaft at Hanging Chadder Pit, and this seems to have been a timber structure, probably pitch pine. This is the downcast shaft in ventilation, and a small squat chimney nearby possible served as a 'cupola' or furnace shaft. A boiler at the bottom of this shaft would heat the air around it, causing it to rise, which would draw fresh air down the other shaft. On a map of 1909, the colliery is simply listed as 'disused'. The colliery in its productive days worked the Royley Seam (the local name for the Arley Mine) at a depth of 270ft. The origins of the name 'Hanging Chadder' come from the Welsh 'Cadr' meaning hill fort; 'hanging' means the downward slope of a hill. Hanging Chadder, therefore, means hill fort on a downward slope.

A tragic and disturbing story is reported in the *Manchester Guardian*, 22 August 1846:

On Thursday last an inquest was held at the Turk's Head public-house, Gravel Hole, Thornham by the coroner for the Rochdale District respecting the death of a youth aged 17 years named Thomas Harrison. On Saturday last whilst the lad was at work in the colliery at Hanging Chadder, Thornham belonging to Messrs Holt and Co. a large quantity of earth suddenly fell on him from the roof of the mine, and he was instantly killed. The deceased was an orphan, and the story is currently in the neighbourhood that the child was purchased by his adopted father for a shilling. A verdict of 'accidental death' was recorded.

Another fatal accident is recorded in the *Rochdale Observer*, 16 November 1861: 'John Driver, aged 54, collier who resides at Thornham was killed on Tuesday morning whilst at his work on the Hanging Chadder Colliery by a stone falling from the roof'.

Hardy Field: Oldham

This pit is marked on a map of 1851, north-west of Higginshaw, and is listed in the Catalogue of Plans of Abandoned Mines: Hardy Field (a) Royton; (b) COAL; (d) 97 NW (122) D9. This is the location of the mine entrance only. An explosion here is reported in the *Manchester Guardian*, 9 May 1840:

On Saturday forenoon last, a serious explosion of carburated hydrogen gas occurred in a coal-pit belonging to Messrs Barker, Evans and Co. at Hardy Fields, Grimbies, Oldham by which two boys, James Taylor, aged 13, and John Taylor, aged 11, brothers, who were at work in the pit within a short distance of the main shaft, with lighted candles were shockingly injured and burnt. They survived until Sunday afternoon, when they died in the pitiable state, being totally insensible. The foul air is supposed to have burst from some old works, as it exploded near the main shaft, though all the draw-ways seemed quite free.

Hartford: Oldham, SD 907 042

A colliery worked by the Oldham, Middleton & Rochdale Colliery Co. in 1869, 1879 and 1884. Prior to this, the pit was worked by Mills, Lees & Co. in 1854. The colliery is marked on an OS map of 1892, and was at the bottom of Wright Street, and behind the Commercial Hotel at Nibble Nook. On the colliery site was a shaft, an air shaft, a smithy, and a reservoir to the north. The pit appears to have been abandoned in the early to mid-1880s, but is listed in 1880 when still being worked by the Oldham, Middleton & Rochdale Colliery Co. Ltd.

The following information is from the Catalogue of Plans of Abandoned Mines (1928): Hartford (a) Oldham; (b) COAL Lower Two (abandoned October 1884); (d) 97 NW (1922) F5, 6: G6: H6. There is also an entry for Hartford and Robin Hill as follows: Hartford and Robin Hill (a) Oldham: Chadderton; (b) COAL (abandoned December 1881); (d) 97 NW (1922) B3, 4: C3, 4: D3, 4, 5, 6, 7: E4, 5, 6, 7: G5, 6, 7, 8: H5, 6, 7: 97 SW (1922) A6, 7.

There are two Mines Inspectors Reports: 'August 29th. Edge Lane and Dry Clough Colliery Company Ltd. William Ogden killed through roof fall in Hartford Pit' (1863); 'February 17th. Hartford Colliery. Charles Ashworth killed through roof fall' (1869).

Hartshead: Ashton-under-Lyne

Mainly a fireclay mine, worked by John Hall & Son (Dukinfield) Ltd, of Dukinfield, Cheshire in 1940, when it employed just five men underground and one surface worker. However, it had a long history. On 3 May 1862, there is a report in the *Colliery Guardian*:

> At the Ashton-under-Lyne County Sessions, on Wednesday, Joseph Horsfall was summoned on the information of Mr Joseph Dickinson, the Government Inspector of Mines for having on the 17th of March last as the agent for the Hartshead mine belonging to Messrs Lees and Booth (The Fairbottom Colliery Co.) neglected to give notice within 24 hours after of the personal injury to Patrick Ruhan had taken place from an explosion. Mr Littler appeared for the defendant, or rather to watch this case and others on behalf of the company. He suggested that all cases should be taken before any decision was come to. Mr Dickinson said they were each specific offences. Mr Littler said with regard to this summons and another of a similar character (not giving notice to the Inspector) without entering into any technical defence, he would submit to penalties, admitting that the law was not complied with, if Mr Dickinson would withdraw the other offences. Mr Dickinson said that he thought there had been such a degree of neglect as to the ventilation that he could not settle the case. Mr Littler replied that after no settlement could be come to, he was sorry so strong an expression should be made by one of her Majesty's inspectors, but he would show that such a charge was unfounded. Mr Dickinson then stated that an explosion had taken place at the Hartshead Colliery on 17th of March, by which Mr Ruhan was burnt, and from the effects he had died. Notice should have been given to the Secretary of State within 24 hours, but it was not given until ten days later, and if the man had not been likely to die, neither the Secretary nor he would probably had noticed. There was nothing, which showed the skill, and management of managers were anxious that owners' names should appear in such a list of accidents. Other information was for not giving notice to the Inspector of the explosion. Thomas Partington stated that he was the underlooker at the Hartshead Pit. He said that the notice of the accident was not given at the time, it was so slight, and he was ignorant that it was necessary to give notice unless the accident was fatal. The case was proved.

Hathershaw Moor: Thornham, SD 909 094

This colliery was the pit that was off Thornham Old Road, to the west, near its junction with the 'Summit'. The pit was recorded as being 80 yards in depth to the Royley Mine. The colliery in the 1840s was worked by Messrs Wild & Co.

and Andrew Wild & Co. in 1848, and Wild & Lord during the early 1850s. In 1853 the colliery was worked by James Stott, Milnes & Co., but this is the last mention of the pit in any mines index. The pit is mentioned in the Catalogue of Plans of Abandoned Mines: Hathershaw Moor (a) Royton; (b) COAL; (d) 89 SW (1910) D4. Note the last entry is the mine entrance only.

The *Manchester Guardian,* 4 April 1846, reports a fatal roof fall:

Colliery Accident. On Thursday last, Mr Dearden, coroner held an inquest at the Yew Tree public-house on the body of Abraham Ashworth, coal miner, aged 29 years, a resident of Buersill, Castleton. It appears that on Tuesday evening last, the deceased was at work at the bottom of one of the coal pits at Hathershaw Moor Colliery, belonging to Messrs Wild and Co. when the roof fell upon him, and he was killed on the spot. He has left a wife and three small children. The jury returned a verdict of 'accidental death'.

There is a report in the *Manchester Guardian*, 17 July 1850, relating to events surrounding an industrial dispute at the site:

The Colliers' Turn-Out. At Rochdale petty sessions, on Monday last, before Messrs William Chadwick and William Fenton, magistrates, and a crowded court, Abraham Howarth, one of the turn-out colliers at Messrs Wild and Lords' coal pits at Thornham and Buersill, was placed in the dock. The 'miners' solicitor general' Mr W.P. Roberts, of Manchester, appeared for the defendant, and Mr Hunt solicitor, appeared for the prosecution. It appears that there has been a turn-out of the colliers for about 13 weeks, for an advance of wage, or dispute as to the amount paid. A number of new hands from various places have been working at the pits, and on the morning of the 11th. inst, defendant met William Lee, late of Leeds, and Joseph Ashton, of Burnley, going to their work at the colliery. He told them dark and short nights would come, and if they continue to work, blood would be shed. Mr Roberts on behalf of the defendant, attributed the language used to a want of education, and said his client was sorry for what he had said. There had been a strike at the pits for 13 weeks, and this was the first case brought before them. Defendant was bound himself in £10, and two securities of £5 each, to keep the peace for twelve months.

Haven: Oldham
This colliery was worked by Joseph Lees during the late 1840s, and was probably near Haven, and Haven House on Count Hill, just below Moorside, where an old shaft is marked on a map of 1891, along with numerous other workings. The entry in the Catalogue of Plans of Abandoned Mines says 'see Count hill (Higher and Lower)', which suggests the pit had underground connections with those collieries which are in the vicinity. Joseph Lees junior (colliery proprietor) gave evidence at the Inquiry into Child Labour in 1841:

The coal trade of this district is in a very depressed state, inasmuch that the proprietors yesterday at their meeting seriously debated whether it were not better to cease working part the mines. Some factories are completely stopped, and others working short time, while diminished earnings of the people themselves force them to crowd together into a smaller number of houses, because of their inability to pay their accustomed rents. There are in this township of Oldham alone about 1,800 houses for labouring people, which are now entirely empty, although they were a few years ago fully occupied, or nearly so. This huddling of people together has been going on for some years, and has diminished the demand for coal. Colliers already haven't full work, and there appears to be no chance but to throw a number out altogether. Of course the work of the children is diminished in the same proportion as that of the parents. Oldham is no worse off than other parts of Lancashire, either in trade or its collieries. [Signed] Joseph Lees.

The only other reference is to a fatality, and is found in the *Manchester Guardian*, 8 July 1848:

On Thursday last, an inquest was held at the Collier's Arms, Oldham by Mr Clarke, deputy coroner on the body of Joseph Hinchcliffe, aged 18, collier, in the employ of Mr Joseph Lees, at Haven Pit. The deceased came to his death on Tuesday last, by a large stone accidentally falling on him from the roof, under which he, with several others was getting coal. The stone contained about 1,500 cubic feet, and became detached through a 'fault', which had not previously been discovered by the miners. Verdict 'accidental death'.

Hebers: near Middleton
The only notable reference to this site is in the *Manchester Guardian*, 11 May 1853:

On Monday last, a boy aged 12 years, employed as a drawer in the Hebers Colliery, near Middleton, died in consequence of injuries which he had received on the 4th inst. A wagon in the pit ran against him on that day, by which means his leg was broken, and he was otherwise injured. The boy's name was William Howorth, son of Thomas Howorth, farmer, Hopwood.

Hey: Oldham
A colliery, location unknown, at work in 1854, and operated by Mills, Lees & Co. By 1861, the pit was being worked by John and James Lees and Joseph Hey.

Heys Colliery: Mossley Road, Ashton-under-Lyne
John Kenworthy and Brothers were working this colliery in 1854, with the Fairbottom Colliery Co. working the site in 1869.

An accident here is reported in the *Manchester Guardian*, 28 December 1850:
On Saturday last a fatal accident occurred at Heys Colliery, Ashton. It appears
that it has been the custom for the men to ride up and down a jig brow, which is
traversed by an endless chain. On Saturday last several hands were coming up the
brow, when one of the links of the chain, which is an excellent one, snapped, and
sent several empty and full tubs with the men who were riding them precipitating
to the bottom. Some of the men were bruised, and one young man named William
Miller was killed when the end of the chain struck him on the head. An inquest
was held on Tuesday before Mr Henshall, deputy coroner when a verdict of
'accidental death' was recorded.

An explosion caused by a lamp is reported in the *Manchester Guardian*, 19 March
1851:

On Monday morning another fatal explosion took place at Heys Colliery, Ashton.
It appears from inquiries made on the spot, that about eight o'clock on Monday
morning, the men being nearly all at work, when a young man named William
Joule, a miner took the top off his lamp, and went amongst some other men. An
explosion ensued, and the consequence was that Joule and several others were
severely injured. One man named James Odgen was killed and another named
James Andrew has since died from his injuries. We are also informed that two
others are in a dangerous state, their recovery being doubtful. It appears, that when
Joule was found, he said he could not blame anyone, as he had caused the explosion
himself by taking the top off his lamp…

Another explosion occurred at the colliery in 1857. Looking at the report in the
Manchester Guardian of 1 August, it seems likely that there were many casualties,
though the extent of the disaster is clearly not certain at the time the report was
written:

Colliery Explosion and Loss of Life, at Ashton-under-Lyne. A fearful explosion
attended with loss of life, occurred yesterday at the Heys Colliery, Mossley Road,
Ashton, belonging to Messrs Kenworthy Brothers. There are five seams at the
colliery, two of which are only being worked, those known as the two-feet-mine,
and the new-mine. There are three shafts, one upcast and two downcast. At six
o'clock yesterday morning between thirty and forty men (the exact number is not
yet known) descended the No.1 downcast shaft, and proceeded to work in the
new-mine, this is 225 yards down the shaft. About thirty yards from the shaft there
is an incline, with an upward gradient, of 1 in 2, which is 460 yards long, and onto
this incline the men proceeded to their work. At the head of the incline there is
an engine of 30 horse power, superintended by an engineer named Edward Elliott,
and employed in drawing the coals up the gradient. In the two-feet-mine, about
fifteen men were working. At half past one o'clock a terrific explosion shook

the houses in the immediate vicinity of the pit, and was heard for a considerable distance around. Almost instantaneously volume of dense smoke and dust were shot up the No.1 downcast shaft with such violence as to break up the iron plating at its mouth, and immediately afterwards, the engineer, Elliott ascended, but, being somewhat injured, he was conveyed home at Dukinfield. The men who had been working in the two-feet-mine, ascended by the No.2 downcast shaft as soon as they heard the explosion, and bravely volunteered to descend the No.1 shaft. About ten of them went down with the underlooker, John Garside, and commenced repairing the air roads. Subsequently a number of other men, volunteers from the neighbouring collieries, went down to their assistance, but the operation is a slow one. In the meantime, the great excitement prevailing in the town, hundreds of persons, including of course the relatives of the unfortunate men below, flocked to the spot, and watched with great anxiety the execrations of those at the mouth of the shaft, who under the superintendence of Mr Pearce, the manager were supplying, bricks, mortar, and steam to the underlooker and those below.

Several medical men of the neighbourhood were also in attendance to render aid to those who might be brought up alive. Mr Dickinson, the inspector of collieries for the Manchester District, was also present. Up to nine o'clock last night, the way had been cleared for about 250 yards along the incline. The bodies of five colliers, all-dead, had then been found, and it was feared that none of the remainder, when discovered would be alive. The names of two of the deceased men are George and Robert Thompson, father and son, the others have not yet been identified. It was calculated that a considerable time would elapse before the whole of the men would be discovered. No positive information about the state of the mine, or the cause of the accident were obtainable up to a late hour last night.

The *Manchester Guardian* of the following Monday 3 August, presented a clearer picture of the full extent of the terrible disaster:

The search for the unfortunate men who were in the mine at the time of the explosion, on Friday has been continued since the evening of that day without intermission, and the total number of bodies recovered up to last night [Sunday] was 31, in all of which life was extinct. The underlooker of the mine, John Garside, descended the shaft soon after the explosion, with about ten men, all volunteers. In the course of the evening others offered their assistance, until the exploring parties numbered about 40. Mr Dickinson, the Government Inspector of Mines for this district, arrived about seven o'clock, and having made a few preliminary enquiries, and examined a plan of the mine descended the shaft. He returned in about two hours, but went down again shortly afterwards. He then remained until a late hour, when he ascended the shaft and he stayed during the night at the residence of Mr Pearce, the manager. The underlooker returned to the surface also at a late hour for the purpose of a brief rest.

The intelligence as to the nature of the explosion was then first imparted to those on the surface. It appeared that on entering the mine, the underlooker found that the 'couples' supporting the roof had been blown down, and that the roof had consequently fallen in. It was the work of some labour to renew these supports, and to clear away the debris. Before much time had elapsed, however, the engineer, Edward Elliott was found at the engine at the head of the gradient. He was much burnt about the head and face, but was alive. He was immediately sent to the surface, and conveyed home to Dukinfield, where we learn he is progressing favourably. Having extinguished the fires under the boilers, and stopped the engines, the exploring parties began to repair and stop up the air passages which occur at regular intervals of between ten and twenty yards through the workings.

The material with which these air passages are blocked had all been blown down by the force of the explosion, and it was necessary to repair each as it was arrived at, before the party could safely proceed. On Friday night a point of 250 yards down the gradient was reached, and here five bodies were found. These were sent to the surface at an early hour in the morning, and conveyed to some empty cottages near the New Inn, Mosley Road. They were identified as the following: George Thompson, 30 years of age, married, leaving a wife and six children, Robert Thompson, son of the above, Joseph Brookshaw, 26, married but with no family, John Bramall, 18 and Joseph Green, aged 12 years. The exploration continued without intermission, and early on Saturday morning, Mr Dickinson, and the underlooker again descended. The same kind of work as that of the previous afternoon had to be got through during the whole of the day. During the two hours in which Mr Dickinson then remained, he penetrated the mine further than any other party, having gone to the bottom of the incline, which is 460 yards long, and 600 yards beyond, in a working which is about 900 yards long, and at a right angle to the incline, in a northerly direction. He also superintended and directed the operations of the exploring party, and it is satisfactory to know that he afterwards reported that everything was being done to recover the bodies. During the day, Mr Seddon, underlooker at the Dunkirk Colliery, Dukinfield, Mr Andrews of the Fairbottom Colliery, and Mr Hibbert of the Bardsley Colliery visited the mine and afforded much advice and assistance. Mr Seddon also brought several men from the Dunkirk Colliery, who aided the exploring party.

The volunteers who presented themselves were very numerous, and when found to be competent men, and fit to be trusted with a lamp, they were sent down. At two o'clock it was announced that a heavy fall of roof had taken place, and that there was a great quantity of sulphur in the mine, which rendered it necessary to proceed with caution. At this time a stream of water was turned down the No.2 downcast shaft, and made to fall like rain, so as to drive the air through the workings with a great force. At six o'clock ten more bodies were found in the 900 yards level, and they were removed to the surface. They were identified as follows: Thomas Gosling, 26, married with two children, William Preece, aged 12, William Knowlan, 30, widow and three children, Benjamin Greenwood of Bengall, 25, widow and two children, William Webb, 23, unmarried, Jonathan Webb, brother of the above, William Catlow, 22, unmarried, Joseph Schofield, aged 12, Charles

Motterhead, aged 11 years and Samuel Walker, 18. The search continued with all possible speed throughout the night, and during the whole of yesterday. The roof in the levels was found to be much broken, and the labour of securing it was not only difficult but also dangerous. Large stones in a loose condition hanging over the men as they worked. Up to nine o'clock last evening, sixteen additional bodies had been found and got to the surface.

They are; Benjamin Greenwood, 30, widow and five or six children, George Gilbert, 17, Richard Barrowclough, married, three children, John Barrowclough, brother of the above, 27, widow and three children, Samuel Hopwood, 20, Samuel Saxon, 26, widow and three children, John Tetlow, 21, John Foster, 38, widow and three children, Philip Ousey, aged 12, Henry Holland, 50, widow and five children, Abraham Holland, 18, William Healey, 20, Henry Braithwaite, 20, John Underwood, 27, widow and three children, Thomas Davis, 22, and John Peat, 19. This makes the total number of bodies removed 31, and several others are still missing.

The names of eight are known, these being all colliers, but whether there are any waggoners, they who are employed by the colliers and not by the proprietors of the pit, in the mine at the time of the explosion, it is at present uncertain. The men known to be still missing are as follows: George Corbeck, Samuel Livesey, Frank Smith, Thomas Holland (boy), Josiah Healey (boy), Samuel Garside, Jonas Copley (boy) and John Emmett aged 23. The cause of the explosion is unknown. The mine is considered to be safe by the men working in it, and has the reputation of being well conducted. The last explosion, which occurred in it, was seven or eight years ago. There was known for gas to have been in the workings, but it was always removed as soon as it formed, and the currents of air were well regulated. There is little doubt that the explosion occurred at the end of the long level beyond the gradient. The bodies were found more and more burnt as the exploring parties proceeded. It is supposed that the explosion was caused by the men getting into some old workings at the end of the long level. The force of the explosion must have been very great.

The iron plating at the mouth of the shaft was blown up, although it was a distance of nearly 1,000 yards from the spot where the gas is supposed to have exploded. The conclusion is said to have been felt nearly half a mile away. A carter who was riding in the roadway near the pit, was thrown from one side of his cart to the other. Other persons sitting in a house at a considerable distance felt the shock. On Saturday night, the 15 bodies then recovered were removed to the homes of their respecting families, where coffins had been provided for them by Messrs Kenworthy. At a late hour last evening the exploring party had got to the end of the 900 yard level, and were proceeding to the workings beyond. Only one accident has occurred during the search, namely, that of a man who made a false step whilst working in the gradient. The majority of the men recovered have been burnt very badly, but some of the men appear to have died from suffocation.

In all, it is believed that forty were killed in this explosion, and it is possible even more died from injuries during the following days. Editions of the *Manchester Guardian* later in the week give accounts of the inquest, and details of a fund that was set up to help the bereaved families.

Higginshaw Lane: Royton★

This may be the Higginshaw Colliery at work in 1842, by Staham, Lees. In the Catalogue of Plans of Abandoned Mines, this entry says 'see Edge Lane'. The following is a record in the Mines Inspectors Report of 1859, of a fatality at the pit, at this point worked by Mr Smethurst: 'November 24th. Higginshaw Lane Colliery. Richard Royds killed through explosion of firedamp. Died 25th December'.

The *Rochdale Observer*, 26 November 1859, reports on the results of a lack of precautions regarding firedamp at the pit:

> On Thursday week, John Kay, collier of Higginshaw died from the effects of being burnt on the 2nd inst. by the explosion of firedamp at the Higginshaw Colliery, Royton belonging to Mr Smethurst. On Tuesday last, Mr Dearden, Coroner, held an inquest on the body at the Hare and Hounds Inn. It appeared from the evidence of the brother of the deceased, that the mine was only examined on Monday mornings, and that contrary to Rule 37, a candle had been used in the workings of a certain part of the pit, and in consequence the deceased got burnt very much about the face. Mr Dickinson, Inspector of Mines was present, and the jury returned a verdict of 'accidental death' and censured the management of the owner, and the incompetence of the underlooker.

Highfield: Moorside, Oldham

An old colliery worked by Abraham Clegg in 1834, and the Sunderland Bros in 1869, according to a mines index. See Counthill (Higher and Lower) which, according to the Catalogue of Plans of Abandoned Mines, share underground connections with the pit.

Hill: Oldham, SD 942 056

A pit located off and to the rear of Yorkshire Street, now the Huddersfield Road (A62), between Dunkerley Street and Holt Street, shown on a map of 1851. The colliery is not mentioned in Joseph Dickinson's 'Statistics of the Collieries of Lancashire, Cheshire and North Wales', a paper read 7 March 1854, and could be presumed closed at this date. Nothing else is known of this pit, other than the information given by the Catalogue of Plans of Abandoned Mines (1928): Hill (a) Oldham; (b) COAL; (d) 97 NE (1922) F1. The last reference is the location of the mine entrance only.

Hodge Clough: Sholver, Oldham, 946 073
Colliery worked by Ashton, Booth & Co. in 1837, and Booth, Clegg & Co. in 1842, although another reference gives the owners as Messrs Lees and Hallows in the same year, which perhaps indicates that two collieries of this name were operating at the same time. A Harry Bentley apparently worked a colliery of this name during 1847. A directory of 1861 says that Jesse Ainsworth was working a pit named Hodge Clough. The Hodge Clough Colliery is shown on Dunn's map of 1829, and on the OS map of 1844, reflecting its antiquity. A footpath on the left off Wilkes Street off the Ripponden Road below Moorside, and directly across from Watlington Close, at Oldham, is the place to start. Follow the footpath keeping close to the little brook, (Hodge Clough) and in a short distance you come across a stile. Stop here and look on the other side of the stream, and you will notice a mound of overgrown colliery waste, although it is difficult to spot. However, closer examination reveals pit spoil, and even the odd piece of coal. The colliery took its name from Hodge Clough, through which the little stream flows, and a former farm of that name. The pit is noted in the Catalogue of Plans of Abandoned Mines as follows: Hodge Clough (a) Oldham; (b) COAL; (d) 97 NE (1922) B2. This is the location of the mine entrance only.

A tragic story relating to one of the miners here is reported in the *Manchester Guardian,* 11 September 1830:

> Some time ago a dog in a rabid condition bit a cat belonging to a person named Thomas Owen, a coalminer at Hodge Clough near Sholver at Oldham.
>
> About fourteen days after the cat became restless, and bit the finger of one of the sons of Owen, a boy aged about eight years of age. Two days later the cat bit the thumb of a youth residing with Owen of the name of Dean. This rather alarmed the young man and the family, but he continued his employment in the mines for several weeks after without any inconvenience. On the first of the present month however, he became restless and complained of difficulty of swallowing, particularly of liquids, and on the following day showed the symptoms of hydrophobia. A surgeon, Mr Whittaker of Shaw Chapel was brought in about ten o'clock at night, however he expired under the most dreadful of agonies. The boy whose finger was bit by the cat is now taking medication, the parents still feel considerable alarm.

The *Manchester Guardian,* 4 November 1837, reports:

> On Friday morning last, the underlooker at the colliery of Messrs Ashton, Booth and Co. at Hodge Clough, Sholver near Oldham, went down the shafts at one of the pits and passing along an excavation to the bottom of an adjoining pit, which had not been worked for some time, his object being to see the state of the mine. On reaching the opening to the perpendicular shaft of the un-worked pit, he found the dead body of an elderly man, who appeared to have fallen down the shaft. The person was much disfigured, and his clothes torn. A small bundle containing a

shirt, handkerchief, woollen cloth patches etc., a walking stick and a tobacco pipe lay near him. The pit is seventy three yards in depth, and opens on an eminence several feet above the adjoining turnpike road from Oldham to Halifax, which is several yards distance. Around it is a railing, except at the landing place. Near the pit are several ovens for burning coke, and the unfortunate man is supposed to have gone off the road to the coke fires and probably lost his way and fallen into the pit. A number of papers were found on the person of the deceased, one is a card on which are written the words 'Joseph Cooper, Pilkington, Lancashire, near Prestwich'. Another is a certificate of admission to the Salford and Pendleton Royal Dispensary, for Joseph Cooper, dated May 29th 1837. There are also two letters, one dated Derby, April 24th 1837, and another dated Stockport, May 9th 1837 signed by Thomas Barrington, both relative to the indenture of apprenticeship of a Joseph Cooper, mentioning that he was apprenticed to the fustian trade, in 1779, with John Clough of Failsworth. These letters are addressed to the overseers at Failsworth. Other memorandums, relating to weft received for weaving, dates of birth and deaths of several of the Cooper family were also found. The corpse was brought to the Oldham Workhouse on Friday forenoon, and on the same day, Mr. T.F. Dearden coroner and a respectable jury investigated the affair at the Black Swan Inn, Greenacres Moor. The jury found a verdict of 'Found dead, without any evidence of the person of the deceased'.

A sad and avoidable accident is reported in the *Manchester Guardian,* 17 April 1847:

Fatal Accident at a Colliery. On Tuesday evening last, two men named Walsh and Potts employed at the colliery of Mr Harry Bentley, Hodge Clough, Oldham were ascending from their work in a tub, when the engineer, through some carelessness or casual oversight, suffered them to be wound over the pulleys of the head-stocks of the pit. The consequence was, that both the poor men fell from a considerable height. One of them, Aaron Walsh, an inhabitant of Copster Hill, fell upon the coal pit hill, and was so seriously injured that he died immediately. The other sufferer, a young man named Potts, residing in Crompton fell upon some earth, and was taken up much injured. He was at once removed to his dwelling, where he still remains in a dangerous state. The unfortunate man who was killed was 46 years of age, and has left a family of seven children. The engineer of the colliery appears to be a young man not fully acquainted with his duties.

The Mines Inspectors Report for the year 1858 records: 'August 7th. Hodge Clough Colliery, Oldham. Worked by Abel Rhodes, John Shaw a 17 year old drawer killed through fall of roof in the Mountain Mine'. This accident was also recorded in the *Colliery Guardian,* 14 August 1858: 'On Saturday last an accident occurred at a coal mine at Hodge Clough, occupied by Mr Abel Rhodes, whereby a collier named John Shaw was killed. It appeared that while the deceased was at work in the mine, a stone fell from the roof and fell upon him. No blame appears to attach to anyone. The inquest has been held, and a verdict to that effect recorded. The deceased was about seventeen years of age'.

Mr Rhodes was accused of ignoring regulations, in the *Colliery Guardian*, 11 September 1858:

> Mr Abel Rhodes who rents a mine at Hodgeclough, Oldham from Mr Jesse Ainsworth was summoned before Oldham Borough bench on Monday and charged with not having provided rules for the proper workings of his pit according to the Acts of Parliament. Mr Dickinson, the Government Inspector appeared in support of the charge, and proved the case. He also informed the magistrates that since the information had been laid against Mr Rhodes rules had been made and approved of. The bench inflicted a fine of 50s, and costs.

Hole Bottom (1): Crompton, near Oldham★, SD 949 087

This colliery is the one that was located up Mark Lane, Crompton, past the cricket ground, where an area of disturbed ground can be seen in the field on the left-hand side going towards Cartchief Nook Farm. Milne and Taylor are recorded as working a colliery of this name in 1834, though a lease to coal rights was taken out in 1771 (Abel Crompton, of Crompton, linen weaver, and James Wilde of Crompton, woollen clothier, to John and James Butterworth of Crompton, woollen clothiers (*Oldham Local Studies*, Misc. 1/13)). The pit appears to have had connections with the Bankhouse and Rhodes Bank Collieries according to the Catalogue of Plans of Abandoned Mines.

> Holebottom Pit at Crompton is about 80 yards deep, coal from 22 to 24 inches thick, the rattlers (inferior coal) are 10 to 12 inches thick on the south side. North side are better quality of coals. The quarterage is 10 the score of loads, of one half penny the load. There is 12 hours pumping in the 24, using barrels of 9 and 10 inches. There is a loose (drainage adit), which takes between 20 and 30 yards off, into which they pump the water. They have two pits and the sale is about 30 quarters at one pit, and 20 at the other per week. There is not many coals to get at this concern, from their present loose on levels, and if Clegg and Co. do not meet with much water in the sinking, this concern will be let down, rather than pump the water for a new concern. Clegg and Cos. pit is considered to be about 20 yards on the rise of Holebottom Levels. 1s 2d and 1s the load is the best selling price. Some of the Shaw mills are having coal from a brest eye, at Cote Knowl at 8d the load, and some are having it from Lees and Co. at 5d the load, but these are what they call 'rattlers'. A pit was sunk by Robert Buckley of Besom Hill some years since at or near Crompton Hole [and] was about 60 yards deep. They [went] through a fault in the sinking of about 10 yards, it was down dip of the rise of the mine, and it was found on the south side of the shaft at 25 or 30 distance. Buckley did not cut this fault. The land where the pit is belongs to a person named Farrer

of Shaw. Buckley paid 3s the score for what he got here, and there was some water to pump. July 13th 1843. (Lancashire Records Office, DDX 614/7)

To confuse matters there were two collieries of this name, the other one was worked by Lees, Jones & Co. in Oldham.

A tragedy was averted at the site by the quick-thinking of the miner involved, as recounted in the *Manchester Guardian*, 13 December 1843:

Narrow Escape. On Monday last as Richard Buckley, a coal miner was being drawn up in a tub at Holebottom Colliery, Crompton, the rope scotched or flew out of the pulley. The tub instantly fell down the shaft, and the miner was thrown against the side with great violence. Notwithstanding this, he with extraordinary presence of mind clung to some pieces of timber called 'horse trees'. He remained in this precarious position until he was rescued by one of the men, who descended to him along the ropes and chains of the pit.

A charge is brought against a miner at the site, as reported in the *Manchester Guardian,* 18 March 1846:

Charge against a coal miner. At the petty sessions, on Monday, a coal miner named John Barrett was charged with having left his employment at the colliery of Mrs Taylor and Sons, Holebottom, Crompton without giving the required notice. Mr Hunt, solicitor of Rochdale, appeared for the complainant, and Mr W.P. Roberts, the miners' attorney general for the defendant. Mr Robert Taylor, a partner in the colliery, stated that the man had left on Thursday last without giving any notice whatsoever.

He had worked for them several times before, and had then given a fortnight's notice as was usual. On cross-examination by Mr Roberts, the witness acknowledged that the coal miners in their service, including the defendant, had to go two miles or more to a public-house kept by witnesses brother in law, a person named Broadley to receive their wages each pay day. He also admitted that 6d per fortnight was taken out of the miner's wages to pay for liquor, but he said that the men had made an agreement amongst themselves to that effect. A printed copy of certain rules to be observed by the miners in the service of the complainants was put in, but Mr Roberts argued it at considerable length that these rules were not binding, inasmuch as they placed no obligation on the employer, and as they did not bear the signature of the firm. Mr Roberts commented on the extremely improper conduct of the complainants, in having carried on a gross system of taking 6d per fortnight from each miner's wage for liquor, for five years, besides obliging the hands to walk upwards of two miles to a public-house in Oldham, very properly called the Trap Inn, where they received their wages.

The 5th and 6th Victoria, chap. 69 prohibited the payment of miners wages at public-houses, beerhouses etc.. and any agreement made at such places was not binding. Mr

Roberts concluded by stating, that if the complainants would pledge themselves to abandon the practice of paying the miners at a public-house, and deducting money for liquor, whether the men consented or not, the defendant would willingly return to work, and give the required notice. Mr Hunt on the part of the complainant, made a promise that the practice of paying the wages at a public-house would be discontinued, and under this arrangement, the defendant consented to return to his work.

Hole Bottom (2): Oldham★

This 'Hole Bottom Colliery' is shown on a map of 1851 off Yorkshire Street near the junction of Bradshaw Street and Church Street, Oldham, and to the east of St Mary's Church. There is also shown an 'old coal pit' off Clegg Street at this time. There appears to have been just one shaft at the 'coal pit' as it was called, although a weighing machine at the back of the Sportsmans Arms, may have been used in connection with the pit.

Henry Garforth, aged thirty-seven, late book keeper and cashier for Messrs Lees and Jones, and previously dialling (surveying) mines, gave evidence at the Inquiry into Child Labour on 28 October 1841:

Has been acquainted with the working of coals from his infancy, having commenced working nine years of age in the neighbourhood of Wakefield, in Yorkshire. His father was the manager of a colliery near Keighley, under Mr Dawson, poor and illiterate until he put himself for three years to a night-school, and by learning there to read, write, and plan, he qualified himself to be an underlooker, and take the management of a mine. This was when the witness was about five years of age. Between eight and nine years of age witness commenced work as a trapper, being perhaps the youngest in the pit at that time. Was quite proud to begin trapping, preferring it to play, but soon got tired. The work is second nature, and for an hour and a half he was a trap-door tenter without ever feeling any alarm, except when he had to go past the place where 'Old Johnson' was killed, when the mere dirt behind his feet could make him occasionally feel timid. Had the door nearest to the shaft, and was always joined by his father to caution, was at it 10 or 11 hours

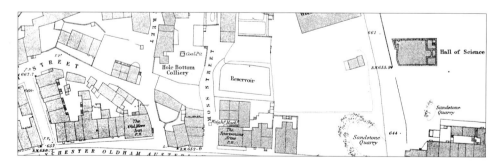

Hole Bottom Colliery, map of 1848.

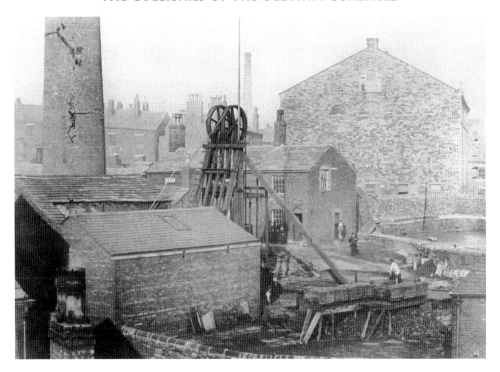

Hole Bottom Pit. (Oldham Library)

a-day. After he had done trapping, which it was usual for the children to begin, he proceeded to the hurrying, which he looked on as a promotion, and was proud of. The trappers are made aware that, upon their attention, their own lives, and those of all the men, depend. If he had the ordering of a colliery in which trappers were regularly required, an old man, at a couple of shillings a day, would be more suitable and understand it, without the giddiness and carelessness that a young child has.

There is many an old collier that is not half a man for work that would be peculiarly qualified for such a job, and when it is required equally for the safety of the men and the advantage for the master, what is 12s a-week? By the time a collier is 50 he is becoming an old man for his work, and yet he might for ten years mind a trap-door with advantage to all parties, or it is a task, which he will both understand and willingly discharge. It was a five-foot seam in which he was working as a hurrier, and there was good room in the ways, in which black-damp, towards the face of the works, was sometimes a very trouble, but not the fire-damp. This hurrying was all by thrusting, and the coal lay level, but the hurrying in this country, called 'waggoning', is different, and not to be liked as he liked that.

An awful accident occurred at the site in 1827, another example of how, in this industry, a momentary lack of concentration can lead to tragedy, *Manchester Guardian,* 22 March 1827:

Dreadful accident at Oldham. On Sunday afternoon the 18th inst. five boys were let down a coalpit belonging to Messrs Lees and Jones and Co. Holebottom, Oldham for the purpose of feeding a horse, which is kept in the mine below. On their giving the usual signal to ascend, the cage was set to work, and the attention of the engineer being directed to some trifling matter, he suffered them to be taken up to the top of the framework above the pit, where the bucket in which the boys were coming up in came in contact with it [the frame-work] was dashed to pieces, and four of its inmates were thrown into the air 40 or 50 feet. Two died the following morning, and a third lies in a very dangerous state, a forth grasped the frame-work above the pit and was saved. An inquest was held on the bodies of the two sufferers, on Tuesday 20th inst. at the Grapes Inn, Yorkshire street. Verdict: 'Accidental death'.

This pit was again mentioned in the evidence taken by John L. Kennedy during his Report on Child Labour in the Coal Mines, 1841:

William Greenhalgh, Holebottom, Oldham — What age are you? — I am 13 years old. What age did you begin working? — When I was 11 years old. What is you employment in the pits? — I am a hurrier, I push wagons of coal in the bottom. What hours do you work? — I go down at six o'clock in the morning, and I come out between five and six o'clock at night. Have you any time allowed for taking your meals? — No, we stop noan (none). Do you work at night? — Ay, week about.

The evidence of Richard Stanley, waggoner, Hole Bottom, tells a similar story:

What age are you? — Going on 13. How long have you been in the pits? — I went down when I was 11 years old first. Have you ever been to school? — No, I never went to school in my life, I can neither read nor write. Do you work day and night? — No, not day and night, I work in the daytime one week, and night the next. I am working the day shift this week. Do you like working in the night? — No, I don't, but I'm liked to do it, everybody else does it. I like working in the day the best. What hours do you work? — From six o'clock in the morning till six at night. Have you any time allowed for meals? — The 'gin' in the 'bottom' stops for half an hour when we work night shift. How far do you wagon your coal? — 150 yards. How many times a day? — 20 times. Do you know how many yards that is in all? — No, I am no reckoner, but it is hard work, I know that. Is the work easier here than at other collieries you have been at? — Yes, I think it is. I have been at Jesse Ainsworth's and Chamber Lane, and Radley's, that is the worst shop, it was up to the knees in water, and we could never tell whether the wagons were off the rails or not.

A young 'hurrier', Samuel Rushworth, paints a grim picture of relentless work in the mines:

What age are you? — I am going on 12. How long have you been a hurrier? — I have been four years in the pit. Can you read or write? — No, I cannot. What hours do you work? — I go down at six o'clock in the morning, and come out at six at night. Do you stop for dinner? — No, we never stop, but we have plenty of time to eat. Do you ever get beaten? — Ay, many a time, but I never get beat much. Do you ever work at night? — Ay, every other week. We should work 8 hour shifts night and day, but we work 12 hours just now. Do the waggoners ever work longer than 12 hours? — No, very seldom, the waggoners change at the same time as the pickmen. How far do you wagon your coal? — I think it will be about 200 yards. How many times a day? — 20 is a regular thing, but I have only brought six today. Do you use the belt and chain? — No, There is no belt and chain used here, they use it at Wrigley's. How do you know that? — Jemmy Mope says so, and his father 'banks' there.

James Thomas, was a thrutcher at the same site:

What age are you? — I am going on 11. How long have you been in the pits? — About a year. What work do you do? — Me and my brother makes a wagon. How old is your brother? — Seventeen. What hours do you work? — We have altered lately, and we are working 12 hour shifts. What time do you go in the morning? — At six o'clock, and I come out at six o'clock at night. Have you any time for meals? — I get my dinner at twelve o'clock, but we don't stop much. Can you read or write? — No, I cannot.

A record in the Mines Inspectors Report, 1853, does not even list the identities of two men killed here: 'April 18th. Holebottom worked by Lees and Jones Co. two men killed through explosion of firedamp. No names given'. Another Mines Inspectors Report, 1856, records another fatality at the site: 'Holebottom, Oldham. J. Whitehead, 38, run over by wagon on jig brow and killed'.

With small communities providing the workforce for a mine, it is common for several members of a family to work together in the same location. The following article reports on an all-too-familiar instance of father and son involved in an accident, *Manchester Guardian*, 5 October 1857:

Accident in a coal mine. On Saturday afternoon an accident occurred at the coal mine in Yorkshire Street, known as Holebottom Pit, by which two men, named David and William Moores (father and son) were dreadfully burned. They were employed in tunnelling in the mine, when from some uncertain cause, the powder for blasting exploded. The noise brought several miners to their assistance, and they were conveyed to the pit mouth, where it was found they were very seriously injured. The usual means of alleviating their sufferings have been adopted, and they were removed to their residence at Edge Lane, Royton, where they have since been attended by Mr Earnshaw, surgeon.

Two Mines Inspectors Reports record two more accidents: 'March 11th. Holebottom Colliery. Peter Pemmington killed through cage descending upon him while he was bricking side of shaft' (1863); 'May 8th. Holebottom Colliery, Oldham. Hugh Nield killed through being caught by wagon' (1868).

Hollins: Hollins, Oldham, SD 915 029
This is probably the colliery that was off the present day Hollins Road (A6104) at Oldham, near the street called 'Mill Gate' and which is marked on the OS map of 1844. Jones & Co. worked the colliery. Mr Cornelius Backhouse, head viewer to Messrs Jones & Co. gave evidence to the Report on Child Labour on 1 November 1841:

Weakly children are not generally put into a pit. In a general way, good strong lads are required for coal-pit work, though there may be exceptions to the rule, in which weakly children are brought down. Some fathers would take a child into the pit, however weakly he was, if he could produce a few shillings a-week, while others would not. The increased use of rails and contrivances has improved the character of the children's labour, and somewhat lessened its amount. The underlookers interfere when they learn of cases of ill usage of children by the men. They feel it part of their duty to protect the weak from the strong those under them, and to preserve decency and order as much as they can in the pit. Abused party will complain to the underlooker, who brings the matter before the head viewer, who has the general management of the pits. There are no engineers under 10 years of age, perhaps not under 12. Several are married men. [Signed] CORNELIUS BACKHOUSE.

The *Manchester Guardian,* 26 June 1847, reports an accident here:

Colliery Accident. On Saturday last, Mr Dearden, coroner, held an inquest at the White Hart Inn, Hollins, on the body of Robert Pearson, a coal miner resident in the vicinity. The day previous, whilst two tubs were passing up and down the colliery of Messrs Jones and Co. at Hollins, they came into contact with each other, and caused a small vessel for lifting stones, known as a 'hoppet' to be detached from the side of the tub. The hoppit fell down the pit, and struck the deceased on the head, and injured him so severely that he died immediately. The deceased was 31 years of age, and has left a wife and two children. Verdict: 'Accidental death'.

A tragic instance of history repeating itself is recorded in the *Manchester Guardian,* 11 March 1848:

Accident in a coal pit. On Wednesday last, Mr Clarke held an inquest at the Wagon and Horses, at Hollinwood, on George Chadderton, nearly 13 years old. He on Monday had for the first time, worked in a coal pit, and was in one belonging to

Jones and Co. when a large stone fell from a height of seventeen feet, and crushed him beneath it. John Hilton, a collier, extricated him in four minutes, but he sobbed twice, and died within five minutes of the accident. Verdict, 'accidental death'. His father was killed nine years ago, in a coal pit, by a similar accident.

A very young miner killed by a wagon had an inquest into his death adjourned due to insufficient evidence, *Manchester Guardian*, 29 September 1856:

Colliery Accident. On Saturday an inquest was held at Hollins, on the body of John Seville, aged ten years of age, son of Julius Seville, who died on the previous Wednesday morning, from the effects of injuries received on Monday. The deceased was at work in a coal pit at Hollins, on Monday morning, when a wagon which was being brought down the 'jig brow' came into contact with him, and passed over his body. He was very severely bruised, and was immediately conveyed home, where he was attended by Mr Earnshaw, the surgeon until Wednesday morning when he died. The evidence given at the inquest was so unsatisfactory a character and threw so little light on the real cause of the accident, that the coroner adjourned the inquest to Friday next, in order that additional witnesses might be in attendance.

Hollows: Oldham
The only report on this pit is in the *Manchester Guardian*, 28 October 1848:

Fatal fall down a coal pit. On Thursday last Mr Clarke held an inquest at the Yew Tree, Buersill Head on Robert Schofield, 44 years of age, an underlooker at the Hollows coal-pit belonging to Wild and Co. On Tuesday last the deceased was descending into the pit in a tub attached to the rope, when the rope broke close to the hooks, and precipitated him down a depth of 80 yards to the bottom of the pit, where he received a fracture of the skull, of which he died instantly. The rope was new three months ago. A verdict of 'accidental death' was recorded.

There is some confusion as to the location of this colliery. I believe it may have been at Rochdale.

Honeywell Lane: Honeywell Lane, Oldham, SD 929 034
Colliery worked by Hibbert and Lees in 1834, Abraham Lees junior, 1842, and Booth and Marland, 1858 and 1869, the partner William Booth living at 53 Ashton Road. John Marland & Co. worked the pit in 1876, and the Chamber Colliery Co. in 1879. Honeywell Lane is also given as the residence of Nathaniel Higgins, a coal master in a directory of 1824. The following is the entry for the Honeywell Lane Colliery in the Catalogue of Plans of Abandoned Mines (1928): Honeywell Lane (a) Oldham; (b) COAL Lower Bent, Higher Bent (abandoned April 1892); (d) 97 SW (1922) B9, 10: C9, 10: D9.

Edmund Stanley, aged thirty-four, was interviewed for the Report into Child Labour on 4 November 1841, and his answers, as well as those of John Gordon, are presented here:

Edmund Stanley, a working collier at the Honeywell pit, sent in his boy between six and seven, and he is now working in the same pit with him, as also are John Gordon's boys with him. Are generally now in the pit by six a.m., and if the winders are prompt they can get out by four o'clock, it will often be five, but very commonly it is six or seven before the children get out, and sometimes as late as eight, when they have to waggon down to the pit a good deal of coal gotten by the men. Have not either of them worked very lately constant night-work, but only occasionally.

John Gordon and Edmund Stanley offer views on the issue:

If he [Gordon] could have afforded it, or had times been good, would have sent his children to school instead of taking them into the pit, and if others had proper feelings for their children they would under such circumstances do the same. Some, however, do seem to be without proper feeling, and without judgement, so that in good times they might not do this, some are entirely wasteful even in the best days. Edmund Stanley took his boy into the pit at a time when he was making only 2s 6d a-day, and thought the 4d a-day, which the lad earned, would be a useful addition. To limit the labour of children in the mines, or the ages at which they should commence labour, would be to reduce the income of a family while its expenses remained the same. The wages of the older waggoners might be increased, but to throw away years of the wages of younger children would be a greater loss in money than could be made good this way. It may be that a great portion of the colliers do not know the value of instruction, and therefore would not, even in good times, avail themselves of the opportunity to give their children time and schooling, I dare say there are many others who would do the same, but that they are prevented by the scantiness of what they earn, and he has himself paid for the day-schooling of his children, each for a short time, when he could ill afford it. Thinks that there are more people than formerly there were who would make sacrifices to get 'learning' for their children, to make them a comfort to their old age, and not merely an advantage for their youth, without any obedience or comfort which might be gained by the other means. A man with understanding knows how to govern himself, a man without understanding doesn't.

Shore Edge is a place chiefly inhabited by colliers taking their children to work at the earliest possible ages into the mountain mines of thin coal, even as soon as six years of age. It has long been noted as a nest of disreputable characters, and no fewer than seven were taken up at once in the last Ashton wakes week. If the colliers, thus brought up, have no perception of the importance of improving their children, knows not how it ought to be brought about for the advantage of the children.

George Gordon is a member of the Primitive Methodist Society, and sends his lads to the Hollinwood Sunday school, and the two biggest to a night school also four night's a-week, for which he pays 4*d* per week to the master … [Edmund Stanley] is in no religious society, but his boy goes to the Primitive Methodist Sunday school in Oldham. There is a good deal of firedamp in the Honeywell-lane Pit at times, but there have been no fatal explosions. Thinks that such young boys should not be entrusted, as engineers, with the lives of a lot of men as they are, they are not 'stayable', and no one under 18 ought to be entrusted with such a job. This is a general opinion among the men themselves. [Signed] EDMUND STANLEY.

A fatality here is reported in the *Manchester Guardian,* 19 March 1858:

Yesterday morning a fatal accident happened at Messrs Booth, Morland, and Co.'s coalpit near Honeywell Lane, Oldham. A number of men are employed in sinking a new shaft, which is already about 80 yards deep. About three o'clock yesterday morning a stone fell from the side of the shaft about 11 yards up, and struck a man named Thomas Lunn, who was working at the bottom of the pit, injuring him very severely. He was got out of the shaft, and conveyed to the house of his sister-in-law, which is a short distance from the pit. Although medical aid was speedily obtained, he died within a short time. Deceased was 21 years of age. (see *Colliery Guardian,* 27 March 1858, p.202)

Two Mines Inspectors Reports are also in existence: 'March 20th. Honeywell Lane Colliery. Joseph Holt killed through fall of roof' (1863); 'July 21st. Honeywell Lane Colliery. James Ainsworth killed by roof fall in the Great Mine' (1866).

Hopwood: Hopwood, Middleton
This pit was worked by Robert Gregg Hopwood in 1854, and the Middleton & Rochdale Colliery Co. in 1869. Catalogue of Plans of Abandoned Mines (1928): Hopwood, Clough, Hatters (a) Middleton; (b) COAL Royley (abandoned 5 February 1904); (d) 88 SE (1910) F4: Last entry mine entrance only. Hopwood, Nancy (a) Middleton; (b) COAL Royley (abandoned prior to 1875); (d) 88 SE (1910) G5, 8: H6, 7, 8: 96 NE (1923) A6, 7, 8: B6, 7, 8, 9: C7, 8.
   A death is recorded in the Mines Inspectors Report, 1854: 'August 26th. Hopwood Colliery, worked by the Trustees of the late R.G. Hopwood. William Nuttall killed through an explosion of firedamp. Died 19th September'.
   The abandonment of the 'Nancy Pit' at Hopwood Colliery, Middleton which was worked by the Oldham, Middleton & Rochdale Colliery Co. was reported in the *Middleton Albion* on 23 October 1875:

Closing of the pit 'Nancy'. This pit, which has been well known in the district, has recently been closed. The miners being unable to find any more good coal in it. The pit which is the property of Captain Hopwood, has been worked by the

Oldham, Middleton and Rochdale Colliery Co. and the proximity of the supply to Middleton rendered it of course less costly than it could otherwise have been. There was little or no carriage to pay by those residing at the top of Middleton. The exhaustion will likely tell heavily upon those who have been accustomed to receiving their supplies from it.

An old man we saw near the depot, seemed to regard the old pit as an affectionate friend who had just passed away. He kept repeating with tears in his eyes 'It's done, It's done, its race has run', 'What shall we do?'. He was told there was plenty more coals to be had. 'Oh aye he said but not at the price'. It is thought that the coal could be got at by cutting to a certain depth below the level now reached, but it is very questionable whether this will be done. The Oldham, Middleton and Rochdale Coal Co. contemplate moving their plant, consisting of trainway etc. to another pit.

Hopwood Hall: Middleton
An early colliery that was worked by R.S. Hopwood, 1842, and Robert Cregg Hopwood in 1848, both probably of Hopwood Hall.

Horrocks Court: Oldham
Pit worked by Exors of Thomas Fogg in 1869, although not mentioned in the Catalogue of Plans of Abandoned Mines.

Hunt Clough: Chadderton
This colliery was worked by the Chamber Colliery Co. in 1879 and 1896, though the colliery existed before this, being marked on a map of 1844. Two 'coal pits' are also shown to the north-east, and the northern-most appears to have had an extensive tramway. The pit worked the Mountain Mine and King Coal, with seventy-two men underground and nine on the surface during 1896, the pit being abandoned the year after. The manager at this time was W.W. Millington, and the undermanager Joseph Taylor. The Hunt Clough Colliery was located to the east of Chadderton Cemetery, and is also marked on a map of 1891. The actual site of the pit was to the rear and right of Chadderton FC, a site now taken by housing.

This is the entry from the Catalogue of Plans of Abandoned Mines (1928): Hunt Clough (a) Chadderton; (b) COAL Royley (abandoned 30 September 1897); (d) 97 NW (1922) C2, 3: D2, 3, 4: E2, 3, 4, 5: F3, 4, 5: G4, 5, 6: H5.

Hunt Lane: Hunt Lane, Chadderton SD 906 054
This colliery is mentioned several times during the coal strike of 1831 (see the Copster Hill Colliery entry). The following is the entry from the Catalogue of Plans of Abandoned Mines: Hunt Lane (a) Chadderton; (b) COAL; (d) 97 NW (1922) G5. The last entry is the location of the mine entrance only.

The colliery is also mentioned in the Report on Child Labour in 1841, with Moses Mills, underlooker at Hunt Lane Mines, providing the first evidence on 4 November 1841:

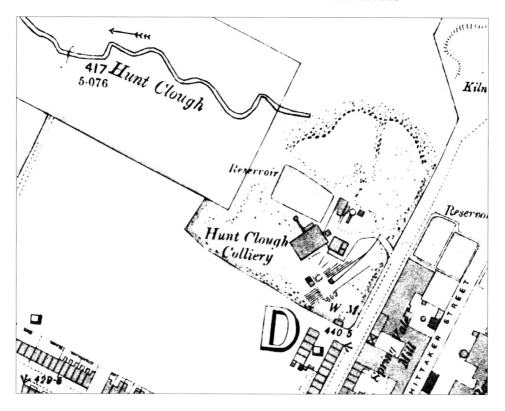

Hunt Clough Colliery, map of 1891.

Formerly, if a child could but learn to manage the engine, they did not look at what age he was. Thinks it has been the case that some might be no more than 10 or 11, they were not so particular as they are now. It is now a rule not to give the management of an engine to any lad under 14. Maybe two months is long enough to learn. The seams worked here are underneath the Oldham slack mine. One seam is 1 foot 7 inch, and the other is 2 foot 5 inch in thickness. They are worked on the same plan as the Chamber lane Pits, and a return of their young hands has already been made. [Signed] M. Mills.

James Woods, engineer, sixteen years of age, 4 November 1841:

Is going in 16. Has been an engineer about four years. Is now working at the Hunt lane Collieries, at the Hor lane Pit. Is busy at his work, is reckoned attentive, in winding has wound over tubs of coals twice; has never wound over men, but was once appointed in place of a lad who wound over three men, and killed them; this was at the Trundley Pit, one of the Chamber-lane Pits, and about two years ago. Gets 9s a week. Cannot read or write. (It is impossible to interrupt him from his work to get his mark).

Thomas Whittaker, engineer, 4 November 1841:

> Is going in 17. Has been engineer about 4 years; learned from John Mills, now turned 18; was with him a month learning, after he gave over driving the horse-engine; has wound over coals once or twice; never any men; gets 7s a-week for six days in the week, and 8s 2d for seven days, which he is now working. The engine works night and day, with a double shift of engineers; it is both drawing and pumping. Can read a bit, but not write. (Cannot be interrupted to sign his evidence).

A dramatic rescue attempt was thankfully successful at the site, as reported in the *Manchester Guardian*, 1 May 1830:

> On Saturday afternoon last as the men and boys at the Hunt Lane Colliery at Chadderton, near Manchester were ascending the pit at the conclusion of their weeks work, the rope attached to the ascending bucket having been lowered hastily, its stiffness and irregularity had detached one of the hooks from the buckets, and the circumstances not being perceived by the coal miners at the time, three boys by the names of John and William Geary and Thomas Buckley entered the bucket to be wound up. They had ascended nearly half way before their perilous situation was discovered (the bucket having turned topsy turvy).
>
> When this was first seen by the workmen below, the boys were clinging to the catch iron and the sides of the bucket for their only support and were suspended over the mouth of the mine. The men at the top seeing the peril in which the boys were placed, durst not venture to attempt winding them up higher, lest they should occasion their fall and nearly all of them deserted the place in dismay running in all directions to raise the alarm with the parents of the boys, so that it was upwards of half an hour before their parents who had previously quit the pit arrived on the spot. On their arrival the people at the top began by words and signals to advise those below as to the means of their deliverance. At last one of the workmen ventured upon the task of rescuing them, and in consequence ascended from the bottom of the pit by means of the conductors and horse trees, and after some considerable difficulty succeeded. The bucket was lowered a little gently and righted, to the great delight of the parents. The boys were at last placed on terra firma.

Hurst: near Ashton-under-Lyne

Two collieries of this name, both at work during the 1840s, one worked by Whittaker and Lees, and one by William Kenworthy. The latter also went by the name of 'Hurst Brook Colliery' and employed thirty-three men and boys underground. Only one Hurst Colliery is listed in the Catalogue of Plans of Abandoned Mines, as follows: Hurst (a) Hurst (b) COAL (d) 105 NE (1923) D2. The last entry is for the location of the mine entrance only.

Mr Kenworthy (the colliery owner) was interviewed by John L. Kennedy for his Report on Child Labour in Coal Mines, 1841:

What means would you take to prevent accidents in coal mines? — I would compel every coal owner who sinks pits to brick the sides the whole way down. A great many accidents happen by pieces coming out of the sides of the pit and falling down. I have seen large portions of rock sticking out of a pit side, which have been pushed out by the pressure from above. It is very common to brick the sides only to the first hard strata. The strong current of air ascending and descending decomposes the rock, and by and by, by the action of the air large portions of the rock are detached. I have seen great ledges in a pit side where stones and rubbish lodge, and when something comes against them they fall down the pit and probably kill one of the boys at the pit-eye. When I first began the coal business, we had pits that were only bricked up to the first strata, and a portion of the rock gave way and a man was killed. Since that time I have had all the pits lined with brick and mortar, and we have not had an accident of that kind. I should recommend as an improvement that there should be side rods for the tubs to go down, and if not, that the tubs should be separated by wooden partition. I have known that many have been thrown out by the tubs or baskets coming in contact with each other in passing. In this neighbourhood, the machinery is usually very good. Have you much carburetted hydrogen or firedamp? — Yes, a great deal, our men use the safety lamp constantly. We are well ventilated, but the gas is generated so fast that the men are obliged to use the lamp almost constantly. Each man is provided with a lamp. Do you find the men anxious to avail themselves of its use? — No, they generally dislike it, the light it affords is scanty, and as soon as they find out they can use a candle with safety they generally do so. Many have been hurt or burnt, that they have become afraid, and are now more careful. We are much troubled with it, and most when we are driving new mines. How long will a rope last? — They are calculated to last 18 months, but some will not last that long. The moment a rope is out of order, the men will come down to the office and say 'Master, we don't like to go down with that rope, it is not safe'. But in some pits the ropes are used when out of order, and generally in the mines belonging to proprietors of small capital, where the expense is grudged. Do you allow the men as much wood for posts as they require? — Yes, certainly, they are never stinted, and go to the underlooker and say how many posts they want. He gives them an order, and they come down to the carpenter's shop for it. This is to prevent waste, but there is no stint of wood, and that is another point I should mention. Some coal proprietors do not allow enough wood for their men. I have heard one of our men say that they have worked where there was not enough wood allowed for posts, and there were great complaints in the neighbourhood about posts and rails in the fields being taken away. But that is many years ago now, and the parties have gone, and I don't think it will happen in this neighbourhood now, but it is so near Oldham and Rochdale. Do you see any way in reducing accidents in coal-pits?

— Why, there must of necessity always be accidents, it is a dangerous trade. But I think that if the underlooker was more careful in compelling the men to draw the posts, and keep them always up to the face, and the men themselves taking a little more care fewer accidents would happen. If a collier neglects to draw his posts, the difficulty increases every yard he advances.

Ten years before this report, there is an article in the *Manchester Guardian*, 3 December 1831, on an accident in the pit:

On Tuesday last the colliers, about thirty in number, at Messrs Kenworthy and Swire's Pit, at Oversteads, near Ashton-under-Lyne were suddenly surprised by an irruption [sic] of water, which came with such impetuosity into the workings, as to wash up the floorings and rails on which the wagons ran. The men barely had time to escape, and before they could be extricated, some of them were immersed up to the breast in water. It appears that since the last turn out of the colliers, some neighbouring pits belonging to Mr Lees, have not been worked, and the water had consequently accumulated in them to such an extent, as at last to break into the workings of Messrs Kenworthy and Swire's in the manner related. Fortunately, no lives were lost, nor was any serious personal injury sustained.

Two accidents are reported by the *Manchester Guardian*, 26 November 1856:

Information of two fatal accidents has reached Mr Rutter, coroner. One at Hurst Brook Colliery belonging to Messrs Kenworthy where Thomas Lamb, aged 16 years was killed by a fall of roof. The other at Glee and Booth's, Broad Oak Colliery.

Hyde (Lane): Hyde
The Hyde Lane Colliery dated from around 1790, ceased production in 1905, and was finally abandoned the following year. There was a serious explosion at the Hyde (Lane) Colliery on 18 January 1889. The colliery then belonged to Messrs Sidebottom and Brother at Hyde in Cheshire, but was later owned by the Dukinfield Coal & Cannel Co. Ltd. The Hyde Colliery was in the heart of the town adjoining a main street. The pit was one of two owned by the same firm, the other being known as Broomstair Colliery, at Denton in Manchester, which was abandoned altogether on 30 July 1898, and dated from at least 1869, when worked by Leigh and Bradbury. Due to flooding at the Broomstair Colliery many of the men and boys were found work at the Hyde Lane Colliery. Thus, on the day of the disaster there were about 200 employed at the pit, being augmented by a number from the Broomstair Colliery. The morning shift, comprising about 80 to 100 men, descended the shaft between half past five and six o'clock. All seemed well until around half past nine when a plume of white smoke was noticed coming from the mouth of the pit. Hastily the cages were lowered into

the mine, and a number of injured men and boys were raised to the surface. The pit was now filling with the deadly afterdamp. From the bottom of the shaft, a steep one in two inclined tunnel dipped away to a level tunnel almost 300 yards long, almost under the village of Haughton. It was here, where thirty-odd men were working, that the explosion took place. Twenty-three of the men working there perished, and another five were seriously injured, burnt and scorched by the hot blast. Other miners working in a lower seam were totally unaware that there had even been an explosion. As always in pit explosions there were many brave acts of heroism, even from those who were already injured. It was even necessary to restrain those eager to assist. A father feared that he had lost his son, another was anxious as to the fate of his brother. The father found the son, charred and mangled. The dead body was carried on a stretcher by two men. Behind, with drooped head and bent frame, walked the father. As soon as it was realised that a blast had occurred, the manager of the colliery, Mr Goodwin, organised a search party. On descending the shaft, the team found it impossible to get to the area of the mine affected. The afterdamp was so thick it was difficult to breathe; in addition many roof falls blocked the way of the rescuers. Progress was slow but, despite the appalling conditions, the obstructions were finally removed. They struggled forward in the foul air. Dr Griffin and Dr Sidebottom, relatives of the mine owners, made their way into the pit a distance of about three quarters of a mile. It was almost two o'clock in the afternoon before they were able to reach the place of the calamity. By this time it was assumed that anyone remaining must have perished. The atmosphere was becoming increasingly hot and the air was bad. Soon they came across six of the dead miners, all in quick succession. The body of one of them, a young lad, was in a sad state, the force of the explosion having hurled him against the side of the pit, which had left a huge gash on the side of his head. Another one of the dead held a cap against his face as if trying to protect himself against the afterdamp. Also among the dead was another young lad named Wildgoose. He and his brother had been working not far from an air passage where the atmosphere was clear. One brother escaped, the other was killed. One lad named Joseph Grattan was doubtless saved by a man named John Haslam. When the explosion occurred, Haslam dragged the boy many yards until the fresh air was reached. However, Haslam lost his own brother, a young man aged twenty. On the surface of the pit there was, not unnaturally, a large gathering of anxious relatives waiting for news of loved ones. Outside the pit gates a greater crowd gathered, waiting, hoping. The first of the bodies was brought out of the pit soon after two o'clock in the afternoon. The cage was lowered time and time again, each time bringing up the bodies of the perished miners. They were covered over in a white cloth, to be taken to the adjoining sawmill in order to be laid out and identified. By seven o'clock the dead numbered seventeen. The final total was to be twenty-three. By eight o'clock the rain started to fall heavily and a strong wind blew across the pit bank, adding even more gloom to the scene. Soon the last of the victims, John

Ridgeway, was brought out of the mine. The list of those who died that day was then issued in the local press:

Frederick Horle, aged 17, of Hyde
Arthur Wildgoose, 15, of 116 Hyde Lane, Hyde
Thomas Davies, 50, Norbury Street, Hyde, married with a family
James Broadhurst, 19, residing at No.6 Charles Street, Hyde
Frank Ashton, 14 of 10 Queen Street, Hyde
Henry Slater, 46, residing at Cheapside, Hyde, married and with a large family
George Henry Wild, 19, son of James Wild residing at 15 Sydall Street, Hyde
Emmanuel Bailey, 50, residing at Waterloo, Ashton, married
Joseph Fish, 23, Stockport Road, Hyde
William Haslam, 20, of Hyde
James Hall, 65, residing at 7 Nelson Street, Hyde, widower
James Bradley, 20, Haughton Green
William Catterall, 70, residing at Reed Street, Hyde, married with three children
Thomas Shaw, 35, Kingston Brow, Hyde, married with three children
John Bailey, 45, residing at Edna Street, Hyde, married with five children
Henry Slater junior, 15, Cheapside, Hyde, son of Henry Slater
Samuel Watson, 24, residing at Catton Street, Hyde, married
Joseph Wild, 31, residing at 7 Port Street, Hyde, married
Joseph Gee, 30, residing at Godley, married with three children
William Slate, 36, residing at White Court, Walter Street, Hyde, married with a large family
Thomas Gee, aged 24, residing at 110 Manchester Road, Hyde
Peter Gee, 30, Moorfield Road, Haughton, married with two children
John Ridgeway, 19, residing at Norfolk Street, Hyde

Many others were injured. John Wild, aged twenty-two was severely burned on his back, face and side. His younger brother, George Henry, perished in the blast. The Hyde Pit was previously considered to be one of the safest in the country, not having had an accident for over twenty-seven years, and that accident was not considered to be serious. 'I felt as safe in this pit as I would by my own fireside' said one of the men. However, the cause of the disaster might well be attributed to the men and management themselves, for the gas was ignited by the naked flames the men were still allowed to use, in spite of frequent explosions of this nature throughout the country at this time. On Tuesday 22 January 1889, twelve of the victims were buried in St George's churchyard. One week later, on Sunday 27 January, a special service was given, complete with a procession through the town headed by the Kingston Mills Band. Two days after the explosion, on Saturday 19 January, the Mayor of Hyde, Alderman Peter Green JP presided over a meeting of ratepayers in the town hall. It was agreed to open a relief fund for the relatives of the deceased. Mr J.W. Sidebotham and Mr Nasmyth Sidebotham, the proprietors, gave £500. Collections were made at the parish church, Stockport, and throughout the region, with many recreational evenings held in memory of the disaster, including a sacred concert presented by the Band of the 4th VBCR at the Volunteer Drill Hall in Stockport. In total, a sum of £6,907 8s 2d was raised for the families – a huge amount in those days, equivalent to £280,000 today. The Hyde Lane Colliery employed nearly 280 men at it peak, and mined the Black Two Feet, Peacock, New, Water and Third Seams, until its abandonment on 28 March 1906. The shafts at the Hyde Lane Colliery were sunk to a depth of 782ft and the Water Mine. Today, a blue plaque on the canal towpath near Manchester Road at Hyde marks the spot of the former colliery, and recalls the disaster there.

Jubilee: Oldham*, SD 943 107

The colliery was located south of Lee Wood, north of Shaw and Crompton and was sunk in 1845 by Edge Lane & Dry Clough Colliery Co. The pit worked the Mountain Mine, though marked Gannister Mine on the geological survey, at a shaft depth of 325ft, passing the Forty Yard and Upper Foot Mines of inferior coals. The Oldham, Middleton & Rochdale Colliery Co. Ltd worked the Jubilee Pit in 1880. In 1883, the colliery was purchased by the Platt Brothers, who coked all the coal produced for their iron-works at Oldham, although the colliery is listed as being under the ownership of the Oldham, Middleton & Rochdale Coal Co. Ltd in 1884.

The colliery closed in 1932, and a mines list records that the pit was being worked by Platt Bros & Co. Ltd, 1924. Also the pit is listed as being worked in 1896 by the Platt Bros & Co. Ltd, Oldham. Robert Evans was the colliery

Jubilee Colliery, Shaw. (Crompton Colliery)

manager at this time, and Joseph Mills the undermanager. The colliery then employed 143 men underground and twenty-nine on the surface.

The coal was used for coking, manufacturing and heating, the seams worked were the Mountain Mine and King Coal. The colliery output was raised at the upcast shaft, watched over by two checkweighmen, one employed by the miners, and the other by the owners of the pit. The coke ovens were charged by means of a tramway above, that left the upcast shaft, the tubs running down by gravity to the ovens. The temperature in the coke ovens could reach as high as 500°C.

The Mountain Mine seam was 30in high at best, and conditions down the pit were harsh and wet. In 1877, it is recorded that some 830 gallons of water per minute were pumped from the workings. The site of the old colliery was opened as a nature reserve in August 1991 by Groundwork in Oldham and Rochdale, and is a fine example of how old industrial sites *can* be preserved, while being allowed to return gradually to nature. The colliery was besides the Jubilee public-house on the Rochdale road (B6194) between Shaw and Milnrow. Many relics of the old pit survive, including the capped upcast and downcast shafts, foundations of the engine houses, and blacksmiths shop.

The cobbled mine access road is still visible, along with a bank of coke ovens, coke oven sidings and the remains of a dynamo house. When the mine closed, the many miles of underground galleries were allowed to flood, from Sholver in the south to Hollingworth Lake in the north. The water, estimated at a thousand million gallons is still pumped out, from the shaft at Butterworth Hall Colliery, with which Jubilee Pit had underground connections.

The colliery is mentioned in Joseph Dickinson's Inspector of Mines list of 1854, when it was worked by Evans Barker & Co. A fatal accident occurred just a year later, as reported in the *Manchester Guardian*, 7 March 1855:

On Sunday last about twelve o'clock, an accident which has been attended with fatal consequences occurred at Crompton. It appears that six men were engaged in turning a capstan to draw the pump rod out of the pump at Jubilee Pit, the property of Messrs Evans and Barker, but when they got the rod up a certain length, they found the weight too much for them. Indeed there should have been fourteen men at the capstan instead of six. The consequence was that they lost all power over it, and were thrown with great violence, and one of them named William Kershaw, a collier, was dashed against a wall of the pit cabin, and had his skull fractured. He died shortly afterwards. Another man, named Joseph Chatham, had his shoulder fractured, and John Gartside was much bruised. The others were more or less bruised and shaken. The deceased left a wife and five or six children.

The site is mentioned in the *Rochdale Observer*, 27 November 1858:

The colliers in the Rochdale area have continued, with one or two exceptions to work steadily. The miners at the Jubilee Pit near Newhey, Milnrow have now been out for about a week. About a month ago the miners at Boarshaw Pit belonging to Messrs Stott, Milne and Co. obtained a slight advance. The number of men at Jubilee is about one hundred.

On 11 March 1920, David Fielding, aged twenty, a banksman at the Jubilee Colliery, Crompton, near Oldham, Lancashire, had his fingers injured while adjusting guard at the pulley.

Kingston Colliery: Kingston, near Hyde

This colliery was located besides the River Tame at Kingston, to the north of Broomstair Bridge on Manchester Road, at the top of Hall Street. The Kingston Colliery was abandoned on 20 October 1925. The pit was formerly worked by the Kingston Colliery Co. Ltd, in 1918 and 1924. This is the only known owner of the colliery. At the former date, the colliery employed eighty men underground and seven surface workers, and was, therefore, a major employer. The pit mined the Mary, Hard, and Colonel, which were abandoned in May 1920, and lastly worked the Town Lane Seam, abandoned in 1925.

Knott Lane: Bardsley, near Oldham

Christopher Jacques is recorded as working the Knott Lane Colliery in 1880. In 1887 it was abandoned. The pit was originally worked with a gin by Kit Jaker.

Knowl: Moorside, Oldham District, SD 956 076

A colliery worked by James Butterworth & Co. in 1867. The pit is also noted on the OS map of 1844, being off Turf Pit Lane, Moorside, on the present-day playing fields, but before Whitehall Lane. A sunken and waterlogged area today indicates the former colliery site, almost opposite the cricket ground. This is marked 'Old Shaft, coal' on a map of 1891. The colliery is mentioned in the Catalogue of Plans of Abandoned Mines (1928): Knowl (a) Oldham; (b) COAL; (d) 97 NE (1923) A4: Last entry is location of mine entrance only.

Lee Pit: Middleton/Chadderton

A colliery, or shaft; part of the Woodside Colliery, worked by the Oldham, Middleton & Rochdale Co. Ltd in 1884. (see also Woodside). Catalogue of Plans of Abandoned Mines gives the following information: Lee, Woodside (a) Middleton/Chadderton; (b) COAL Royley (abandoned 1 January 1903); (d) 97 NW (1922) A1, 2, 3, 4: B1, 2, 3: C2, 3, 4: D3.

A Mines Inspectors Report for the year 1866 records: 'May 2nd. Lee Pit, Chadderton. John Farron [Farrow?] killed through roof fall, died on the 25th'.

Lees: Oldham

A colliery that was either in the Lees District of Oldham, or worked by a person of that name, such as Abraham Lees. It was probably the former, as a directory of 1824-1825 tells us that Beckett and Winterbottom were coal masters of a Lees Colliery at this time. This may be the entry in the Catalogue of Plans of Abandoned Mines listed as: Lees and Hallows (a) Oldham; (b) COAL Seam unnamed; (c) Whittaker and Bradburn, King Edward Street, Macclesfield, Cheshire; (d) 97 NE (1922) A2: B2.

Limehurst: Bardsley

This colliery was worked by John George Newton in 1854, and the Limehurst Colliery Co. in 1869 and 1879. The New Limehurst Colliery Co. Ltd, Ashton-under-Lyne, worked the pit in 1896, when it was mining the Peacock and Two Foot seams with 293 men underground and thirty-eight on the surface in 1896. Owen Henry was the manager at this time; this was a large colliery for the Bardsley/Limehurst area, and a major employer.

The following information is from the Catalogue of Plans of Abandoned Mines: Limehurst (a) Waterloo, Bardsley, Hartshead, Hurst; (b) COAL Black (abandoned 1884); (d) 105 NW (1923) A9, 10, 11, 12: B9, 10, 11, 12: C9, 10, 11. Limehurst (a) Waterloo; (b) COAL New Fairbottom (abandoned December 1894); (d) 105 NW (1923) B10. Last entry is for mine entrance only.

A Mines Inspectors Report for the year 1869 records the death of a boy: 'May 20th. Limehurst Colliery. John Howard, 12 years, killed through stone falling from roof.'

Limehurst New: Bardsley

This pit is mentioned in the Catalogue of Plans for Abandoned Mines (1928): Limehurst New (a) Waterloo, Hurst, Hartshead; (b) COAL two Feet, Peacock (abandoned 21 December 1898); (d) 97 SW G12: H11, 12: 97 SE (1922) G1: H1: 109 NW (1923) A11, 12: B10, 11, 12> 105 NE (1923) A1: B1.

Limeside: Limeside, near Oldham

A colliery worked by John Evans in 1834, and E. Evans, no doubt some relation, in 1842. Thomas Ramsbottom & Sons worked the colliery in 1869. The pit is not mentioned in a mines list of 1880. The colliery was off the Limeside Road at Hollinwood. Information from the Catalogue of Plans of Abandoned Mines: Limeside (a) Oldham, Woodhouses; (b) COAL Foxholes (1826); (c) Chamber Colliery Co. Ltd, Hollinwood, Oldham; (d) 97 SW (1922) F5, 6: G5, 6.

Little End: Oldham

Worked by Abraham Crompton in 1861, and by Kay and Wilks in 1869. Nothing else is known. The colliery is not even mentioned in the Catalogue of Plans of Abandoned Mines (1928).

Little Green: Middleton★

This pit was worked by Messrs Wild, Andrews and Haigh during the late 1840s, and worked by Wyld, Andrews & Co. in 1854. Note that the record names 'Wyld', which should be 'Wild'.

The *Manchester Guardian* reports an explosion at the site, 23 September 1848:

On Saturday last, Mr Dearden held an inquest at the Black Bull Inn, Middleton, on the body of James Wild, miner, nearly 26 years of age. William Mitchell, coal miner, said that about half past seven on Wednesday morning last, he and others went to their work at the Little Green coal-pit belonging to Messrs Wild, Andrews, and Haigh. The pit was about 70 yards in depth, and the seam 30 inches in thickness. There were four seams at the pit. He had worked there above two years. They use safety lamps when required. The men had all been told not to go into that part of the mine where the accident occurred, it was about 50 yards from the shafts. The deceased, Thomas Cheetham and a boy aged about 13 years, went into that part of the mine. Cheetham had a candle with him, when the explosion took place. He was very badly burnt, though the boy was not injured. The deceased was very much burnt, and also injured on the left side, so that he died at four o'clock Friday morning. The boy, Nathaniel Wood, said that he was four yards from Wild when the explosion took place. They all had candles. He had a spade in his hand, and it was blown out of it, but he was not hurt. The 'blaze' went over his head. The boy corroborated the evidence of the last witness, relative to the previous caution not to enter that part of the mine. The jury returned a verdict of 'accidental death'. Cheetham, the other miner who was injured, died on Monday morning.

Littletown: Werneth, Oldham

This pit was in the Littletown area of Werneth, and behind the Wagon and Horses Inn. The following is a reference, in the *Annals of Oldham 1783-1839*, to a coal pit in Werneth, which may or may not be the Littletown Colliery:

April 27th 1808, A lamentable accident occurred at Werneth, as John Bradley, Robert Cardwell and Thomas Hawkins were repairing some damage to a coal-pit about half way down, when the fire damp took fire and went off with such velocity that they were literally mashed to pieces. It was several hours before anyone durst venture to fetch the bodies out.

Lodge: Middleton

An early colliery worked by Wild and Andrews, 1842, but not mentioned in the Catalogue of Plans.

Lords Field: Oldham Road, Ashton-under-Lyne

This colliery appears in a list of mines of 1880, and was being worked by the Lords Field Colliery Co. The last fatal accident appears to have occurred in

1875, and the pit is recorded as being abandoned in 1877, which contradicts the information that the pit was being worked in 1880! The following information is from the Catalogue of Plans of Abandoned Mines (1928): Lords Field (a) Ashton-under-Lyne, Waterloo, Hurst; (b) COAL Great Roger, Furness (abandoned 1877); (d) 105 NW (1913) D10, 11, 12: E10, 11, 12: G10, 11.

Low Crompton: Crompton, Oldham*, SD 924 091
Worked by James Clegg & Co. in 1851, James Stott, Milne & Co. in 1854, James Wild in 1857, and the Oldham, Middleton & Rochdale Colliery Co. in 1869 and 1879. This colliery was situated on the east side of Low Crompton Road between Low and High Crompton. A large area of colliery spoil indicates the site, and the small lodge now used by an angling club was used as a colliery reservoir to supply the steam engines.

The pit appears to have closed around 1885. Evidence in the pit heaps indicates that fireclay was also mined here. The farmer at Low Crompton Farm has an unusual but effective means of protecting the public from the dangers of the old mineworkings: large mounds of steaming farmyard manure cover the pit head.

Two men at the site were charged with incautious behaviour, as recorded in the *Manchester Guardian*, 4 September 1857:

> Caution to Colliers. At the petty sessions yesterday, two colliers named John Watmough and Stephen Clegg, were charged with violating the regulations of Mr James Wild's colliery at Lower Crompton, on the 22nd August, by working with a naked light. Robert Fitton, underlooker in the mine, stated that on the day in question, between eleven and twelve o'clock, he saw the defendants working with their Davy-lamps uncovered. The chairman, Rev. T.S. Mills, commented on the recklessness displayed by the defendants, and ordered them to be committed for a month with hard labour.

The Mines Inspectors Report for the year 1867 recorded: 'April 17th. Low Crompton Colliery. James Taylor aged 16 years caught by his wagon while going down incline and killed'.

The following information is taken from the Catalogue of Plans of Abandoned Mines: Low Crompton (a) Crompton; (b) COAL Top, Bottom (1852); (c) Winstanley and Ashworth, 42, Deansgate, Manchester; (d) 89 SW E8: Last entry is location of mine entrance only.

Lower Moor: Edge Lane Road, Sarah Moor, Oldham, SD 927 060
Worked by Mayall and Leach in 1861, and Mayall and Seddon in 1869. John Mayall was working the colliery in his own right in 1875 and the trustees of John Mayall worked the site in 1879. The colliery is marked 'disused' on the OS map of 1891, and was located off Edge Lane Road, just above Charter Street but on the other side. The Lowermoor Brick Works was within a short distance of

the colliery, so it is possible fireclay was also mined here. Some old coal shafts are marked on the map of 1891 to the north of Lowermoor Colliery, but a new housing scheme now covers this area. Today, the site of Lowermoor Colliery appears to have been on a grassed portion of land at the junction of Edge Lane Road and the present day Wimpole Street. There were a number of fatal accidents at the colliery.

The Mines Inspectors Report for the year 1867 states: 'November 8th. Low Moor Colliery. John Kerry crushed to death by wagon'. A few months later, the Mines Inspectors Report records another accident: 'April 22nd. Low Moor Colliery. William Lowe killed through roof fall and other injuries incurred while being taken out of pit' (1868).

The *Manchester Guardian*, 26 May 1868, reports on a dangerous breach of regulations at the colliery:

> At the Oldham Police Station yesterday a miner named William Lees was charged with a breach of the colliery rules at Messrs Mayall and Seddon's Colliery, Lower Moor. It appears that on Friday morning the fireman inspected the workings at the colliery, and having discovered the presence of gas in the upper level, he put up signals marked 'fire' as a warning to parties going down the mine. Later Mr Dickinson, Inspector of Mines visited the colliery, and when he went in to the workings he discovered the signal had been removed, and some of the men were working in the level. The defendant was charged with the removal of the signal.

Lowside: Glodwick, Oldham*, SD 938 043
A colliery of some antiquity worked by William Rigby in 1824 (trade directory) and William Wrighley (written 'Wrighley' in the source, but should be 'Wrigley') in 1841. Messrs W. Blackburne and Co. worked the mine in 1863, as did John G. Blackburne in 1869, when he lived at Dry Clough. John Ashworth was working the colliery in 1879. The parish records of Ashton record a burial on 15 December 1663 of 'John Taylor, Alt, found in a cole pitt at Lowside and fell on the 17th day at night as was sayd'. The pit was on Warren Lane in the Lowside Drive area of Glodwick, and consisted of a number of shafts including two named 'Starkie' and 'Britannia'. Samuel Walkden, collier in the employment of Mr Wrigley, at the Low Side Mine, for between eighteen and twenty years, gave evidence at the Report into Child Labour on 29 October 1841, as this summary shows:

> Will be 65 years of age next March, and has been a collier all his life; at first at the Duke of Bridgewater's works at Walkden Moor. Has worked at Bolton and in other parts of the county, and has worked up in the neighbourhood of Oldham for 23 years. Two bits of lads' working with him have to draw the tubs of 3cwt each down the 'broo' for 40 yards, dipping about two yards in seven on sleds. In some places, in the same pit, the coal will dip one yard in two; when the lads get the tubs into the main-way, one by one, they load two on a waggonbody, and push that on

four wheels on the rails to the pit-bottom. The tubs are sledded down the 40 yards incline by the belt and chain. The two lads working for him will be one 13 years of age next Christmas, the other is going in 15; to the first he is grandfather. The first has been three years in the pit; the other may have been six or seven years in the pit, but he cannot say.

Poverty makes the parents bring them in very soon. They bring children down about nine years of age to receive wages at 9d or 10d a-day. Where there is a great family they will bring them from their cradle, if they can. They bring them to learn a bit at first and see how the other lads get on; and then they begin thrutching, till they are bald with wearing the hair off their heads. Is himself an old 'fellow', who works at easy places, that yet require judgement to get no more than is required from the pillars without letting them down, and requires two boys to take away his coals. Never knew in this district more than one woman at work and this was at Squire Greave's for a week, where he was himself under-looker; but the men said they would leave work if she continued, and so both she and the husband had to go. Gave her 14s out of the club to carry her own. But down in Worsley district, under the Duke's (now Lord Francis Egerton's) women work in the pits common enough, and little girls, too, heaving up with a belt and chain. The men [would] send them anywhere for something to eat. When in full work the lads at the pit where he is at work are at it for 12 working hours. The men can come out a bit sooner, an hour or two sometimes. Works regular at double sets, night and day, having done that for six years or more. The night set goes down about seven, or sometimes nearer eight, but sometimes they are up next morning at seven, sometimes five, but sometimes not until after seven. The day set go down between seven and eight regularly, and they come up, the men at four or five, but the lads will not until seven or eight. The night set one week, is the day set the next, except that old men like himself work only the day set. The children, when bed-time comes upon them begin to be drowsy and sleepy, and the only way to keep them awake is to give them a good sowse on the side of the head, and kick their —, or give them a good shake. When demand has been very busy, the Saturday night set have worked on until Sunday morning, 'cheating the Lord, as they thought'. But generally the men, who finish their night shift on Saturday morning, go next into the pit as the day shift on Monday morning. But if there is work to be done, it must be done, Sunday or workday. A return of the number of children has been made to the Commission, by the proprietor of the pit where he works. The master wants them to keep off drinking, pay their way, and follow their work. Are now making only four days a week or three and a half in summertime, and yet are working night shifts and day shifts. Men are now making less than a pound a week. A full days work is reckoned at 5s. His two lads get 3s a day, one having 1s 9d and the other 1s 3d. Sometimes, two have 1s 3d a piece, sometimes one has 9d and the other 2s 3d all according to their strength. If you ill-use a child in our pit, you must take your tools and be off. The underlooker will allow neither swearing nor fighting. 'Them as is religious would tell the underlooker, aye, by George, sure'. The lads are mostly well done at home, else they could not follow their work. They seem to be as well fed as their wages allow. Is certain parents bring children into the pits than they did sin masters began bating their wages. Some are sent to the factory first, and then brought into the pit afterwards. Even if the children can merely sit down, and keep the rats from the dinners, they will bring them down. Children cannot see their own danger, but their parents take care of them. [Signed] Samuel (X) Walkden [his mark].

There are five entries listed in the Catalogue of Plans of Abandoned Mines for Lowside Pit: Lowside (a) Oldham; (b) COAL Little (abandoned January 1909); (d) 94 SW (1909) F1, 2: G2: H3. Lowside (a) Oldham; (b) COAL Blendfire (abandoned July 1894); (d) 97 SW (1922) B12: Last entry is location of mine entrance only. Lowside (Estate) (a) Oldham; (b) COAL Lower bent; (c) R. and F. Buckley, Lowside Colliery, Oldham; (d) 97 SE (1922) B1 C1.

There is also this entry: Lowside, Abbey Hills, Britannia, Fenny Hill (a) Oldham; (b) COAL Black, Lower Bent, Higher Bent, Great, Little, (abandoned 15 October 1880); (d) 97 SW (1922) probably A11, 12: B11, 12: C11, 12; D11, 12; 97 SE (1922) A1: B1, 2: C1, 2: D1. Lowside, Lunn (a) Oldham; (b) COAL Blendfire, Little; (c) B. and F. Buckley, Lowside Colliery, Oldham; (d) 97 SE (1922) B1: C1: The Mines Inspectors Report below appears to indicate that William Wrigley, one time owner of the pit, was killed there in 1858: 'June 28th. Low Side Colliery. William Wrigley and John Winterbottom killed through falling out of box while examining the pumps'. Another report records another fatality in 1861: 'January 1st. Lowside Colliery. R. Kidger, aged 30, killed through fall of stone from roof'. And again, in 1863, a Mines Inspectors Report notes a death at the site: 'April 29th. Lowside Colliery worked by William Blackburne and Co. James Spencer, aged 18, killed through roof fall in Higher Bent Mine. Died 12th August'.

A serious accident is reported at the colliery in the *Manchester Guardian*, 8 June 1863:

Fatal Colliery Accident, Two Men Killed. On Saturday morning an accident occurred at the Britannia Pit, Lowside Colliery, Oldham belonging to Messrs W. Blackburn and Co., which resulted in the death of two miners and serious injury to a third. It appears that Joseph Lee, Joseph Saxon, and George Blakeman went to work at the Britannia Pit, and were in the lowest level on the south side at the bottom of the engine incline, when part of the roof fell upon them. Lee was partly covered by the stone and rubbish, and after vainly attempting to extricate himself he lay still for more than an hour, until he heard a boy come from another part of the pit, and then he called for help. Assistance was procured, and Lee was removed. Saxon and Blakeman were found dead.

And later that year, a Mines Inspectors Report records a final fatality: 'December 21st. Lowside Colliery. Aaron Tatlock killed through fall of roof in Starkie Pit'.

Marlfield: High Crompton

Nothing is known of this pit, although it did exist. 'Marl' is soil consisting of clay and lime, often used as a fertiliser to sweeten poorer soil.

Maygate: near Oldham, SD 917 058

Worked by Abraham Clegg during the early 1840s. There is a 'Maygate' today off the Chadderton Way (A627) at Oldham, and the colliery would probably have been in this location. However, this area has been extensively built-up and there are no remains of the old pit. The pit is not listed in the Catalogue of Plans of Abandoned Mines (1928).

Midge Holme: Crompton

A pit mentioned in the court case concerning Bank House Pit, and was apparently located above the latter. Nothing else known of this colliery, which was used as an underground reservoir by Oldham Corporation.

Mill Bottom: Paulden Wood, Oldham

This pit is mentioned in the Report on Child Labour in 1841, when William Dronsfield gave evidence:

> William Dronsfield, going in 18, November 4th, 1841. Saw his father killed in the pit, by a fall of coals crushing him against a post, has ever since been afraid of his own life in the pit. Has gone three Sundays to t' Dippers' Sunday school, on the Ashton road. Scarcely ever went to Sunday-school before, because he has had to work a deal on Sundays; was like to work on Sundays, because he had to 'wind t' water out o' men's way agen Monday'. Cannot read or write. If he had a full week's work would make, as a waggoner, 10s; only once made so much; made lately 7s 6d. Was at Ryley's for five years, working with the belt and chain, in his trousers, clogs, and cap, bringing the sledge-boxes down the bays to a truck in the main-way, and drawing this truck, loaded with two boxes, along the main-way to the pit-bottom. They work there still in this way, although it is Black Mine (a thick seam).
>
> Has since worked at several places, first trying the Mill Bottom Pit of Mr James Clay's, at Paulden Wood, about two miles from Oldham, on the Saddleworth road, where the seam is about 21 inches thick. This was so small that he could not work in it. They take the children there at six and seven years of age, they do so at all the mountain-seam mines. The drawers in these pits work perfectly naked, but the thrutchers have their caps on, that their heads may not be galled in pushing the tubs with them. The ways are generally two feet and a half and three feet high; the bays are the height only of the seam. The Mill Bottom Pit is very wet but the lads are merry. They 'jumpen about like cats' when in the pit, and like their rest-day when out of it. Some are so young they go in their bed-gowns, some in jacket and trousers. They like to go i' pit, they are proud on it, [Has] cried himsel' many a time to go in with his father, now could cry to get out on it. In the mines,

as at Mr Clegg's, the men work perfectly naked, lying on one side. Has worked at Wrigley's once, from between six and seven in the morning till ten o'clock at night, sometimes till nine, very often till eight. The pits not so very dry either. Has often been so tired that he could scarcely stir, his knees and thighs felt as though they were broken. Very often felt so in the week-time, was so tired with the long hours, would drop asleep the moment he was in an easy position. Worked night-sets in Mr Wrigley's pits, which are still regularly worked by alternate night and day shifts. Did not like the night-work, nobody does, would prefer work six days than five nights, for the same money. Felt always quite muzzy and sleepy in the night, when working, felt just heavy at first and tired— morning after, but later in the day would get quite hearty. [Signed] WILLIAM (X) DRONSFIELD [mark].

Moor Field: Moor Side, Sholver
The only record relating to the colliery is a report in the *Manchester Guardian*, 14 December 1844:

Boy Killed By A Colliery Engine. On Thursday last, Mr Molesworth, deputy coroner of Rochdale, held an inquest at the Collier's Arms, Moor Side, Sholver, on the body of John Inchcliffe, aged 13 years the son of John Inchcliffe, joiner of Counthill, who was employed as an engine tenter at the colliery at Moor Field, Moor Side, belonging to Mr Job Lees, and who had been working there during the night. About four o'clock on Tuesday morning, another engine tenter, who was on the premises, was surprised to see the engine suddenly stop, whilst winding up a tub containing a miner ascending from his work. On examination of the wheel race of the engine wheel, the body of the deceased was found entangled in the machinery, shockingly mutilated. He is supposed to have fallen asleep whilst sitting on the stool near the engine, and having accidentally dropped into the wheel race, which is unprotected by any railing or guard whatever. He must have been killed instantly.

Had he continued asleep, in a safe position, it is probable that a fatal accident might have occurred to the miner who was ascending the shaft, for he would very likely have been drawn over the top of the pit stocks, and then thrown out with great violence, but the fall of the body of the deceased against the engine wheel stopped the engine at once. Though the deceased was only 13 years of age, he is stated to have been employed as a colliery engine tenter for two or three years. According to the evidence of one of the witnesses, he had been asleep in a dangerous situation near the boiler-house for a hour and a half the same night. The owner of the colliery was very properly blamed for suffering the engine wheel race to be without any guard whatsoever. The jury returned a verdict of 'accidental death'.

Moorside: Moorside
A colliery worked by Messrs Lees in 1841, and Thomas Mellodew in 1875, according to a trade's directory. James Jones gave evidence in the Report on

Child Labour on 29 October 1841, and the summary of his responses mentions the Moorside Pit:

Is going in 13, has been five years in the pit, is drawing for William Burgess, Has been about three years drawing, first thrutched for one of James Miles's lads, (and) got for thrutching for him 3s 6d a-week and 4s was paid by George Hewitt, or Buckey Hewitt, the man as Miles's lad was drawing for had wages the third week after going into the pit. This was at a pit of Messrs Lees's, at Moorside. (He) has worked at several other pits before he came to this, where he has been two years. His father is a joiner, about a quarter of a mile off, stops only just long enough to eat his dinner. It 'comes' (is sent), and is sometimes a bread and butter cake (wheaten bread and butter) gets his breakfast before he comes, of oatmeal porridge and oatcake; will have his porridge and oatcake as soon as he gets home now, when he has just left work, and some bread and butter cake before he goes to bed at nine o'clock. Works in his shirt and cap, needs no 'plodding' to cover his back with. (He) works with belt and chain, it does not hurt him, about a week it hurt him, but not after. Pit is dry as pepper, and warm too, couldn't abide to have aught else on him while working, would be too hot. Has thrutching for him his little brother, Henry Jones, who is going in six, and has been in the pit three months. He gets 1s 6d a-week, (and) gets himself 5s a-week. It is sometimes 16 yards from the working into the mainroad, and it is more than 200 yards to the bottom of the pit, (He) goes sometimes fourteen times a-day; to go fourteen times tires him, if he plays too, plays a good deal, plays now about three days a-week, plays at knurr sometimes, football, and marbles. They never lick him in pit, some they do, sometimes the lads deserve it, they get a piece of cord and hit them on the —, holding them with the other hand. Sometimes the lads do it for one another, sometimes they fight at pit bottom about hooking on, or in the railroad, because they don't go fast enough. Has no other clothes besides the very dirty and ragged ones he has on, (but) goes nevertheless to Sunday-school. Some goes i' waur (work) clothes na' these. It is called Sholver-lane Sunday-school. Will wash himself so soon as he gets home and has had his porridge, will wash then his hands and face. Washes himself all over every Sunday morning, standing beside a tub of water, and rubbing himself 'as white as snow'; if he did not his mother would beat him, goes sometimes to night-school.

After exhibiting some impatience, he here exclaimed that 'he wanted to go woam (home) for his porridge', and ran off as fast as he could into the dark. (Signed) James (X) Jones (his mark)'. Henry Jones also gave evidence on 29 October 1841, the summary running: 'Is going in six, thrutches with his brother; works with his clothes on, has not doffed them yet. HENRY (X) JONES'. John Jones, junior also took part: 'Is brother of the two last, is going in eight, is thrutching, gets half-a-crown a-week; works in the same place and for the same hours with his brothers, never went to any school; does not know his letters. (Signed) JOHN (X) JONES junior (mark)'.

Moston: Moston
Worked by John Stanley in 1854, Exors of John Stanley, 1869, Platt Bros & Co., 1879, Platt Bros & Co. Ltd, Oldham, in 1940, and the National Coal Board from 1947. Seams worked included Big Mine, Colonel, Fox Holes, Mary Mine in 1896, and the Pumping Station in 1960. The colliery employed 402 underground and 136 on the surface in 1896, and twenty-two underground and twenty-seven on the surface in 1951, during salvage. Managers include Richard Purdy, 1896 and F. Tootle, 1951. The colliery was abandoned 5 June 1950, when it employed 650 men. The original pit (No.1) was sunk in 1840 near to Nuthurst railway bridge to a depth of 326ft. A serious flooding of the mine on 9 November 1884, caused the pit to be abandoned and new sinkings undertaken, at what then became the New Moston Colliery.

This is probably the reference to the Moston Old Pit listed in the Catalogue of Plans of Abandoned Mines: Moston Old (a) Manchester; (b) COAL Seven Feet; (c) Divisional Engineers Office LMS Railway Co. Ltd, Hunts Bank, Manchester; (d) 96 SE (1923) F10, 11: G10, 11.

An example of the sometimes reckless attitude some displayed can be seen in a report in the *Manchester Guardian*, 23 October 1857:

Working in a coal mine with a naked candle. Thomas Waterhouse, a miner employed at Moston Colliery was summoned for working in the mine with a naked candle contrary to the rules of the colliery.

The defendant admitted having used the candle, but said it was common practice in the mine. Mr Trafford fined him 20s and costs, and remarked that it was an extraordinary thing that he should be obliged to fine a man in order to make him take care of his own life.

A tragic accident at the site is reported in the *Manchester Guardian*, 1 March 1861:

Fatal Accident in a Coal-Pit. A collier named Robert Clough, in the employ of Mr Stanley, at the Moston Colliery was killed on Friday morning last. About half past nine o'clock, Clough was at work in the pit and was about to put up a prop for the support of a stone in the roof. When he had made the necessary hole, he knelt down in order to introduce the end of the prop, and when this was in position the stone, which was about three yards square and a foot in thickness fell upon him. A man who was working near the place, obtained assistance and the stone was raised, but Clough was found to be dead. It was stated that the deceased had examined the stone on the previous day, and was then about to place some props under it, but as they were too short, he said he would do it in the morning. An inquest was held yesterday before Mr W.S. Rutter, the district coroner, at the Woodman Inn, Newton Heath. The verdict was 'accidental death'. The deceased was 24 years of age and was married. His widow had been the wife of another man, who was also killed in the pit.

A report on the final days of the site is to be found in the *Oldham Evening Chronicle,* 25 February 1953:

> Moston Pit ceased production in June 1950, but a skeleton staff was kept on to salvage equipment and materials. The last of this 'ghost' crew finished last week-end. Among them was a maintenance fitter, 69 year old Simpson Middleton, of Northfield Avenue, New Moston, who has spent 56 years there. He is now 69, and is retiring. Two other men with 53 years of service, Jack Cunliffe, winding engineman of Ainsworth Street, Newton Heath, and deputy Harry Langford, of Mather Street, Failsworth, both of whom are 68, also retired on Saturday. The pit belonged to Platt Brothers before nationalisation, and there was a stay down strike when it was announced that it was to be closed. Most of those employed there, however were found other jobs at other pits in the Manchester area.

Netherhey: Oldham, SD 938 039
This colliery was located at the bottom of Netherhey Street, just beyond its junction with Tate Street in the Glodwick area of Oldham. The area has been reclaimed and landscaped, and there are no apparent remains of the colliery. The pit is marked as 'old colliery' in the 1890s, and was shown with two shafts and a number of small buildings along with a reservoir.

New Bailey: Chadderton
This colliery was at Thompson Lane, Butler Green, Chadderton, and worked by Messrs William Jones & Co. during the 1840s. The shaft depth was 450ft, probably to the Royley Mine (Arley Seam). A terrible and gruesome accident occurred here in 1848, and is recorded in the *Manchester Guardian,* 1 January 1848:

> Shocking accident at a colliery. On Thursday last, Mr Clarke, deputy coroner opened an inquest at Chadderton, on the body of Thomas Whitehead, a banksman, or colliery workman. On Wednesday afternoon last, the deceased was at work near the mouth of the shaft at the New Bailey Colliery, Thompson Lane, Chadderton belonging to Messrs William Jones and Co. when he pushed a wagon too far over the pit mouth, over-balanced himself, and fell down the shaft, a depth of 150 yards. He was instantly killed, his head being severed from his body, and thrown some distance from it. The deceased was 26 years of age, and unmarried. Verdict: 'Accidental death'.

New Earth: Greenacres Moor, Oldham
Worked by Abraham Lees and Sons in 1842, and the sinking of the colliery dates from this time. The 'Greenacres Moor' reference is given in directory, however, the pit was more than likely located at New Earth off the Roundthorn Road, Oldham. The Chamber Colliery Co. Ltd was working

this pit in 1880, when it is listed as being at Lees. There are two accidents reported here, both recorded in the *Manchester Guardian*. The first appears in the 11 May 1842 edition: 'On Friday last, a young man named Samuel Brierley, who was employed in sinking a colliery at New Earth, Oldham when a large stone fell on his head, and he was instantly killed. He was unmarried, 26 years of age and resided at Red Tan Nook'. The second accident is in the *Manchester Guardian* of 28 July 1847: 'On Saturday last, Mr Dearden held an inquest at Red Tan Nook, Oldham, respecting the death of Daniel Tattersall, a coal miner. On Friday last, whilst the deceased was at work in the colliery of Mr Abraham Lees, New Earth, Side of Moor, a large stone accidentally fell from the roof of the mine upon his head, and killed him on the spot. The deceased who resided at Red Tan Nook, was 43 years of age, and has left a widow and several children'.

New Engine: Butler Green, Oldham, SD 908 037
This colliery was located off Old Lane and Engine Street, Butler Green, near the Oldham/Chadderton district and is shown on the OS map of 1844, but the sinking of this pit dates from 1803. Locally this pit was named 'Slack', and the shaft depth is recorded as being 65 yards to the Black Mine. Two shafts near here, one named 'Cupola' in the aptly named 'Cupola Field' were filled prior to 1840. The output from the colliery was transported by canal. There are a number of accidents recorded at this location. In the *Manchester Guardian*, 13 November 1830, there is a report of an accident which left a man severely injured: 'On Thursday morning last a collier by the name of Kay, working at the New Engine Coal Pits, Oldham mistaking the situation he was in the pit fell nearly 20 yards from a higher level to a lower level, and a coal bucket falling upon him injured him very seriously. He still survives, but there is little hope of him recovering'. A boy was killed in 1850, and this was recorded in the *Manchester Guardian*, 3 July 1850: 'Fatal Accident at a Colliery. On Friday morning an accident occurred at the New Engine Pit, Old Lane, Chadderton, whereby a boy named Joseph Ashcroft [?] aged about twelve years was killed'. A horrific accident at the site is reported in the *Manchester Guardian*, 30 April 1853:

> Shocking Accident. On Thursday an inquest was held at Hollinwood, on the body of John Scholes, aged 71 years, who came to his death by falling into a vat of boiling copperas at the New Engine Colliery Works, on the 23rd inst. It appears that he was walking on a plank that was improperly placed, and that he fell from it. He got out of the vat without assistance, and when found he was taking off some portions of his clothing. He was so dreadfully scalded that he lingered only until the following day. He had been employed a long time on the premises. A verdict of 'accidental death' was returned.

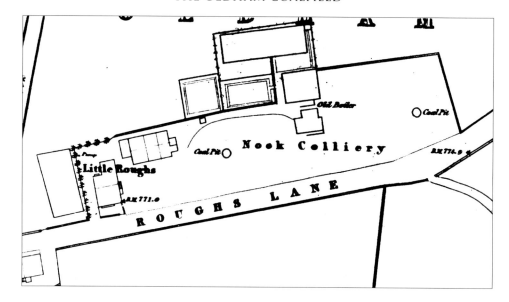

Nook Colliery, map of 1848.

Nook: Oldham
A colliery off Old Edge Lane, Oldham. The colliery is clearly marked on a map of 1851. The pit is shown with two shafts and 'an old boiler'. However, the colliery is not mentioned in Joseph Dickinson's 'Statistics of the Collieries of Lancashire, Cheshire, and North Wales', a paper read on 7 March 1854.

A fatality occurred at the pit, as reported in *Manchester Guardian,* 15 July 1848:

> On Tuesday last, Mr Clarke held an inquest at the Engine Inn, Edge Lane, near Royton on the body of William, son of William Beswick, of Holden Fold, coal miner aged 19 years. At eight o'clock on Tuesday morning last, the deceased went to work in one of Mr Evan's coal-pits, Edge Lane, and soon after he had got into the mine, a large stone, from the roof of the pit fell and killed him on the spot. Verdict: 'Accidental death'.

An accident, apparently caused by the 'carelessness' of the victim, according to a jury, is reported in the *Manchester Guardian,* 2 December 1848:

> An inquest was held yesterday morning at the Sun Inn, Red Town Nook, Oldham, on the body of Joseph Garforth, aged 18 years, late engineer at Nook Colliery. It appeared that he came to his death about half past eleven o'clock on Wednesday night last, by falling down the coal pit – a depth of about 139 yards. He remained at work when the night shift commenced, merely to be ready to draw up the men if required, and as there was but a few coal wagons to be wound up during the

night, it was considered unnecessary to have a banksman there, and the deceased undertook to attend to his engine, and to bank the wagons as well. The banksman left about ten o'clock, and was the last person to see the deceased alive. He saw him in the morning acting very imprudently, in order to save him walking from the pit mouth to the engine-house, and cautioned him not to do it again, and as no one saw the accident, it is supposed that the same conduct, having been repeated caused the fatal catastrophe. He was seen on the previous morning, when he had taken the full wagon from the cage, to throw back the shoulders, which caused the cage to hang about 14 inches below the surface, and in that position he pushed the empty wagon onto the cage, which was evidently dangerous, as being iron, it might have over balanced and dragged him into the pit. Such appears to have been the cause of the calamity, for when the banksman reached the place in the morning, he found the cage hanging as above described, and the engineer no where near.

The men at the bottom were aware of it, but could neither give the alarm nor get out, as no one was on the premises. The first person who was aware of the accident, was a lad about 13 years of age, who was at work at the bottom of the shaft, and hearing a wagon falling down, he ran out of the way, and when it reached the bottom, he heard something else fall, which on returning to the spot, he found to be the lifeless body, but so mutilated about the head and face, that it was a long time before he could be recognised. The jury returned a verdict of 'accidental death caused by his own carelessness'. They also cautioned the owner of the pit against allowing the engineer, or any other person to act in the same way again.

The *Manchester Guardian*, 17 May 1851, reports on the case of a man caught sleeping in the pit:

Sleeping at Coal-pits. On Wednesday last at the petty sessions held at Rochdale, Robert Holt was charged with sleeping at Nook coal-pit. It was considered a dangerous practice to allow persons to sleep in such places, and the owners of collieries have made complaints concerning it. The men were committed to prison for 14 days.

Northgate: Sholver Hey, Oldham

A colliery noted on a map of the 1870s as being south of Sholver Hey, when the pit is shown with a bank of coke ovens. There still is a Northgate Lane between the Ripponden Road (A672) and Sholver Lane, Sholver. There is but a brief mention in the Catalogue of Plans of Abandoned Mines (1928): Northgate (a) Oldham; (b) COAL; (d) 97 NE (1922) A2: Last entry location of mine entrance only.

Oaks: Hollins Road, Oldham

This pit was opened on 27 December 1848, and was worked by: William Jones & Co. in 1854; Chamber Colliery Co. in 1869 and 1879; Chamber Colliery Co. Ltd,

Albert Pit, Oak Colliery. (Oldham Library)

Hollinwood, Oldham, in 1896 and 1924; National Coal Board from 1947. The seams worked were the Bent in 1896, and the Colonel and Furnace in 1951. Men employed: 146 underground, twenty-one surface in 1896; 277 underground, and eighty-seven on surface in 1951. Undermanager was George Sumner, in 1896, and manager was W.W. Millington.

In 1913, when Chamber Colliery Co. Ltd owned the site, the pit employed 340 below ground and fifty-nine on the surface. This entry is taken from the Catalogue of Plans of Abandoned Mines (1928): Oak, Albert, Victoria (a) Oldham, Woodhouses, Bardsley; (b) COAL Black (1883) Higher Bent (1906) Lower bent or Peacock (1906); (c) Chamber Colliery Co. Ltd, Hollinwood, Oldham; (d) 97 SW (1922) C4, 5: D4, 5, 6, 7, 8, 9, 10: E4, 5, 6, 7, 8, 9, 10: F5, 6, 7, 8, 9, 10.

Oak Colliery, Hollins Road, Oldham, was situated within the borough of Oldham. There were three shafts at the colliery, each 40 yards from each other. The downcast and drawing shaft was 10ft 8in in diameter, and 318 yards down to the Bent Seam. The upcast shaft was 10ft diameter, and also 318 yards to the same seam. The third shaft, the pumping shaft, was 11ft in diameter and 358 yards deep, being 10 yards below the Black Seam. All these shafts were lined throughout with 9in brick walling. The winding engine there had one vertical cylinder 36in by 60in with an overhead drum for flat ropes, 9ft diameter at the beginning, and 14ft at the end of the lift. This engine raised two tubs of 7cwt capacity in each cage one above the other. There were two rope conductors for the thimbles on the outside of each cage, and two ropes between them, against which the rubbers of the cage slide to prevent any contact. The pumping engine was of the Cornish type, with one vertical cylinder 80in by 120in equal beam, Cornish valves and condenser which was constructed by Messrs Fairbairn & Co. This engine was in operation for twelve hours per day, delivering to the surface 390 gallons of water per minute. The pit was ventilated by a Guibal fan, 40ft by 12ft driven by a 28in horizontal engine and duplicate. This fan made thirty-four revolutions and produced a circulation of 40,000 cubic feet per minute. An engine operating the underground haulage was placed on the surface, and had two horizontal cylinders 14in by 28in geared 1 to 3. One drum 7ft in diameter worked a west engine plane, or downbrow in the Bent Seam, the length of which was 700 yards. From the downbrow the levels were turned every 50 yards, and from these the coal was cleared out to the rise up to the old workings. The gateways were 12 yards apart, and after building substantial pack walls on each side of them, the hollows between them were also filled in close with stone. The two layers of coal were obtained by two distinct workings, the Lower Bent 2ft 3in thick was taken first. The Upper Bent 1ft 8in thick was taken some yards behind. The measures between them were rock and shale. The colliery was abandoned 13 July 1956, when it was mining the Colonel and Furnace Seams, at that time it employing over 350 men. The three shafts at Oak Colliery were The Victoria, The Albert and The Duke. At the Duke shaft, evidently older than the 'Victoria' and 'Albert' pits there was a beam engine, and a stone tablet bore the date 1845. The height of the beam engine above ground was about 30ft, and the drums were outside in the open yard. The engine was in use until around 1914, when it was discarded and an electric pump installed in its place. One of the earlier coal cutting machines was installed at the Albert Pit, a Siskol or Champion made by the International Coal Co. This worked like a pneumatic machine with two handles on the side and a percussion valve that was fixed on a stand. A five chiselled pick at the end of a rod worked with a rotary motion, about 15ft wide and around 4ft deep. The Oak Colliery had a tramway, known locally as the 'Oak Incline' that ran from the pit down to the Manchester and Ashton-under-Lyne Canal on the Hollinwood Branch of the canal.

The opening of the pit was recorded in the *Manchester Guardian,* 30 December 1848, as follows:

The Oak Colliery, Hollinwood. The opening of this new concern, the property of Messrs William Jones and Co. at Hollinwood was formerly celebrated on Wednesday last by the workmen who have been employed in sinking the shafts to the Black Mine, giving their employers a dinner, on the successful reaching of the mine, in both pits, and with scarce an accident.

Three Mines Inspectors Reports record separate accidents: 'December 7th. Oak Colliery, worked by William Jones and Co. James Broome, waggoner, killed through fall of roof' (1852); 'December 9th. John Cooper killed through fall of roof' (1852); 'January 3rd. Oak Colliery, J. Willowship, hooker-on, killed by brick falling from side of shaft' (1856).

A roof fall in the 'Albert' pit was recorded in the *Manchester Guardian*, 27 August 1856:

> On Saturday last an accident occurred at the Prince Albert Pit, at Oak Colliery, Hollins by which a miner named John Thornley, about 50 years of age was seriously hurt, and narrowly escaped death. Thornley was at work in the pit, when a portion of the roof in the place in which he was gave way and buried him in the rubbish. Some of the workmen who saw the accident immediately came to his assistance, and when he was extricated it was found that his leg and foot were frightfully crushed. He was conveyed home and has been attended to since the accident by Mr Leach, surgeon. Yesterday it was considered that amputation would be necessary.

A falling stone caused a fatality at the site, as reported in the *Manchester Guardian*, 29 April 1857:

> Fatal Colliery Accident. On Tuesday, Mr Ferrand Dearden, coroner held an inquest at the Dog and Partridge Inn, on the body of Joseph Turner, aged 50, of Bower Lane, Hollinwood. He was a coal miner and worked at the Albert Colliery, Hollinwood, of Messrs William Jones and Co. On the 8th inst. while he was at work, a stone fell upon him from the roof and caused severe injuries on his thigh and ribs. He died on the 23rd inst. Verdict: 'Accidental death'.

An inquest, dealing with a fatal firedamp explosion is reported in the *Colliery Guardian*, 11 January 1862:

> An inquest was held on Monday at the Bridgewater Arms, Hollinwood (Oldham) on the body of Robert Price aged 23, burnt to death by an explosion of firedamp on Friday week at the Oaks Colliery, belonging to the Chamber Colliery Company. Mr Dickinson, inspector of mines, who had inspected the colliery was present. The explosion it appears took place in the Lower Bent Mine, which was well known to give off large quantities of firedamp, and in all parts of the workings, except the main levels where air was entering, safety lamps were in use. The jury returned a verdict of 'accidental death'.

Several Mines Inspectors Report for the years 1864-1869 record further deaths: 'April 26th. Oak Colliery, Hollinwood. William Hilton and James Wright killed through stone falling in the Albert Pit' (1864); 'February 3rd. Oak Colliery, Oldham. Abraham Taylor aged 46 killed through roof fall' (1869); 'February 13th. Oak Colliery, Oldham. Joseph Heap killed through being caught between cog wheels' (1869).

A major accident occurred, in which four were killed, at the Albert pit in 1884, as recounted in the *Oldham Evening Observer* of 14 August:

Frightful Colliery Accident at Albert Pit. Four Men Killed. This morning, about six o'clock, a fearful accident occurred at Albert Pit, Hollinwood, by which four men have lost their lives. This pit has preserved considerable immunity from any accident of a grievous nature until the fateful events of today. The previous evening everything was reported right, and this morning, the underlooker, Andrew Ogden, examined the pit in the usual way, and found all right. The men assembled for their work at the usual hour, and the descent of the shaft was made safely. The pit is one of the most considerable in the district, and has various ramifications. Amongst those who prepared for work were two brothers, named James and Joseph Leach, and John Wright and Eli Greaves. These men were employed at a distant part of the working, many hundreds of yards from the shaft, and in order to reach their destination, they got into two wagons, the two Leaches occupying the first conveyance, and the other men in the second. The wagons were drawn by a pony, and they ran along on a tramway. Over three hundred yards of the distance was traversed, without any incident, but the men appeared to have kept a look-out for any giving way of the roof, occurrences of which, we understand, are more frequent at this time of the year. When about three hundred yards of the way had been covered, a portion of the roof seems to have given way, and one of the men, at least seems to have come aware of the alarming fact, for he jumped out of the wagon, but, alas, too late. With a heavy smash, masses of rock fell upon the moving wagons, and instantly arrested their progress. As we have said, one of the men tried to escape. We believe it was Joseph Leach, whose injuries were of a different character, to those of his ill fated companions. But he was caught between the shoulders and head, and jammed between the stone and the edge of the wagon.

Not a cry was raised, the accident being so sudden, but that an accident had occurred was soon conveyed to other parts of the pit, and assistance came. As soon as possible assistance was rendered, and the men were extricated, but human aid was out of the question, as the men, if not dead, were at the last gasp. Joseph Leach presented the saddest spectacle, and his injuries were more of an external nature. His head was badly disfigured, and blood flowed profusely. As soon as possible the bodies were taken to the top, and taken to their homes on spring carts. James Leach resided at Hollinwood, and is about 45 years of age, married. John Wright, about 65 years of age, resided at Ashfield Street, Hollinwood, and leaves a widow and several members of family. Eli Greaves, 50, resided at Aaron Street, Hollinwood and leaves a widow. Joseph Leach, who lives at Hollinwood has left a widow and four children to mourn his loss. The Leach family consists of several miners, another brother being employed at another pit in the locality. The stone that fell upon them was of considerable size, being three yards long and eight inches thick. It fell in one mass, and not only killed the men but crushed the wagon. The pony escaped injury. The pit where the accident happened was the 'Victoria' No.1 and is 290 yards deep. The sad accident caused the work to be suspended for the day.

An intriguing account of the nationalisation of the site is reported in the *Oldham Standard*, 11 January 1947:

> Two minutes before eleven o'clock on Sunday morning, the buzzers at Oak Pit, Hollins Road sounded a rather noisy introduction to the 'Vesting Day' ceremony which was to mark the handing over of the pit to the nation. Then, on the first stroke of the hour, the colliery manager, Mr J.T. Hughes hoisted the Union Jack. The flag of the National Coal Board was also hung over the pit head. He received the flags from 15 year old trainee, George Wood. A plaque which stated 'This colliery is now managed by the National Coal Board on behalf of the people, January 1st 1947' was handed over by Mr James Berry, an old collier, to Mr Thomas Harris who placed it at the entrance to the colliery. There were present at the ceremony, two colliers who are 71 years of age, and who have been 61 years in the mining industry, Mr Richard Morris, who is in the New Years Honours list was awarded the BEM and Mr William Berry. Mr Morris was born near Wrexham, and has been engaged at the Oak Pit for 42 years. Mr Berry, an official for 51 years, he is a native of Hindley. There was a large attendance of the miners from the three pits of the former Chamber Colliery Co. and Moston and Bradford at an open air meeting held in the afternoon in the yard at Oak Pit. The Mayor (Councillor J. Berry) who presided said the colliery was about 120 years old. At one time coal mining was one of Oldham's chief industries. No doubt some of those present remembered the closing of the pits at Crompton, Royton, Hollinwood, and Chamber Road. Coal mining was followed by the hatting trade, which eventually went to Denton, and then cotton doubling followed, which trade eventually went to Stockport. Those industries were followed by the cotton spinning trade, and manufacture of textile machinery, and engineering generally.

Old Brook: Crompton

Evidently a drift mine worked during the 1840s, and was located below Browns Barn on Slences, above Brushes Clough. Possibly worked by John and Thomas Mills, who also worked Browns Colliery nearby, and Brushes Colliery. Old Brook Colliery was located to the north-east of Brook Colliery, and is shown on a tithe map for 1847. The record in the Catalogue of Plans of Abandoned Mines (1928) runs as follows: Brook Old (a) Crompton; (b) COAL; (d) 89 SE (1910) C3. Last entry location of mine entrance only.

Old Tame Mine: Denshaw, near Oldham

This coal pit was listed in the *Guide to the Coalfields* (1948), when worked by F. Wood & Sons of Old Tame, Denshaw, Oldham. However, it went on to say 'Not worked during 1947'. Old Tame is to the south-west of Denshaw on the Oldham Ripponden Road, behind the Golden Fleece Inn. There were a number of mills in this area, and perhaps the colliery supplied these with fuel. The mills included Old Tame Mill, Horest Mill and Slackcote Mill. Nothing else is known.

Park: Crompton, Oldham★

Colliery worked by Evans, Barker & Co. in 1854, and Bailey and Dronsfield in 1869. This pit shows up on the tithe map dated 1848, and was across from the Crompton tollgate, before Crompton Fold. The pit is marked 'old shaft' in 1890, and located between the Park Inn and the former Angel Inn, on the Buckstones Road, Shaw and Crompton. Information taken from the Catalogue of Plans of Abandoned Mines (1928): Park (a) Oldham; (b) COAL Higher Bent, Lower Bent (1869); (c) Divisional Engineers Office LMS Railway Co. Ltd, Hunts Bank, Manchester; (d) 97 SW (1922) A9; B9.

A Mines Inspectors Report for the year 1867 records: 'August 7th. Park Colliery. Joseph Ward and Joel Hall [killed] and two others burnt by an explosion of firedamp while sinking shaft'.

Paulden (Wood): Oldham★, SD 955 062

Worked by James Clegg during the early 1840s when the colliery employed eighty-three men and boys. In 1854, Mills, Lees & Co. worked the pit. The pit was located to the east of Waterworks Road, Waterhead, Oldham, below the reservoir near Lowbrook Lane, and besides the River Medlock. The shaft here was 52 yards from the Gannister Mine. Catalogue of Plans of Abandoned Mines (a) Oldham; (b) COAL; (d) 97 NE (1922) E4.

The following is evidence taken by John L. Kennedy during his Report on Child Labour in the Coal Mines (1841):

> Henry Jones, at Mr Clegg's Paulden Wood, near Oldham. What age are you? — I am going on six years old. Are you the youngest in the pit? — Yes, excepting Jack Jones. How long have you been at work? — I have only been at work a week or two. What time do you go to work in the morning? — I go down about four o'clock in the morning. What work are you put to? — I am a thrutcher. What time do you come up? — I should come out at twelve, but sometimes it is later, we are working two shifts of eight hours. Do you stop for meals? — No, we stop noan (none) we keep worchink (working) all the time.

James Jones also took part, at Mr Clegg's, Paulden Wood, near Oldham:

> What age are you? — I shall be twelve at Oldham Wakes. What hours do you work? — Sometimes I go down at four o'clock in the morning and worch (work) till twelve, and another shift works from 12 in the day till 6 at night — we change week about. Have you ever worked longer hours? — The longest time I have worked was ten hours, none of the children work longer. Do you stop to take your food? — No, we don't stop, we eat when we have the time. Do you take your food down with you? — No, we have it sent down. What do you get to eat? — I get butter-cakes for breakfast, I have nothing to drink, and butter-cakes for dinner, except on Sundays, then I have bacon and potatoes, or meat. I have thick porridge

and another butter-cake for supper. Are you ever beaten? — No, they never thrash me. How many boys are there in the pit? — About thirty thrutchers and drawers. What is the height of the main road? — It is a yard high. What height are the roads in the workings? — In the workings the roads are 20 to 23 inches. Then you will have to crawl on your hands and feet? — Yes. What is the weight of the tubs? — We draw two and a half cwt. Are the tubs and sledges on wheels? — On wheels, there are rails laid through out the workings. Do you use a belt and chain? — Yes, one pulls in front with a belt and chain, and one thrutcher behind, sometimes two thrutchers behind. What is the distance you bring the coals? — Sometimes 800 or 900 yards. Is the mine steep? — There is a rise of one yard in six. How long have you been in the pit? — I have been six or seven years in the pit. I have worked here twice, and I have worked in the Fairbottom Company. What made you leave the Fairbottom Company? — There was not regular work, and my father didn't like us to work there, there was so much sulphur, it takes fire very oft. What hours do you work in the pit? — I work the same hours as James Wild. What time do you have meals? — We stop an hour for dinner, and we eat our breakfast before we go down. Do you get plenty to eat? — I never wanted in my life. Have you ever been beaten? — I was only thrashed twice with his fists. Do you ever go to Sunday-School? — Yes, I go regular, my father sends me every Sunday. Do you go to church? — The schoolmaster takes us sometimes, but I do not go regularly. Have you ever been to day-school? — Yes, I have been to two schools. Have you ever been hurt? — No, never. How many of a family have you got at your house? — I have one sister, 16 years old, four lads besides myself, and an apprentice between 17 and 18. The lads are all younger than me. How many bedrooms have you in the house? — Two bedrooms and three beds. Mary Ann and Martha and Henry sleep in one bed, father and mother and little James in another bed, me, George, and the apprentice in the other. Have you any clothes besides those you have got on? — Yes, I have two pairs of trousers, and two jackets, and one singlet. I have one pit shirt made out of linsey wool. I have a clean one at home. I change every night when I go home, and wash my face ears and head, but I do not wash my feet, legs and body, except when I bathe in summertime. The apprentice washes himself same as me, and my mother makes George wash the same as we do.

Pea Croft: Werneth, Oldham
This was a colliery of some antiquity, and the only evidence of it appears in this remarkable report in the *Manchester Guardian*, 18 September 1850:

Extraordinary Ride. We often hear of exploits in horsemanship, but there was one about half a century ago which the most expert jockey would hesitate to venture on. Near the garden fence of the ancient hall at Werneth, near Oldham, a coal pit called Pea Croft Pit was at work by means of a gin, worked by a horse which was driven by a boy from ten to twelve years old. It was customary on an evening, when the labours of the day had concluded, for the lad to have a ride back to the stable. On one of these occasions, the horse began to move backwards, and went right down the pit with the boy on its back. The shaft was about one hundred yards in depth, and one of the widest. It had just been filled up in order to make the street behind the new houses, in what is now called Werneth Park. On descending to ascertain the results of this fearful descent, it was found that the boy had received little more harm than the breaking of his thigh, but the horse was smashed to pieces. The rider was living a few years ago.

Pit Bank: Oldham, 934 063 approx.

This colliery is marked on Dunn's map of 1829, and on the OS map of 1844, and it appears to have been in the Frances Street/Acre Lane area of Acre, east of Oldham Edge. 'Old Pit Bank' is also shown. In 1824 Samuel Haugh, a gentleman, lived at Pittbank House, and is listed in a directory for that year. The colliery was worked by Ainsworth and Lees during the early 1840s, when twenty men and boys aged eighteen years upwards, four aged thirteen to eighteen years and three under thirteen years were employed there. The Royley Seam was worked at the Pit Bank Colliery, at a depth of 102 yards. Catalogue of Plans of Abandoned Mines: (a) Oldham; (b) COAL; (d) 97 NW (1922) D11. The area has long since been built-up, and it is with some difficulty that one has to locate the exact position of the old colliery. However, there are a number of other references to the pit, and other pits at Oldham Edge.

A record of an incident which occurred over two centuries ago can be found in the *Annals of Oldham 1787-1830*: 'October 10th 1802, Thomas Greaves of Northmoor, who this evening fell into a coal-pit at Oldham Edge, which was several yards deep in water, but a piece of old wood which was in the water prevented him from sinking until persons released him from his perilous position'.

The *Manchester Guardian*, 8 April 1843 reports: 'Explosion of Firedamp. On Tuesday afternoon last, an explosion of firedamp took place at Mr Jesse Ainsworth's Colliery, Pit Bank, Oldham. Eight of the miners, men and boys were severely burned. They were using candles instead of safety lamps'. And on 22 April, the paper records: 'On Wednesday last, Mr Dearden, coroner held an inquest at the Bull's Head Inn on the body of Robert Leach, who died on Saturday morning in consequence of being severely scorched on the face and breast by the explosion of firedamp in the Pit Bank Colliery on the 4th inst. The deceased was a single man aged between thirty and forty years of age'.

The Report on Child Labour, 1841, stated: 'Only four parish apprentices appear in the returns that have been made. Their total numbers on the collieries of this neighbourhood is believed to be small. Nearly all the boys in the pits are natives of the immediate neighbourhood, to which their manners are assuredly native'.

However, the 'parish apprentice' practice continued, with the inevitable fatal results. It may have been the case that few 'parish apprentices' were employed in the Oldham collieries, but the case below highlights the danger which the children faced. In this particular case, reported in the *Manchester Guardian*, 10 February 1844, the lad in question lost his life at the tender age of just over seven years, notwithstanding that the accident took place two years after the Act was passed forbidding the employment of boys under ten years of age underground:

Dreadful Accident to a Boy. On Monday evening last, a boy of only seven years and nine months, named James Bradley, was accidentally killed in Pit Bank Colliery, Oldham under the following circumstances: There is a short incline of about eight yards at the bottom of the mine, which rises one yard in every four and a half. The deceased had got upon a wagon at the top of the brow, and before it could be stopped it descended the incline at a rapid rate. The boy was thrown off, and fell against the side of the mine, his head was shockingly injured, and he was instantly killed. The deceased was the son of a single woman named Caroline Bradley, an inmate of the Oldham Workhouse. According to the Act of Parliament, recently passed respecting collieries, it is illegal to employ so young a boy as the deceased in a colliery. At the coroner's inquest, held Wednesday last at the Collier's Arms, Moor Side, a verdict of 'accidental death' was returned.

Miners from Pit Bank were charged with intimidation, apparently linked to a union industrial action, as the *Manchester Guardian* reports on 8 June 1844:

Charge of Intimidation. At the petty sessions on Thursday, four coal miners, lately in the employment of Mr Jesse Ainsworth, of Pit Bank, namely James Ogden, John Morris, Joseph Turner and George Lees were charged with having used threats or other means of intimidation to deter a young man named Nathaniel Gill from working for Mr Ainsworth. The court was crowded by a large number of coal miners, many of whom assembled outside the town hall. Among the spectators in the courts rooms were several colliery proprietors. Mr Ascroft was retained on the part of Mr Ainsworth, and Mr Halsall, solicitor appeared for the defendants. Gill, the coal miner who had been intimidated, stated that on Wednesday morning week, the defendants had suddenly rushed upon him from behind a wall near the Blue Coat School, and had stood before him in a body to prevent him passing. Ogden said he had better turn back, lest he should get his limbs broken, but they did not strike him, nor had he ever been obstructed by the defendants before. He had been called a 'knobstick' by several of the unionists. Mr Halsall contended that there was no evidence as to three of the defendants being guilty of acts of intimidation, and the evidence against the fourth defendant was of light nature. Mr Ascroft argued that the defendants obstructed Gill, and therefore were guilty of an act of intimidation. The bench were of the opinion that the accused were concealed behind the wall for an unlawful purpose, that of stopping the man Gill by improper means from going to his work, Ogden, Turner and Morris were sentenced to two months imprisonment and hard labour. But as they gave notice of appeal to the Salford Sessions, and entered securities for that purpose, they were set at liberty. The fourth defendant Lees, was bound over to keep the peace for six months.

Pleasant Springs: Oldham Edge, Oldham

A pit worked by Joseph Jones junior & Co. during the 1840s. A robbery here is recorded in the *Manchester Guardian*, 21 May 1845: 'During the night of Sunday last, or the early hours of Monday, the colliery engine-house of Messrs Joseph Jones junior and Co. was broken in to, at the Pleasant Springs Colliery, Oldham Edge. They got through the roof by removing several slates, various fixtures belonging to the engine were removed and stolen'.

Priory: Bank Top, Oldham, SD 924 046

This old colliery, marked on the OS map of 1848, appears to have been buried under the A627 and A62 ring roads around Oldham. Nothing else is known, as this part of Oldham has changed dramatically over the last 150 years or so. Street names often give an indication of where a particular colliery might have been located. However, in this case, Priory Close and Priory Grove, both streets in Oldham, are misleading, for the colliery was located besides the railway. The Catalogue of Plans of Abandoned Mines records: (a) Oldham; (b) COAL; (d) 97 SW (1922) A9.

Red Tan Nook: Oldham Edge, Oldham

A colliery worked by Lees, Jones & Co. during the 1850s. An attempt at convening a meeting of miners is reported in the *Manchester Guardian*, 30 August 1843:

> A meeting of the coal miners of Oldham and the surrounding district, to consider the propriety of joining the general turn out had been announced to take place on Oldham Edge, on Monday forenoon last, at ten o'clock, but the day proved extremely wet, very few persons met at the place appointed.
>
> A group of individuals, however, did ultimately assemble, but they speedily adjourned to a club room at the Old Mess House, in Oldham. The number assembled being considered too small to proceed with any important business for which the meeting at Oldham Edge had been convened.

A more successful attempt is recorded in the *Manchester Guardian* a few days later, on 2 September 1843:

> On Monday evening a meeting took place of the coal miners at Oldham Edge for the purpose of forming an organisation for the district. Five men were elected as delegates to attend the meeting of the miners which is to be held in a few days time at Newcastle-upon-Tyne.

A fatal explosion of firedamp is reported in the *Manchester Guardian*, 24 March 1855:

> On Thursday last Mr T. Dearden, coroner held an inquest at the Bay Horse public-house, Oldham Edge on the body of Eli Barrett, who was employed at the Red Tan Nook Colliery, belonging to Messrs Lees, Jones and Co. and who died on Monday morning from the effects of the injuries he received by an explosion of firedamp. It appears that on the preceding Friday, a collier named Samuel Jackson, and the deceased were working in the pit, when the former took the top off his lamp, and for some purpose which has not been explained went into an old working, in which there seems to have been an accumulation of firedamp, for on his entrance to there immediately followed an explosion. The deceased was so severely burnt that he died on Monday, Jackson was also seriously burnt, and he now lies in a very perilous state. As he is the only person who can give any explanation of the affair the inquest was adjourned till Thursday 14th April. By one of the rules of the company, any person taking the top off his safety lamp is liable to dismissal from the works.

Rhodes Bank: Rhodes Bank, Oldham, SD 929 047
Pit worked by Lees, Jones & Co. in 1869 and 1875, and the Chamber Colliery Co. in 1879, but dates from at least the early 1840s. The colliery was located besides the Lancashire and Yorkshire Railway line at Rhodes Bank, Oldham, and is shown on a map of 1851. There were two shafts at the colliery, a reservoir and a smithy. The Black Mine was worked at Rhodes Bank at a depth of 128 yards.

The Catalogue of Plans of Abandoned Mines lists: Rhodes Bank (a) Oldham; (b) COAL Black, Lower Bent, Royley, Blend Fire, Higher Bent (abandoned 1887); (d) 97 NW (1922) G9, 10: H9, 10, 11: 97 SW (1922) A9, 10, 11: B9, 10, 11. Rhodes Bank (a) Oldham; (b) COAL: Rowley; (c) Divisional Engineer's Office LMS Railway Co. Ltd, Hunts Bank, Manchester; (d) 97 NW (1922) H10. Rhodes Bank, Nelson (a) Oldham; (b) COAL: seam unnamed (1842); (c) Whittaker and Bradburn, King Edward Street, Macclesfield, Cheshire; (d) 97 NW (1922) H10. Rhodes Bank, Holebottom, Nelson, Shut (a) Oldham; (b) COAL: Blendfire, Higher Bent or Peacock, Lower Bent, Royley, Black, Great (about 1879); (c) Chamber Colliery Co. Ltd, Hollinwood near Oldham; (d) 97 NW (1922) G9, 10: H9, 10, 11: 97 NW (1922) A10, 11: B11.

Readers of the *Manchester Guardian*, 3 July 1841, were offered confirmation of rumours of a terrible accident at the site:

> Lamentable coal pit accident. Yesterday, at noon, considerable excitement and alarm pervaded the neighbourhood of Waterloo, Oldham, by the report that an explosion of firedamp had occurred in the coal pit of Messrs Jones and Co. of that place. The report proved too true and we regret to learn that three individuals were killed (one of them the underlooker of the pit) and three others dreadfully burnt, and some others had not been got out of the pit when our account left.

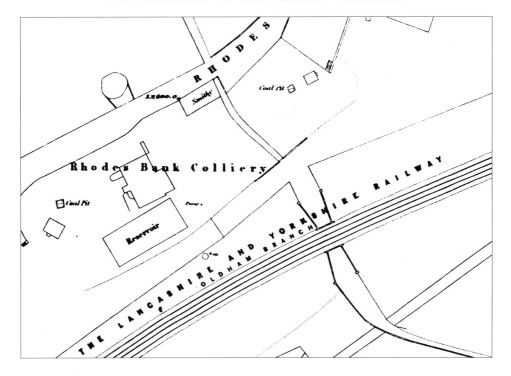

Rhodes Bank Colliery, map of 1848.

The *Manchester Guardian* reports another tragic accident on 27 February 1847:

Fatal Accident at a Colliery. On Monday last, a young man named John Haigh, a coal miner, in Rhodes Bank Colliery, belonging to Messrs Lees, Jones and Co. had occasion to go to the outlet of one of the passages opening into the perpendicular shaft of the mine. A wagon was going down the pit at the time, and struck him on the head and body so severely, that he died the same night at the house of his mother, George Street, Oldham. The deceased was a single man, 27 years of age.

And almost two years later the *Manchester Guardian* again reports, on 14 February 1849, on a miner killed by a falling roof:

Colliery Accident. On Friday the 9th inst. at the Spread Eagle Inn, an inquest was held by Mr Clarke, on the body of Robert Jackson, a miner who was killed on Tuesday the 6th inst. by the falling of a part of the roof at the Nelson Pit, Rhodes Bank. At the time of the accident, the deceased was engaged in the very dangerous task of post drawing, when a portion of the roof fell upon his legs, and wedged him against the side. He was not killed by this fall, but remained fast, and in great agony for six hours, during which time every effort was made to extricate him, until at last another fall of the roof put an end to his sufferings. It was not until 24 hours after the first fall that the body was recovered. Verdict 'accidental death'. The jury expressed great sympathy for the case of the deceased, and wished to record their opinion that the drawing of posts ought not to be allowed in cases attended with danger.

The *Manchester Guardian*, 22 May 1850, reports:

Death from Explosion of Firedamp in a Coal-pit. On Saturday an inquest was held at the Spread Eagle Inn, Manchester Street, by Mr Dearden, coroner on the body of George Ashworth, aged 32 years, who had been seriously burnt by an explosion of firedamp in Rhodes Bank Pit, on Friday the 10th inst. He lingered until Thursday, when he died. It appeared from the evidence that no blame was to be attached to the proprietors of the pit, or to the underlooker, but that there had been want of proper caution on the part of the deceased. A verdict of 'accidental death' was returned.

A man was found hiding at the colliery, and was charged, as reported in the *Manchester Guardian,* 19 February 1851:

Intent to commit a felony. At the petty sessions on Saturday, John Clegg, was charged with concealing himself, with intent to commit a felony in the engine house at Rhodes Bank Colliery. The engineer stated that about seven o'clock on Friday evening he had locked the engine house door, and left all safe. He went again about half past twelve, when he found the door still locked, and he would not have known if anyone was in, had his dog not found the man concealed. He called for assistance, and a man presumed to be Clegg's accomplice, who was inside ran off. Clegg was committed to hard labour for three months.

A horrific accident, in which one man was killed, is described in the *Manchester Guardian*, 28 April 1852:

Fatal Accident in a Coal Pit. On the afternoon of Saturday last, a man named Marsh Howarth was at work at the bottom of the shaft at Rhodes Bank Colliery, and was employed in loading a wagon which was attached to the rope with broken props. While he was so engaged the engine started, and Howarth who was leaning over the side of the tub, was carried up and wedged for a distance of sixty yards between the tub and the side of the pit. The tub, then coming to a part of the pit that was wider, he fell to the bottom, and was found quite dead and dreadfully mangled. He was 40 years of age, and has left a wife and four children.

The Mines Inspectors Report for 1861 records: 'August 4th. Rhodes Bank Colliery. S. Schofield fell out of sinking bucket in shaft and killed'. And an entry in 1867 runs: 'January 11th. Rhodes Bank Colliery. James Ashworth killed by stone falling while drawing props'.

A number of charges were brought against Mr Lees, of Lees & Co., as described in the *Colliery Guardian*, 17 August 1861:

> On Thursday at the Oldham Borough Court, Mr Joseph Dickinson, Government Inspector of Mines appeared to prefer three charges of breaches of the Mines Acts against Mr Lees (Lees and Co.) Rhodes Bank Colliery, Oldham. Mr Dickinson said that he visited the pit on 6th of August, and found the ventilation in a bad sate. In one part of the mine the gas was in an explosive state. Men were at work not far from the place, though the first general rule was that men should not work in mines unless they were properly ventilated. The second charge was for not having that portion of the mine where the gas was fenced off, and the third was for allowing lamps that were unlocked to be used in the pit. The charges were proved, and fines of £7 10s and costs were imposed.

Robin Hill, Oldham

This pit was located in the Coldhurst/North Moor area of Oldham, and is shown on a map for the 1850s. The pit at this time had two banks of coke ovens and two shafts. Robin Street now exists besides the Rochdale Road (A671) in Oldham, and doubtless the colliery was nearby. The colliery was worked by Messrs Evans and a combination of Barker, Evans & Co. during the 1840s and 1850s and the Oldham, Middleton & Rochdale Colliery Co. in 1869, 1879 and 1884.

James Taylor, alias 'Lump Lad', going on eleven years of age, gave evidence at the Inquiry into Child Labour on 31 October 1841, and it is reported below:

> The old colliers call his father Old Lump, and so they call him Young Lump. Is going on 11 years of age, and working in Messrs Evans's pit, up Royton Road, at Robin Hill Pit. Has just begun to work there, but has been waggoning for two years for Messrs Lees. Before that was in the pit two years with his father, playing and helping to load the tubs for his father at Hardy Field's Pit, one of Messrs Lees, in the 'Black Mine', there a yard thick. Had not then any wages. Him and James Broadbent now makes a waggoner. Is not working full time any more than the men. If he were, the two would earn in their stint, 3s 6d a day, of which he would have 1s 3d being the least of the two. He had been earning 2s 8d, and 4s a week. Two of the lads working in the pit where he is working are younger than himself. One is going on 8, and one going on 10. There's 24 waggoners i' that pit. Some of 'em are quite big uns, one was a getter. Where he was last working used to go at half-past five in the morning, and thought it early if he got out at six at night. The men come out about four, and if one waggoner had done before another they helped one another, and if they played it was quietly, and not long. Was working full time there, but was forced to leave because his 'butty', or leader, went away, on' his brother, for whom he waggoned, (for) thrashing him in the pit. Used to work at the pit he was last in, T'waymark, on Oldham Edge, one of Abraham Lees's on the night-shift when it was his master's turn, but commonly in the day-shift, one week after another.

Went at six o'clock at night into the pit, and stayed till eight in the morning; but the men came out at six. Him and the other lads stayed to waggon out the coals they had got. Liked working in the day-set best, because when he had been working at night could not sleep in the day, not more than two hours, and then they ran a playing him. Felt when he slept as though he were waggoning, and dreamt that the waggons were all coming on t'butty and him, that the roof was tumbling in on them, or that George Whitehead, his butty, was 'puncing' (or beating) him. He was a wicked lad, and one time wouldn't let him eat his dinner. Then when he got up to run about th' loan (lane) after t' other lads, he felt 'queer, and kept shuttin' his een (eyes) and runnin'. He couldn't feel well after working all t' neet (night). Could keep awake all night constantly working, but if he stopped work he would go to sleep, and then he would have a clout i' the mouth.

Used to take his dinner down with him when he had any, and eat at it as he could, working. Never had anything but butter-cakes (bread and butter) to his dinner. Many a time has gone without both breakfast and dinner altogether, and felt sickly like, and mazy. His mother had nowt to give him, because she could na' get nowt. Hur said hur had nowt for him. Hur said if hur could get a bit for him hur would but his father, who was a collier, drank a good deal of his wages. His father used to give his mother about 20s a fortnight. Has three younger brothers, and three were buried. They're all little ones the oldest going on seven. He'd a' been i' th' pit now if he'd been worth aught. But he is na' so strong as himself wa' at that age, and would na' ha' th' sense to get out o' road if aught fell.

If he'd been worth aught he would a' been doin i' th' little mine (some narrow seam). Often went to the night-set without his butter cakes for supper than with them, and felt sickly and mazy then. Was working for David Whitehead, an' ye know him. He never axed if he'd come with his butter-cakes, an' he never told him. He ne'er gied him nought. The waggoners, neither, wouldn't gie one another a bit o' butter-cake if they were clamm'd to dead. It was only at times he had to work in the night set, because he engine was not going in the night, and it was only a night's work for one collier in turn, with his drawer, to fill all the empty tubs. Now thrutches the waggons with his head and hands, as is the common fashion. The waggons hold three baskets (6cwt), and are filled by the biggest waggoner. It was 800 yards at the pit bottom that he had to thrutch where he was last working, and has now to thrutch 1,300. Would bring a waggon 16 times the 800 yards for a full day's work, but did not do that oft, about a day in a week. Sometimes would do only a quarter, or a half, or three-quarters of those journeys, according as coal was in demand. In the Robin Hill Pit has now to go about 400 yards of the distance over the clog tops in sludge and water.

The main road is a yard six inches high, and there are no jigs but slants (inclines) where he puts on a thrasher to the wheel of the waggon, which locks it. Have still to pull back a little. The big lad goes in the front with his 'yead' (head) to the waggon, and walking backwards, to keep it coming down fast. They work only in their clogs, stockings, trousers and cap. Saw a lad run over at Black Ridings Pit by a waggon and have his leg broke, but this does not often happen. Has never had any accident himself. Was once at Robin Hill Pit, going to Tommy Farrer, and knocking at th' sounding rod to let down the tub, when a man, who had been wound over t' pulley, fell down t' pit close to him, almost on him. He were kilt before he leet (alighted or readied the bottom). He was only a big lad, though they called old. Old Frost wound him o'er. He ran out o' the engine-house woam (home), but th' master fetched him back. He went on winding there till th' next morning, when he was taken to th' Waterloo Pit, under the same firm, where he is now winding. The waggon broke two of his fingers by going over them, and he had to play him a fortnight with 'em, but did na' think much about that. Has no holidays but Christmas day, unless work be slack.

Him that he waggons for draws the money for both, and then comes to pay him. He gives it to his mother, but it does na' pay for his keep. Father lives in Lord-street, Oldham. There are two rooms i' th' house, the chamber and the house. The chamber is above th' house. They all sleep in the chamber, which has one bed, in which all four children sleep with their father and mother. There is one chair in the room besides, but nothing else. In the house there is nothing but one chair and two stools. Father is only just out of work, as a collier, and nothing has lately been sold away. He had an accident by being buried in earth from the falling from the roof.

Mother does nought for him when he gets home but give him something to eat if she has it. Washes his hands and face every day, and his whole body once a-week. Has only one shirt, one pair of stockings, and the ragged and dirty coat, waistcoat, and trousers he has on. When he has had something to eat runs into the street and plays. Always finds somebody to play wi', and can play at aught as they can plays at 'trinnill' and 'th' hammer and block' these oftener than aught else. Goes in home early, because he has to get up early, goes in about eight o'clock, (and) then sleeps and, without dreaming, until he gets up every workday morning at five o'clock.

Has porridge and treacle to breakfast when he has any, bread and butter cakes to dinner, if can get them. Porridge and milk when he comes home, never any potatoes nor any bread, but what is in his bread and butter cakes. Never was kept from work by illness, but has often felt sick. Goes to no school, never went to a day-school, went to the Old Methodist Sunday-school five months ago, but his father took him off three months ago, because he had such ragged clothes. Went before for a week or two to a Sunday school i' th' Bunk (Bank). Cannot say letters (Adds a few smaller numbers, but has no notion of subtraction). Has never heard of Jesus Christ, has never heard of God, but in the pit when the men swear, has heard the men in the pit say 'God damn thee'. Does not know what county he is in has never been anywhere but here, i' th' pit, and at Rochdale; never heard of London, never heard of the Queen, and dunnot know who he is. [Signed] JAMES (X) TAYLOR [his mark].

A serious accident here injured a miner, who later died at home. The *Manchester Guardian,* 1 June 1844, reports on the tragedy:

Colliery Accident. On Monday an inquest was held before Mr Molesworth at the Hare and Hounds Inn, Royton on the body of James Lees, a coal miner. On Friday morning last, whilst the deceased was at work in the colliery at Robin Hill, Coldhurst, belonging to Messrs Barker, Evans and Co. a large quantity of coal shale fell upon him, by which his thigh was broken, and his loins severely crushed. All the poor man's body was covered by the fallen coal, except his hands. He was taken out alive, and survived until Monday morning, when he died at his house in Royton. The deceased was a widower, of 42 years of age, and has left two children. A verdict of 'accidental death' was returned.

The *Manchester Guardian*, 4 July 1846, reports on an accident at the site in which a father and son were badly burned:

Serious explosion of firedamp. On Monday morning last, three men and two boys employed at the Robin Hill Colliery, North Moor, the property of Messrs Evans, Barker and Co. were severely injured by an accidental explosion of firedamp.

One of the miners named Croxon, the father of one of the injured boys persisted in going into some of the old works, with an uncovered candle, although cautioned as to the consequences. On going a second time, the inflammable air exploded to the great injury of the three men and two boys working in that part of the mine. Croxon was severely burnt in several parts of the body, and his son most dreadfully scorched, particularly about the head and ears. Croxon and his sons are in an extremely precarious situation, but the other sufferers seem much more likely to recover.

A tragic death resulting from another explosion at the site is recorded in the *Manchester Guardian*, 2 June 1847:

Colliery Accident. On Saturday last, Mr J.S. Clarke, deputy coroner, held an inquest at the Gaping Goose public-house, Coldhurst on the body of Isaac Holden, a coal miner who a fortnight previous was severely burnt by an accidental explosion of firedamp in the colliery of Messrs Evans, Barker and Co. Robin Hill, North Moor. The poor man lingered in extreme agony until Friday last, when he died at his lodgings near North Moor toll bar. The deceased, who was 37 years of age has not left any wife or family. Verdict; 'Accidentally killed by an explosion of firedamp'.

A very similar incident, in which a man endured a prolonged period of suffering before he died, is described in the *Manchester Guardian,* 3 November 1847:

On Thursday last, Mr Dearden, coroner held an inquest at the Dog and Partridge public-house, Shudehill, Oldham on the body of George Evans, a coal miner. On Tuesday fortnight, whilst the deceased was at work in the colliery of Messrs Barker, Evans and Co., Robin Hill, North Moor. He was accidentally burnt by an explosion of firedamp occasioned by the incautious manner in which one of the miners used a light. Several boys were more or less injuries by the same explosion, but they are in the course of recovering. The unfortunate man lingered in extreme agony till Tuesday last, when he died. The deceased who was a resident of Back Hanover Street, was 50 years of age, and has left a grown up family. Verdict: 'Burnt by firedamp'.

It is clear that the mine was dangerously prone to firedamp, as indicated by another explosion at the site. The accident is reported in the *Manchester Guardian, 2 October 1850:*

Explosion of Firedamp. A serious accident occurred at the Robin Hill Colliery on Monday. It appears that about seven o'clock in the morning, Mr John Evans, son of Mr Edward Evans, the proprietor, accompanied by Henry Got, the underlooker descended the pit to inspect a tunnel, of which the driving had begun, but which had been suspended for some time in consequence of the turn-out colliers. When they had gone some distance, they left their candles and proceeded without them, but the motion of the two men seems to have caused a current of gas, which came into contact with the candles, and an explosion ensued. Both men were seriously injured, but it is hoped they are out of danger. Other men in another part of the mine felt the rush of air consequent of the explosion and rushed to their aid.

An indication of the aggression which industrial disputes could provoke is provided by a report in the *Manchester Guardian, 23 November 1850:*

Intimidation. At the petty sessions, on Thursday, Robert Mellor and John Butterworth were charged with going to the house of Robert Johnson, and calling him a 'knobstick' and telling him, that unless he went to where he came from (Wigan) it would not be long before his life was taken. It appears that the complainant had come to work for Mr Evans, coal proprietor, and the defendants are turn-outs. As great annoyance has been offered to the new hands, the bench considered it necessary to mark the illegality of such proceedings, by committing the prisoners for two months hard labour.

A tragic incident is recorded in the *Manchester Guardian, 28 May 1851:*

An explosion which caused the loss of one life and seriously endangering many others took place at the Robin Hill coal-pit on Friday morning. The miners descended the shaft about six o'clock in the morning as usual and found one portion of the works was not clear, as a door which ought to have been closed had been left open the previous night. The deceased, John Hewitt, who was an experienced miner, and aged about 49 years, observed these circumstances, and said all the danger was on his side. He was cautioned by another miner, John Mills not to go up, or at least to go in another direction, which was clear. He left the deceased sitting on some bricks with a lighted candle in his hand. They had not proceeded very far when they heard a dreadful explosion, and on returning they found the deceased lying quite dead a few yards from the spot where they had left him. Another man had his thigh broken. The deceased left a wife and family.

The following accident is apparently attributed to Edge Lane Pit in the Mines Inspectors Report. It is reported in the *Manchester Guardian*, 12 February 1853:

Colliery Accident. On Tuesday, a man named Jonathan Motley, (spelt 'Wottley' in Mines Inspectors Report) aged about 50 years, was killed at Robin Hill coal pit, by the falling of a portion of roof in the form of what the miners call a 'pothole' which is caused by a piece of roof dropping out, and leaving a cavity like a mug. The rock fell upon him, and killed him on the spot.

With the history of explosions at the site, it is disturbing that a miner would use a lamp incautiously, but a miner was charged with this offence, as recorded in the *Manchester Guardian*, 6 January 1857:

Caution to Colliers. James Crompton, a collier in the employ of Messrs Evans, Barker and Co. colliery owners, was brought up at the petty sessions yesterday, on a charge of infringement of the regulations put up at the colliery, under the provisions of the act for the prevention of accidents in coalmines. The underlooker of the Riley Mine in the Robin Hill Colliery stated, that on Wednesday the 24th December, the defendant took the top off his safety lamp, in a part of the mine, which was regarded, as dangerous.

All the workmen in the mine were cautioned on the 12th of December, and the regulations, one of which forbade any of them to uncover their lamp, were exposed in different parts of the works. The defendant said, he thought there was no danger, and the underlooker gave him good character. The mayor reproved the defendant for his recklessness of his conduct, which might have attended great loss of life and property. He was fined 20s and costs, or in default, one month in prison.

A fire here is reported in the *Manchester Guardian*, 15 January 1857:

On Monday last a fire was discovered to have broken out in the Robin Hill Pit, on Royton Road, belonging to Messrs Evans, Barker and Co. There is a flue from the engine at the bottom of the blowing pit to the upcast shaft, a distance of 60 yards, it is supposed to have become overheated, and set fire to the coals, which must have become very dry, the flue having been in use for some dozen years. Steps at once were taken to put it out by turning water into the flue, but this was found to have no effect. Yesterday operations were commenced to smother it out by walling up the airways leading to the upcast shaft. Last night this had been partly accomplished, and was so far successful, and it is expected it will be completed in a day or two. Fortunately, the loss will be comparatively inconsiderable, as there are two other workings connected with the mine. By cutting off the upcast shaft, which was formerly the blowing pit of the mine, which has been worked up, the present blowing pit will be converted into use as the upcast shaft. No person has sustained any serious injury, but on Tuesday night, the underlooker had a narrow escape from suffocation, having proceeded too far into the smoke. He was however, taken out, and recovered in a short time. The men who are employed at the pit, will probably be thrown out of work for a fortnight by the occurrence.

Roundthorn: Roundthorn, Oldham, SD 943 041

A colliery worked by Messrs William Evans in 1879, and the Glodwick Coal, Brick & Fireclay Co. Ltd, Glodwick, Oldham, 1896, when Mr J.W. Needham was the colliery manager who employed seven men underground and two on the surface. The coal output from the Blendfire Mine was used for manufacturing purposes. In 1934, Mr R.E. Buckley worked a colliery of this name, and again in 1938, when there were ten men underground and one surface worker. The Roundthorn Colliery was almost to the rear of the Dog and Partridge public house at Roundthorn, where an access road further back towards Lowside led on to the pit site. Large amounts of colliery waste can be seen in this area, which has also been extensively quarried. There is no apparent trace of the two 'old coal shafts' one to the rear of the pit, and one at the back of Roundthorn Primary School. The pit is marked on a map of 1879.

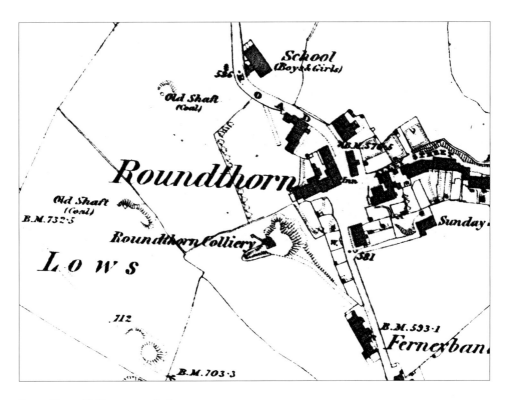

Roundthorn Colliery, map of 1879.

The Catalogue of Plans of Abandoned Mines lists: Roundthorn (a) Oldham; (b) COAL Blendfire, Great (abandoned 24 September 1894); (d) 97 SW (1922) B12: C12: 97 SE (1922) B1: C1: Roundthorn; (a) Oldham; (b) COAL Great, Blendfire (1894); (c) R and F Buckley, Lowside Colliery, Oldham; (d) 97 SE (1922) B1: C1; Roundthorn, Abbey Hills (a) Oldham; (b) COAL Lindsay (abandoned June 1922); (d) 97 SE (1909) H12.

Royley: Royley, near Royton
The *Annals of Oldham* record: 'September 10th 1790, a boy of nine years was killed at the Royley coal-pit'. Also, in the same source: '26th July 1792, James Maddock of Royton, banksman in doing his work at the coal-pit at Royley had the misfortune to fall down, and was killed on the spot'. Royley is also the local name for the Arley Seam of coal, which is normally of excellent quality.

Royton: Royton, SD 920 080
Colliery worked by the Oldham, Middleton & Rochdale Coal Co. 1879, and the Oldham & Rochdale Coal Co. Ltd, 1896. Pit employed 160 men underground, twenty surface in 1896, when Walter Evans was the manager and Thomas Scholes, was the undermanager. The pit is shown on a map of 1890. The colliery worked a number of seams including the Higher Twos Mine at shaft depth 208ft, the Bottom Neddy Mine at 495ft and the Arley Mine (Royley locally) at 756ft.

The site is listed in the Catalogue of Plans of Abandoned Mines: Royton, Chain, Dean, Hanging Chadder, Low Crompton (a) Crompton, Royton, Rochdale, Milnrow; (b) COAL; Royley, Glebe (abandoned 1 June 1903); (d) 89 SW (1910) B5, 6: C3, 4, 5, 6, 7, 8: D3, 4, 5, 6, 7, 8, 9: E4, 5, 6, 7, 8, 9: F5, 6, 7, 8, 9: G5, 6, 7, 8, 9, 10: H6, 7, 8, 9, 10: 97 NW (1922) A6, 7, 8, 9, 10: B7, 8, 9, 10: C8.

Many of the mines around here connected underground, and this had benefits and disadvantages. Many early pits left no records of their workings. The Royton Mine was apparently flooded out by some uncharted workings. The water at Fenny Hill Colliery, Glodwick, was said to have subsided between 20 and 30ft! The last tub of coal at the Royton Colliery was raised on 14 April 1901. The Oldham coal owners are said to have approached Lord Stamford with a view of establishing a pumping station at Ashton-under-Lyne which was hoped to have saved the Oldham pits from such flooding. However, nothing materialised. Royton Park, opened on Coronation Day, 22 June 1911, was built on the site of Royton Colliery. The colliery chimney was demolished shortly after the flooding of the pit. There is a comprehensive account of this in the *Bacup Times*, 8 February 1902:

> The chimney at Royton Colliery belonging to the Oldham, Middleton and Rochdale Coal Co. was razed on Saturday afternoon in the presence of thousands of people. The pit was flooded some months ago, and this necessitated the stopping of the mining operations there, the result being that about 200 colliers whose

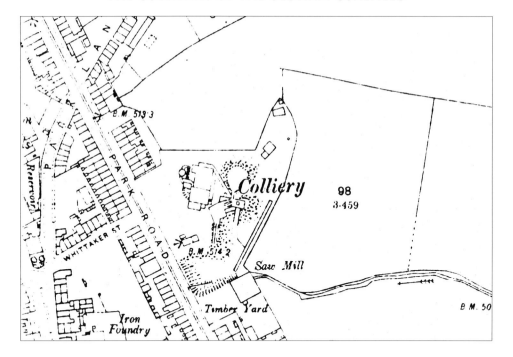

Royton Colliery, map of 1890.

wages amounted to about £400 per week, were thrown out of employment. After the closing of the pit the whole of the stock above ground was bought by Mr G. Butterworth, broker of Rochdale, who employed Mr Kay, of Middleton Junction to raze the chimney. This was 56 yards high, with a base diameter of about six yards. It was built in 1872 – 29 years ago. The estimated weight being 600 tons. The preparations for razing, Mr Kay and his men made three large holes in half the circumference at the base of the chimney and inserted supports, between which were placed six charges of dynamite.

On Saturday afternoon these were fired by means of time fuses. After the explosion of the dynamite, the chimney was seen to sway, as if about to fall headlong, but suddenly the base gave way and the remainder telescoped completely, the top dropping within thirty yards of the foundations. Then a hearty cheer was given by the crowd, and most of the spectators rushed forward to see the debris. Superintendent McQueen, with a staff of police, rendered good service in keeping the people at a safe distance until the chimney fell.

Royton Park

The only information I have on this pit is from the Catalogue of Plans of Abandoned Mines: (a) Royton; (b) COAL, Royley (about 1885); (c) Divisional Engineer's Office, LMS Railway Co. Ltd, Hunts Bank, Manchester; (d) 97 NW (1922) A7, 8: B7.

Sally Kay Pits: Werneth

This was the name given to two pits worked by William Jones 'near the Railway Inn, Manchester Street and Worthington Street' according to a correspondent in the *Oldham Chronicle* in January 1885. The correspondent went on to say:

> They stood back from the road about opposite the western end of Mr Mannock's old mill, being adjacent to the public house now known as the Railway Inn, but then under another name, which was kept by a worthy hostess named Sally Kay, and the colliery was known as 'Sally Kay Pits'. She was famed for keeping an excellent tap, and I have heard of many lively scenes taking place there on a 'reckoning' Saturday, when the hewers of the black diamond were washing their dusty throttles with prime home-brewed ale. At one of these pits there was a lifting engine for pumping the water, and at the other they wound the coal. There was also a 'beast ee' (tunnel pit driven into the hillside) higher up on the brow side above 'Sally Kay Pits' where the Dirt Mine was got, which was continued working down to a much later period, and will be well remembered by many persons now living in Oldham.

Salmon Field: Royton, Oldham

Worked by John Smethurst in 1869, and doubtless the colliery was off Salmon Field which runs off the Shaw Road (A663). Another probable site would be close by Salmon Fields Farm, off the Higginshaw Lane. The colliery was abandoned in 1895. The Catalogue of Plans of Abandoned Mines lists: Salmonfield (a) Royton; (b) COAL Little: (abandoned May 1895); (d) 97 NW (1922) C9: D9; Salmonfield (a) Royton; (b) COAL Big (abandoned May 1895); (d) 97 NW (1922) C9: D9.

Sarah Moor: Sarah Moor

Evidently in the Sarah Moor district of Oldham, the only other information is taken from the Catalogue of Plans of Abandoned Mines: Sarah Moor (a) Oldham; (b) COAL Great (abandoned prior to May 1884); (d) 97 NW (1922) F9.

Scowcroft: Middleton★

Worked by Wyld (should read Wild), Andrews & Co. in 1854, nothing else known.

Shaw Street

A pit which by all accounts was located on Shaw Street, Oldham, and was abandoned in 1923, however it does not appear in a mines list for 1896. The only other information is from the Catalogue of Plans of Abandoned Mines which should give the location of the colliery for those interested in further research: Shaw Street (a) Oldham; (b) COAL Great (abandoned 2 April 1923); (d) 97 NW (1922) E9, 10: F9, 10. The pit shows up in a list of mines for the year 1918, when it was worked by G.B. Waite & Co., 82 Fisher Street, Oldham. It was not a large pit, it only employed five men underground and two surface workers, and was perhaps a fireclay mine.

Sholver: Sholver, Oldham, SD 943 076

The Oldham, Middleton & Rochdale Coal Co. Ltd worked the pit, according to a directory of 1884. This colliery is the one marked on the OS map of 1891 on Cop Road, Sholver to the south of Old Bank Farm. Where Cop Lane descends steeply from Sholver Lane and through a cutting is an area of colliery waste on the tree-lined side of the road. A reservoir and airshaft are shown to have been on the Sholver side of the pit, and it is marked as 'disused' on a map of 1909. A new housing estate is fast covering this area.

Sholver Fold: Oldham*

A colliery worked by Abraham Lees, 1854. The most notable reference to the colliery is in the *Manchester Guardian*, 5 May 1845. The report details a dispute related to union issues:

Charge against a union miner. At the petty sessions on Monday, the charge of assault against Robert Whitworth, secretary of the Miner's Union, adjourned from Thursday last, was resumed. Emanuel Taylor, the complainant, called a witness, named John Midgley, who stated that both Taylor and Whitworth had used hard words against each other, on the occasion referred to, which was a dispute that had taken place in a cabin, at the colliery of Mr Abraham Lees, Oldham Edge. But he did not recollect Whitworth having used any threatening language. Taylor said Midgley had been bribed by the union miners not to tell the truth, although he had promised him several times that he would come forward as a witness. In answer to various questions put to the witness by the magistrate, Mr Mills, he stated that he had paid money to the miner's union, about a fortnight ago. He had sometimes paid 1s 10d per fortnight, and once paid five shillings for a fortnight. He had never heard Whitworth call Taylor a 'knobstick' or threaten to throw him into the pit. At this stage of the proceedings a respectable looking man applied to the magistrates to be permitted to say some thing, stating he was clerk to Mr Roberts, 'the miner's attorney general'. Mr Mills asked the gentleman if he was an articled clerk. The reply seemed to have been in the negative, for immediately afterwards Mr Roberts's representative enquired if he was allowed to take notes. This request was granted. The defendant next called two witnesses, the first being Thomas Jones, a union miner. He said he had merely heard Whitworth ask Taylor, the complainant why he had not paid anything to the union the Saturday night before. On hearing this, Taylor uttered several oaths to Whitworth, and used other abusive epithets.

He had not heard the defendant threaten he would do anything to injure the complainant. David Whitehead, a union miner, the second witness, stated that there was a great deal of squabbling and quarrelling going on amongst the parties in the coal pit. He was very near both Taylor and Whitworth, and he heard the latter ask the former why he had not paid his union money on the Saturday night before, on which Midgley used a great deal of abusive language. He had never heard Whitworth use any threats to Taylor, neither had he refused to go to work because Taylor and Midgley did not pay the union. Witness had paid as much as five shillings one fortnight to the union. Taylor stated that he was afraid of Whitworth and others doing him some bodily harm. The witness, Whitehead, on being re-questioned, added that if Whitworth had used any threatening language to Taylor, he must have heard it. Whitworth was ultimately required to find sureties to keep the peace for three months, himself in £10, and two in £5 each.

Sholver Lane

A colliery worked by T. Mellodew & Co. in 1879. The Mellodew family were also extensive mill owners in this area. It is they who built the cottages known as 'Old Turf Pits' on Turf Pit Lane. The Catalogue of Plans of Abandoned Mines lists: Sholver Lane, Nos.1, 2, 3, 4 (a) Oldham; (b) COAL Foot (abandoned 2 July 1887); (d) 89 SE (1910) H2, 3: 97 NE (1922) A2, 3.

Sholver Moor: Oldham★, SD 944 080

Two collieries of this name working in 1854, one owned by James Buckley and the other by George Hallas. One of these pits is shown on the OS map of 1844, at the above grid reference. A sad story of the death of a young miner by falling is reported in the *Manchester Guardian,* 13 October 1847:

> Yesterday week, Mr Dearden held an inquest at the Black Horse, Watersheddings, on the body of William Crossley, a coal miner. The deceased when ascending from his work at Sholver Colliery, on Saturday week, was suddenly seized, when near the top with a fit and fell out of the tub, unperceived by his companions. He fell to the bottom of the pit, and was so injured that he died immediately. The deceased was an unmarried man, and aged 21 years. Verdict: 'Accidental injuries from falling down a coal-pit shaft'.

An even younger miner was killed here in March 1848 and, according to the *Manchester Guardian*, 15 March 1848, there had been another such incident in the same week:

> Boy killed in a colliery. On Saturday forenoon last, whilst a boy nearly twelve years of age, named Israel Wadsworth, was at work in a colliery on Sholver Moor, a quantity of shaly stone fell from the roof and sides of the mine upon him, by which he was immediately killed. This is the second instance which has occurred during the last week of boys being killed in the immediate neighbourhood of Oldham.

The following report, in the *Manchester Guardian*, 18 November 1848, may be a reference to this pit, or one of the many others that worked on Sholver Moor:

On Tuesday last, Mr Clarke held an inquest at the Collier's Arms, Sholver Moor, on Joseph Bridge, collier, aged 22 years. On Saturday last, at half past ten, he was in a coal works at Sholver Moor, and was in the act of removing a prop, when it fell on his neck and knocked him down covering his head and right arm. A boy named William Hales tried to pull off the prop, and the earth came with it, he shouted for assistance. John Armstrong arrived after Bridge had lain about ten minutes under the weight, and when extricated by Armstrong, he was quite dead. A verdict of 'accidental death' was recorded.

Shooting Butts: Werneth Brow, Oldham

A colliery that opened in about 1790, it closed soon after, when the lease on the workings ran out in 1812. Some years later the colliery was re-opened under the management of Radley, Clegg and Co. The Shooting Butts Pit was described prior to 1822 as 'being one of the worst pits belonging to the company'. Twenty yards down the shaft rock was constantly flaking away from the shaft sides, on one occasion hundreds of tons fell smashing scaffold over the sump at the pit bottom.

The repairs consisted of wooden rings and patched brickwork, which themselves became rotten and liable to get dislocated. However, the sides of the pit never fell while men were being raised or lowered, and no injuries were ever caused from this. The engine at the Shooting Butts Pit was some 140 yards away from the shaft mouth. It was said that the engine driver could not see the pit unless it was a clear day. The only way to tell when the cage was at the top of the shaft was by a piece of rag tied around the rope or chain, the engine driver had to keep an eye out for as it approached the winding drum. On abandonment the pit shafts were filled in, but around 1885 the shafts opened up again with a large landslip, and caused much alarm and sensation in the area.

Slibber Pits

Cyrus Taylor, engineer at one of the Slibber Pits, aged thirteen, gave evidence for the Report on Child Labour, 5 November 1841, and it was recorded as follows:

Is past 13, and has been five weeks next Saturday learning to be engineer at the Slibber Pits, of the company of Messrs Jones. (Is at this hour by himself winding coals, also one cargo of a boy and three men). Was working at the bottom, but got two fingers cut off showing the stumps on the left hand. Winds men as well as coals. The proper engineer is Samuel Taylor, no relation of his, and who is somewhere about, mending waggons. Samuel Taylor always comes into the engine-house to be with him when he is winding men. He is about 18 years old. Learned to read at Sunday school; cannot write.

Mr Joseph Wild, chief constable of Oldham, also gave evidence, which related to children being in charge of the winding engines at the collieries, and is also an intriguing and useful summary of many of the causes of accidents in the area. The evidence was taken on 1 November 1841:

Has been chief constable of Oldham nearly six years, and ten years altogether a constable in this neighbourhood. The children are taken down to thrutch, draw, and waggon about seven or eight years of age generally. It is chiefly in regard to the fatal accidents that his attention is directed to their occupations in the mines, having to collect the witnesses for the coroner in all cases occurring in the township of Oldham. The neighbourhood of Oldham is the most fruitful to the coroner of this part of the county, Mr Dearden, because of the number of the population and the nature or their employment in mines and factories. There have been a deal of accidents to children and young people, as well as to men, in the mines here, during the last five or six years. The chief accidents are from fire-damp, and from falling in of roofs, or of stones from the roof; the former chiefly through incaution on the part or the men or of the children; and the latter from the ignorance of unpractised getters, or a stinginess in the smaller employers as to their supply of wood for props.

A cause, which is more general than, is usually made to appear at the coroner's inquests, because the feelings and interests of the witnesses tend to conceal it. Parties, after giving their own account of accidents in conversation, could not be got to depose to the same facts before the coroner. A common thing is for a master to leave the men to 'rob the post wood', as it is termed, to supply the wants of their hewing; or in other words to fetch away the wood from old workings to an extent which, in the want of any other supply, has been carried to an extreme of great danger. This has repeatedly been given in evidence before the coroner. It is more up grown men that are killed this way than children, who are for the most of the time in the main and securer ways of the pits drawing, thrutching, and waggoning. Many accidents have occurred from firedamp. About 12 months ago two young brothers, named Taylor, aged about 11 and 13, were burnt to death by fire-damp in Evans's colliery, on Oldham Edge, saw them himself. Three years ago three or four young people were similarly burnt to death, and others much injured, in Messrs Jones's colliery at Werneth. In this same colliery there were two other serious explosions about that time, one after another. There are numerous occasions in which one may be killed, and one or two seriously injured; but those already mentioned are the occasions on which the greatest number of young people he recollects to have been burnt at once have lost their lives. There have been many instances in the neighbourhood of two or three persons of more advanced years being burnt together, of whom some would die, and some recover. In the case at Werneth the fathers of the children (it being Monday) did not go down to work, but sent the children down to clear the roads and get the place ready, and it was while doing this that, in their ignorance and incaution, they incurred death.

On the 3rd day of July last, in the Holebottom Pit, close to the town, four men, including the underlooker, were killed. This was through the wilful carelessness of one of them, who had been duly cautioned by his fellow workmen before he went in. There are scores of cases in which individuals are badly burned, who do not die, but are made cripples for life. Mere children are not to be trusted where such casualties may occur in a moment's thoughtlessness. It is probably the younger and most inexperienced getters who are most injured by the firedamp. But there is a class of accidents of which children employed at coal-works in this neighbourhood are the cause to persons of all ages. These occur in the winding up by the steam machinery of all persons out of the pit.

It is a general system here to employ mere children to attend these engines, and stop them at the proper moment; and if they be not stopped the two or three or four or five persons wound up together are thrown over the beam down into the pit again. The inducement to employ these children in circumstances where life and death depend on their momentary attention is merry that their services can be obtained for perhaps 5s or 7s a-week instead of the 30s a-week, which the proprietors would perhaps have to pay to a man of full years and discretion. There have been people wound over at Oldham Edge, at Werneth, at Chamber-lane, at Robin Hill, at Oldbottom [perhaps Holebottom], and on Union Ground here, within the last six or seven years to his recollection. Does not know a case in which children were not the engineers; and though he cannot speak to all of them being such, it was generally the case in these instances.

The coroner's juries having to give verdicts in cases where such young people were concerned, and in which to attribute gross neglect would be subjecting them to a charge of manslaughter, have always leaned to the side of extenuation, but have expressed their dissatisfaction with the master's employing children in such a service, and for so indefensible a reason; and on one occasion lie was desired by the coroner and jury to go to the master, and tell him so. Three or four boys were killed in this way at the Chamber-lane Colliery of Messrs Jones, two or three years since, by the momentary neglect of a little boy, who he thinks was only nine years of age, and who he heard, after the worst was over, had turned away from the engine when it was winding up, on his attention being attracted by a mouse on the hearth. In this case a deodand of 100s was levied on the engine, and returned by the coroner to the Court of Exchequer, but it was never recovered from the parties.

It is certainly observable in the ease of colliers that there is a great amount of rude callous-less on the subject of accidents among them and their families; they are quite an uneducated set of people, who go to cockpits, and races, and fights; and many are gamblers and drinkers. In a day or two's time, among such people, even their wives and children seem to have forgotten it. They will say at the time, 'Oh, I am not a bit surprised, I expected it – I expected it'; and it soon passes by. There are so many killed that it becomes quite customary to expect such things. The chief talk is just at the moment, until the body gets home, and then there is no more talk about it. People generally feel, 'Oh, it's only a collier!' There would be more feeling a hundred times if a policeman were to kill a dog in the street. In different neighbourhoods here there would be more bother and talk, is sure there would, about killing a dog than killing a collier. The colliers even amongst themselves say so. There have been cases of the maltreatment of children in collieries brought before the magistrates, perhaps one or two a year. The maltreatment was always according to barbarous rules among the workers themselves, inflicting punishment on supposed delinquents, generally by holding the head fast between the legs of another, and inflicting each a certain number of blows on the bare posteriors with pieces of wood, called 'cuts', about a foot long and an inch in diameter, used as tokens to distinguish one man's tubs from another. However the one punished may cry, they stick to him, and in the last case, where a hungry lad had stolen a pit-dinner, they mangled his body seriously. In other cases the injured parties could not work at all for some time. In the case mentioned, the offenders were made to placard the town with an apology, and to render some compensation in money to the party, and promise not to follow any such course in future. There have been a very few instances of parish apprentices to collier's ill used by their masters, and in one case the magistrates cancelled the indentures. The colliery lads are a wickeder race than the factory children, swearing and cursing.

Children as well as men appear to have superior muscular power about the arms and chest and the collier children generally beat the factory children in apparent health and strength it is a healthful job, if they get their bellyful of meat, but they are a rougher set. If they come to fighting, they have no mercy in punching, even in the face, or biting or 'damping' (throttling) or anything else. They have no feeling for others, as the factory lads have, compared to them. The fighting here is at any advantage, but fighting is nothing to compare with what it used to be, where there is one fight now there used to be a hundred, and every case that comes to the knowledge of the police is brought before the magistrates. The factory lads are 'neisher' (more delicate) than the collier-lads, who are altogether more robust. As they grow up they are very rough. They marry more often before than after 20, but the factory people marry altogether sooner. Of late years the colliers have not neglected their work, when they could get any, because it has been scarce, but formerly they used to drink every-thing. They would not work on a Monday, but only send the lads into the pit to clear it, and go themselves to cock fighting or a race, or keep to drinking. The most improvident would often continue drinking as long as they had anything to drink. They have much more vigour than the factory people, and if angered by any of these, when ill licked drive all before them. The colliers have had a friendly society, with a stock in the master's hands, but have heard that this is going out.

The hands of different employers subscribe, however, to pay the funeral expenses of a comrade, 1s from every collier, and 6d from every waggoner. The only other clubs into which they enter are lodges of the Foresters, Shepherds, Druids, Odd Fellows, and other societies, including members from other occupations, but the articles of which are commonly not enrolled. These are subject to much abuse by the parties in trust, who get byelaws passed to suit their own purposes, and the magistrates are debarred from any means of rendering justice to a dissentient individual. The colliers, at the turnout last winter, although they assembled in large numbers, exhibited a surprising peaceableness of demeanour. There were threats to individuals quarrelling with them, but there was not a single special constable sworn or required, [signed] Joseph Wild.

Spaw: Oldham

A colliery noted on Dunn's map of 1829, and located between Roundthorn and Lees Brook, but nothing else known.

Stablefield: Werneth Brow, Oldham

This early colliery was at Werneth Brow, about 100 yards east from the Shooting Butts Pit. A hand geared engine stationed between the Shooting Butts and Stablefield Pits wound coal from both shafts as well as the Bye Pit, some 15 yards away (see 'Werneth Coal Mines' by Fred M. Bickerton, *Oldham Weekly Chronicle*, 15 June 1968).

Stampstone: Lower Moor, Oldham

A colliery at work on a street named Gould Street in the Acre area of Oldham during the mid-1850s, near Stampstone Street, off the Shaw Road (B6194). Leeses & Co. were working the colliery in 1871.

Catalogue of Plans of Abandoned Mines, Stampstone, (a) Oldham; (b) COAL, Royley (1865); (c) Chamber Colliery Co. Ltd, Hollinwood, Oldham; (d) 97 NW (1922) F11, 12: G11, 12: H12: 97 NW (1922) G1: H1. The only other reference I have come across is the report of an explosion in the *Manchester Guardian*, 11 February 1856:

> Colliery Accident. An inquest was held on Friday evening, before Mr Dearden, coroner, on the body of George Wolfenden, a boy aged about twelve years, son of a collier at Greenacres, who died in consequence of injuries received about six weeks ago, from an explosion at Stampstone Colliery, Lower Moor. The deceased along with another boy worked for his father, and being sent by the latter in to a part of the pit which had not been examined, an explosion took place, when they were both severely burned, but the other boy recovered. The jury after hearing the evidence returned a verdict of 'accidentally killed by an explosion of firedamp' and the coroner severely reprimanded the father for sending the boys into a part of the works without having first examined them to see that all was safe.

Stockfield: Chadderton, SD 907 047

Stockfield Colliery is described in the *Colliery Guardian* in 1892:

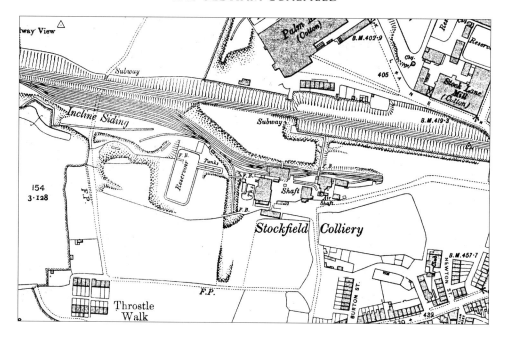

Stockfield Colliery, map of 1906.

This colliery was situated about one and a half miles west of Oldham station, two shafts were sunk 30 yards apart. The downcast, also the drawing shaft, was 13ft in diameter, and the upcast 12ft in diameter. Both these shaft were sunk down to the Royley Seam at a depth of 341 yards, and lined with 9in brickwork. The dip in this seam varied from 1 in 6 to 1 in 9. The winding engine had two horizontal cylinders, 26in by 60in with a 15ft plain drum, this engine raised two tubs in each cage on one deck. This same engine raised some water from the pit bottom at night time, the conductors in the shaft were of wood, two to cage. Ventilation was achieved by means of a Guibal fan, 36ft by 12ft driven by an engine and duplicate, single cylinder 24in by 45in. In addition to ventilating the Stockfield colliery, the same engine ventilated the Denton Lane and Fernyfield collieries. The Stockfield colliery sidings were in connection with the Lancashire and Yorkshire Railway. The colliery was worked by the Chamber Colliery Co.

A coal cutting machine was in use at the Stockfield Colliery around 1904. This was the Pickquick 6ft. A steel bar coal cutter with a taper of 9in to 4in. The machine was about 12ft long and 4ft wide, and weighed about 4 tons. When it was dismantled it was taken to the Wood Park Colliery on skids.

Stockfield Colliery closed in 1914, when the pit was working towards Royton in the Royley Mine. The Stockfield Colliery at one time broke into some old workings that led from around St Luke's Church, Chadderton, towards Middleton Junction. It was thought that these old workings belonged to an old mine situated near the junction of Stockfield Road and Cobden Street, a few hundred yards from Stockfield Pit. The Chamber Colliery Co. Ltd, Hollinwood, Oldham, worked the colliery in the 1890s. W. W. Millington is listed as the colliery manager and Isaac Turner the undermanager. Underground, 181 men were employed, and twenty-five were employed on the surface. The output was used for gas making, heating and manufacture, and the seam worked was the Royley Mine.

The site is listed in the Catalogue of Plans of Abandoned Mines: Stockfield (a) Chadderton; (b) COAL, Royley (abandoned 29 October 1914); (d) 96 NE (1928) E11, 12: F12: G12: 97 NW (1922) E1: F1, 2, 3, 4: G1, 2, 3, 4: H1, 2, 3, 4, 5: 97 SW (1922)A3, 4, 5, 6: B5, 6; Stockfield (a) Chadderton; (b) COAL, Lower Two (abandoned 29 October 1914); (d) 97 NW (1922) H4: 97 SW (1922) A4.

The *Colliery Guardian*, 25 March 1870, records a death here: 'John Marlow was killed at the Stockfield Colliery at Chadderton near Oldham in a shaft accident'.

A dreadful accident occurred at the colliery, as reported in the *Manchester Guardian*, 12 February 1880:

> Colliery Accident near Oldham, Two Men Killed. On Tuesday afternoon, a shocking accident occurred at Stockfield Colliery, Chadderton, near Oldham. The pit is owned by the Chamber Colliery Company. It appears that two men, Thomas Needham, 29, and James Williams, 24, were getting coal when a portion of the roof fell. Henry Jones who was working near gave an alarm, and steps were taken to extricate the men, who were buried under a large mass of stones. After some difficulty they were extricated, but it was found that they were both dead. Needham having his back broken, and Williams his head crushed. About two tons of coal fell upon them. The roof was propped with four supports, and no danger was apprehended. The men had just finished in the old workings, and were commencing in the new one when the stone fell. Williams was married, and leaves a wife and one child. Needham was single.

Sunfield: Moorside, Oldham, SD 953 071
Worked by Thomas Mellodew & Co. in 1879, the colliery is marked on the OS map of 1891, but as 'disused'. The pit was on the right of the continuation of Counthill Road (Moorside Oldham) and is the second noticeable spoil heap. In the middle of this spoil can be seen clearly the circular depression of the old shaft, where a few inches of the red bricked lining is exposed. Also in close proximity is the reed-filled old lodge belonging to the colliery. This, of course, was used to supply the steam engine that raised the coal. The Catalogue of Plans of Abandoned Mines lists: Sunfield (a) Oldham; (b) COAL, Foot (abandoned 1885); (d) 97 NE (1922) A4: B4, 5.

A number of collieries on Count Hill were in close proximity. From this spot can be seen the Count Hill Colliery, Turf Pits Colliery, and an un-named colliery to the west of the present day cricket ground. Little wonder that the mine owners and colliers often ventured into each other's working. This occasionally led to court action. See Count Hill Colliery.

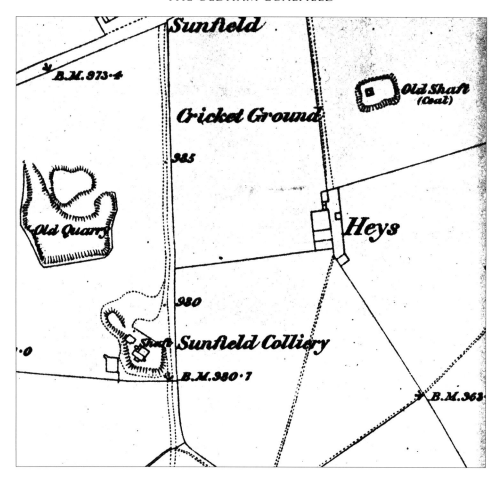

Map of Sunfield Colliery.

Swine Clough: Greenacres Moor, Oldham
A colliery worked by Abraham Lees & Co. in 1834 and 1837, though the pit existed before this, being shown on Dunn's map of 1829.

The tragic death of a young miner here is reported in the *Manchester Guardian*, 2 December 1837:

> On Sunday morning a boy by the name of Street, about 15 years of age, whose father is an inhabitant of Side of Greenacres Moor, Oldham died in consequence of injuries he received on Monday week in one of the coal pits at Swine Clough, belonging to Mr Abraham Lees. He was ascending the shaft in a tub, and on reaching the platform or landing place at the opening of the mine, he stepped on to it, but fell through an aperture that he did not perceive. He was precipitated to a depth of eighteen yards, by which both his arms were broken and he was otherwise injured to such an extent as to cause his death.

The Hill: Greenacres, Oldham

I have little information on this coal mine, other than it is marked on the OS map of 1844-48. The colliery was located at a place called 'The Hill' on Greenacres Road, but does not show up in any mines index, before or after this date! The Hill Colliery is recorded as being 60 yards deep to the Royley Mine.

Thornley: Thornley, Oldham

Worked mostly for fireclay, though a small amount of coal was mined by the Lancashire Firebrick Co. Ltd, Thornley, Lees, Oldham, 1896. The pit employed just two underground and three on the surface in 1896, when William Liversage was the manager.

Tonge (Lane): Middleton

This was a colliery worked by Whitehead & Co. in 1848, and Whitehead & Andrews in 1854, though there is much evidence that coal was worked in this area long before this time. One of the pit shafts here was named 'The Little Green Pit' (see entry) and worked towards the canal at Boarshaw Bridge. Two other shafts were sunk in this area to the north-west of Little Green Pit, but were soon abandoned, possibly due to water conditions. The last shaft to be sunk was named the New Pit, which remained in production until its abandonment in 1857. This pit had a curious tradition behind it, which says that one of the manager's sons hanged himself from the colliery headstocks. From that time the locals always referred to this pit as the 'Gallows Pit' (see *Middleton Guardian*, 24 February 1994, for the article on mining at Middleton by Joe Pimlott).

A lucky escape is reported in the *Blackburn Gazette*, 2 August 1832: 'On Tuesday last while a number of colliers were at work in a coal mine at Tonge, near Middleton (Manchester) they were alarmed by the 'rough' giving way. They escaped and in less than half a minute their clothes and packages were buried'.

An instance of the use of candles resulting in disaster is recorded in the *Manchester Guardian*, 17 October 1840:

Coal Pit Accident. On Monday morning last four brothers named Gregory, and a young man named Ingham, were seriously burnt by an explosion of firedamp, in Messrs Andrew and Whitehead's coal-pit, Tonge near Middleton. We understand that the young men had candles, instead of lamps otherwise the above accident would not have occurred. The men are likely to recover, but three of them are very much burnt.

There is news of a pay dispute in the *Manchester Guardian*, 13 January 1844: 'Collier's Turnout. On Tuesday morning the men at Tonge Lane Colliery, near Middleton turned out for an advance of 8*d* per quarter in their wage. The men are yet out'.

The *Manchester Guardian*, 25 March 1846, reports the tragic death of a girl near the colliery:

On Friday last, Mr Rutter held an inquest at the Lamb Inn, Tonge Lane, Middleton on the body of Mary, daughter of William Horton, coal miner, aged five and a half years. It appeared that the deceased and other children were playing on the banks of the reservoir belonging to Tonge Colliery when she fell into the water on Thursday afternoon and drowned. Verdict: 'Accidental death'.

The death of a miner who survived for nine months after suffering extensive burns is reported in the *Manchester Guardian*, 1 July 1848:

Death from an explosion of firedamp. On Tuesday last, Mr Clarke, deputy coroner held an inquest, at Middleton, on James Andrew Newton, 16 years old, a waggoner in Mr Whitehead's engine-pit, at Tonge. On the 4th of October last, he went to a place to be worked that day, with a lighted candle in his hand, having been told by the overlooker on no account to go there with a light. The result was that an explosion of firedamp took place, and he was severely burnt on the face and arms. Richard Gregory, a collier went with him to his mother's house, having previously sent for Mr Moore. The surgeon came ten minutes after Newton was brought home, and applied plasters to the burns, and visited him every day till he died, nine months after the accident. Verdict: 'Accidentally killed by fire-damp'.

An unusual story, relating to the theft of colliery candles, is recounted in the *Manchester Guardian*, 5 May 1856:

On Saturday last, a collier named Joseph Shepherd in the employ of Roscow and Wild at Tonge was charged before the magistrates for stealing a pound of candles belonging to his employers. On the previous Thursday, another worker examined the prisoner's coat, which was hung up in the engine house, and a pound of candles were found in a pocket. When the prisoner left work he was called into the counting house and accused of the theft. He produced the candles and begged for forgiveness. He was committed to jail for a month.

Turf Pits: Oldham*, SD 945 074

A colliery worked by Job Lees 1854, and the one marked on the OS map of 1891. The pit was to the south of Turf Pit Lane, Moorside (Oldham) almost directly across from the present day Sunfield Avenue. Here is 'Old Turf Pits', a group of old cottages dating from the mid-1700s. A public footpath passes in front of these cottages, where a noticeable spoil heap can be seen in the field. This is the site of Turf Pits Colliery. The 'Turf Pits' themselves are probably the small quarry-like depression (marked 'old quarry' on the map) below the cricket ground further up Turf Pits Lane. The Turf Pits Colliery is noted as 'disused' on a map of 1909, though at this time there is still an 'old shaft' in front of the Old Turf Pits Cottages.

Victoria: Ashton-under-Lyne

The Victoria Colliery was an old pit, even in the 1860s, and worked from just one shaft when in the hands of Mr F. D. P. Astley. It later came into the possession of the Dukinfield Colliery Co., of which Mr Astley was a director. The older single shaft later became the downcast pit and was also used for pumping purposes, becoming known to the men as the 'Old Pit'. A new shaft was sunk around 1860, upcast with a furnace for ventilation. Here, the men descended and ascended to pit, and the coal was also raised here. The working hours were long; the night shift worked from eight o'clock at night until six o'clock in the morning, and the day shift from eight in the morning until six in the evening. From the bottom of the shaft, a level road ran for around 700 yards to a point known as the 'Dip Workings'. Here the tunnel dipped steeply away, downwards, so much so that a windlass was in use to haul the tubs of coal to the top. It was here at around ten minutes to eight on the morning of Thursday 14 June 1866 that one of the most disastrous explosions ever to occur in Dukinfield took place. At six o'clock that fateful day, seventy-two men descended the new pit, which was 500 yards deep, to start their day's work. The explosion took place less than two hours later. There was a great deal of damage done in the blast; tubs were upturned, airways were broken, and brattice littered the tunnels. However, the pit was not fired, and the shaft remained intact. As soon as was possible, the pit manager, Isaac Wilding, and a large number of willing helpers, were able to descend and begin the rescue work. By ten o'clock, nineteen men and boys were brought to the surface, most of whom were unhurt, and were able to walk home without assistance. Four hours later, and from the deeper workings, another eleven men were recovered, each suffering to some extent from the deadly afterdamp. Two of these men were also badly burned. Their names were: James Winterbottom, of Astley Street; Edward Hodgkiss; Samuel Ramsbottom; James M'Hugh; James Bullock; Joseph Wilde; Martin Birtenshaw; and John Brooks, who was much burned. All were from Dukinfield. Next came Joseph Phillip of Newton, brother to the underlooker at the pit, a man named Pickup, of Ashton-under-Lyne, and John Walker of Hurst Brook, who was very much burned. Surgeons on the pit bank attended to those in need as large anxious crowds gathered. Deep underground further exploration parties struggled through the debris and foul air which got thicker as they neared the source of the blast. It was soon realised that few of those still below could have survived in such conditions. By late evening, thirty-seven dead bodies, including a number of young souls, had been recovered from the hell below:

John Lomas, aged 20 of Dukinfield, unmarried
Henry Noble, 14, of Victoria Street, Dukinfield
William King, 26, of Dukinfield, married with two young children
James Pickup, of Dukinfield
Terence M'Hugh, 20, of Dukinfield

John Armfield, about 12, of Dukinfield

Thomas Smethurst, about 12, of Dukinfield

Samuel Hodson, 14, of Dukinfield

Richard France, a married man with a family, of Hyde

John Thomas Buckley, a boy of Dukinfield

William Mellor, a married man with a family, of Dukinfield

John Gee, a married man with a family, Dukinfield

Thomas Gregson, adult, of Newton

James Morrissey, adult, of Dukinfield

W. Harrott, married man with several children, of Dukinfield

W. Chorley, an old man living at Dukinfield

John Elliott, married man with a family, of Newton

James Haslam, a youth, of Dukinfield

George Phillips, the underlooker at the pit, married, of Newton Wood

Luke Warren, a boy, of Dukinfield

James Brannon of Hyde, whose body was not identified

John Rickson, of Flowery Field

Charles Booth, Dukinfield

William Martin, Dukinfield

William Booth, Dukinfield

George Robinson, of Hyde

Samuel Johnson, of Hyde

William Ashton, of Newton

William Garratt, of Dukinfield

James Hill, Dukinfield

David Clayton, of Dukinfield

Samuel Norton, a boy, of Newton

Joseph Kay, a boy, Dukinfield

John Shore, of Flowery Field

Thomas Honson, of Newton

Robert Armfield, Dukinfield

One man was not identified in first reports. Besides the thirty-seven who were killed, another thirty were injured, and one or two of these were not expected to survive. The remaining six men managed to escape unscathed by going up the old shaft at the colliery. The pit bank was soon crowded by an anxious and eager flock waiting for news of their loved ones. As each cage came to the bank, the crowds rushed forwards. Those beyond help were covered over in a white cloth and taken to a temporary mortuary close by. The injured were quickly placed on a waiting cart, or sped away in a cab for surgical aid. Dukinfield and the surrounding area were left grieving and mourning the appalling events of the day. The following Monday a public meeting was held at Dukinfield to take into consideration the best means of alleviating to terrible suffering of the mothers, widows and orphans of those who lost their lives at the Victoria Colliery the previous Thursday. In the chair was the Revd Hopps, and presiding was Mr Hyde. The Revd Hopps at the meeting then made the following resolution: 'That this meeting, whilst expressing its deep sympathy with the suffering and bereaved, hears with satisfaction and pleasure, that it is the intension of Mr F.D.P. Astley to adequately relieve the sufferers through the late accident, and that, in accordance with his wish, as reported to the meeting, the contemplated public subscription was not to be proceeded with'. A vote of thanks was given to the medical men who attended the pit on the day of the disaster and the meeting was terminated with a further vote of thanks to the chairman. The terrible events of Thursday 14 June 1866 slowly faded into the cobwebs of time and history – just another coal mining disaster! The Victoria Colliery, also known as 'Lakes Pit' was located to the rear, in a south-east direction, of the Angel Inn on the Hyde Road at Dukinfield. Close by to the west and near the railway was the Astley Deep Pit, and on the other side of the railway was the Dewsnap Colliery, the group known collectively as the 'Dukinfield Collieries'. The Victoria Colliery was being worked by the Dukinfield Coal & Cannel Co. Ltd in the 1880s, and the abandonment plans are included with those of the Astley and Chapel Pits. See also Dukinfield Colliery for area worked.

Warmbly Wood: Limeside, Oldham, SD 917 081
This colliery appears to have been on, or at least very near, the site of the Limehurst Infant and Junior School and The Holy Family RC Infant and Junior Schools at Limeside, Oldham. The colliery is marked on the OS map of 1844, and was 'about 100 yards deep to the Cannel Seam'.

Waterhead Mill: Waterhead, Oldham
Exact location unknown, probably close to Waterhead Mill, but definitely in the Waterhead district of Oldham. The colliery is listed in a trade directory for 1834, when Stopherd and Wareing were working it.

Waterloo: Royton, SD 911 071
A colliery worked by Barker, Evans & Co. during the 1840s. The pit may, however, have dated from 1815, if its name is anything to go by. The colliery is marked on a map of 1844, and was in the Holden Fold area, roughly at the end of Mendip Close. The Catalogue of Plans of Abandoned Mines lists: Waterloo (a) Royton; (b) COAL (d) 97 NW (1922) C5: The latter is the location of the mine entrance only.

A fatal accident here is reported in the *Manchester Guardian*, 20 June 1844:

Serious Colliery Accident. On Saturday forenoon last, a large fall of earth and stones accidentally occurred in Waterloo Colliery, Royton, belonging to Messrs Barker, Evans and Co. whereby a boy of eleven years of age, Benjamin, son of John Johnson, of Haggate, who was working in the mine at the time, was instantly killed being overwhelmed by the falling mass. A coal miner, 48 years of age, named Joseph Mellor, of Ryley Clough, who was also employed in the mine was dreadfully injured by the descent of the materials, and he died on Sunday morning last.

A tragic accident involving the colliery railway is described in the *Manchester Guardian, 7 May 1845:*

On Saturday last an inquest was held at Haggate, Royton on the body of a youth named Samuel Stafford, aged 17 years of age. On Thursday last the deceased not being at his work, namely that of a bleacher at the mill of Mr Hamilton, Birchenlee, Royton, amused himself by helping the boys working on the railway leading to the Waterloo Colliery. Whilst thus occupied, he got on a train of coal wagons, and having kicked the horse, it became restive, and thus threw the wagons in such a position that the legs of the deceased became entangled between the chain and the shafting. He was thrown alongside the wagons and dragged some distance. He ultimately got crushed between wagon and wheels, as the former was placed on boards, and thus detached from the wheels themselves. The unfortunate youth survived the accident for several hours, but in a state of extreme suffering. He resided with his relatives at Haggate. Verdict: 'Accidental death'.

Werneth: Werneth, Oldham
This colliery was worked by Joseph Jones junior in 1842, and shows up on Dunn's map of 1829. The pit was located to the west of Werneth Lodge. Earlier evidence is that Lees, Jones and Ducurst were coal masters at Werneth Colliery in 1824, according to a trade directory. But there also appears to have been a New Werneth Colliery at work at this time, worked by John Radley, who lived at King Street, Oldham.

Whetstone Hill: Royton
This colliery, marked on Dunn's map of 1829, and the 1844 OS map, was at the end of Whetstone Hill Road in the Broadbent area of the Oldham District. In the early 1920s miners working at an unnamed pit off Broadbent Road, near Fitton's Watersheddings Mill came across some old workings thought to have been connected with Whetstone Hill Colliery. The wooden slippers (perhaps sleepers) found under the truck lines indicated that the workings must have existed for over a hundred years before that date. The Catalogue of Plans of Abandoned Mines lists: Whet Stone (a) Oldham; (b) COAL; (d) 97 NW (1922) C11. The latter is the location of the mine entrance only.

White House
This pit, abandoned in 1926, was apparently somewhere in Oldham. The only information I have is from the Catalogue of Plans of Abandoned Mines. The location of the pit can be traced from the map entry: White House (a) Oldham; (b) Blendfire, Great Mine (abandoned 31 January 1926); (d) 97 NW (1922) E9.

Woodpark Pit, 1954. (D.T. Pollitt)

Woodpark: Bardsley, near Oldham

Woodpark Pit (sometimes Wood Park) was worked by Lees and Booth in 1859, the Chamber Colliery Co. Ltd from 1879 until the 1940s, and the National Coal Board from 1947. In 1938, while still under the Chamber Colliery Co., the pit employed 309 men below ground and eighty surface workers. Seams worked included the Peacock and Two Feet in 1896, and Colonel in 1951. The men employed comprised 152 underground and nineteen on the surface in 1896, and 294 underground and eighty-two on the surface in 1951. Managers were W.W. Millington in 1896, R. Crompton in 1951, and under-managers Edward Bradbury in 1896 and Charles Clay in 1951.

The pit was sunk in an area well-known for its valuable coal seams, and the colliery was located besides the main Ashton Road at Bardsley, at its junction with Coal Pit Lane. The colliery took its name from Wood Park Farm and the Wood Park Clough that lay to the south-west of the pit. A tramway ran from the colliery down to the Manchester and Ashton-under-Lyne Canal between Wood Park Clough and Knott Lane.

The Catalogue of Plans of Abandoned Mines lists: Woodpark Oldham: Bardsley: Woodhouses (b) COAL, Peacock, Two Feet (abandoned 28 September 1899); (d) 97 SW (1922) F6, 7, 8, 9, 10, 11: G6, 7, 8, 9, 10, 11: H7, 8, 9, 10, 11: 105 NW (1923) A11.

One of the earliest references to Woodpark Colliery is sadly a report on a double fatality, in the *Manchester Guardian,* 14 June 1859:

Fatal Accident in a Coal Pit, Two Men Killed. An inquest held yesterday before Mr Rutter, coroner, at the Half Way House, Bardsley, near Ashton-under-Lyne, on the bodies of George Billington and Matthew Andrew, coal miners who were killed on Monday morning last, through a portion of roof of the Woodpark Pit falling in upon them. The pit in question belongs to Lees and Booth, the extensive colliery owners. It appears from the evidence that the two men were employed in removing rubbish at the lower end of one of the levels, one side of the roof near them being supported by a stone wall, and the other side by means of posts, six inches apart. It is supposed that whilst thus engaged, the posts got disturbed, ultimately gave way, and the roof, part of which consisted of a large stone of between five and six tons in weight fell upon the unfortunate men, and crushed them to death. The head of Billington, and the arm of Andrew were the only parts of their bodies to be seen when the accident was discovered. The former leaves a widow and five children, and the latter a widow and four children, to relieve whom, a subscription is being set up. A verdict of 'accidental death' was recorded.

The Mines Inspectors Report for the year 1868 records: 'December 17th. Woodpark Colliery. James Chadwick killed by being crushed by wagon'.

There was a fearful accident a few years later when the rope on the cage broke, as reported in the *Manchester Guardian,* 19 January 1873:

Breaking of a pit rope, two men killed and six injured. A little before six o'clock yesterday morning the men employed in the workings began to descend the shaft at the Woodpark Pit, one of the collieries belonging to Messrs Lees, the Fairbottom Coal Company, about midway between Ashton-under-Lyne and Oldham. One cage load consisting of eight men had been deposited at the bottom of the shaft, and a second party of eight men were being lowered when an accident of a frightful character occurred. The pit is 475 yards in depth, or thereabouts. The cage was within about 40 yards of the bottom of the shaft, when the wire rope, without any previous warning snapped asunder in that portion which was being paid out, between the engine house and the drum at the pit head.

It was thought from the violence of the conclusion, and the great weight of the rope, 430 yards, which would follow them down the shaft and coil itself on the poor fellows, that there would be little chance that any of the eight men would be rescued alive. There was promptly a party of volunteers in the cage and on their way to give rescue to their brethren. The rescuers were lowered all right until they came to that point to the bottom of the shaft which the cage fell, and from that point to the bottom of the shaft they were met with many obstacles, here a piece of bratticing, there a piece of old rope, and lower a piece of the cage. This being the case for the last 40 yards, the descent was performed very slowly, and it was nine o'clock before the cage reached the bottom. In the meantime the news of the calamity had been carried to Oldham on one side, and to Ashton on the other, and 300 or 400 persons crowded the pit bank. About half past nine the signal was given for the cage to be lifted. The only persons who came up were two of the men, who had gone down to give aid. The news they brought, although sad, was not as bad as had been looked for. Instead of all the men being killed outright, only two were found to have been killed, although others had received injuries. Efforts were at once made to liberate the sufferers, but this was a work of time. Directly the shaft was cleared, the extrication of the sufferers was commenced, and the poor fellows were liberated in a short time. Soon after ten o'clock, Joseph Taylor was brought to the bank, and the remainder followed in quick succession – James Taylor, James Needham, Joshua Goddard, Joseph Matley, and Francis Hughes.

The body of James Dickinson was next brought up about 11 o'clock. There only remained to find the body of Brooks, and this work was of some difficulty. At twenty past eleven the signal was again given to wind, and the cage arrived at the top, where it was found the remains of Brooks were in it. He was in the bottom portion of the cage, which was covered with water, and he had not a single bruise, but he had been drowned. The man Hughes, who was not hurt much gives the following account of the accident: 'It is usual for the engineer to check the speed of his engine when winding men up or down some little time before they are at their journey end. When he gives the first check to the load, I should think it would be about 40 yards from the bottom. It was then that those in the top part of the cage cried out 'The rope's broke, we're going'. I was in the bottom part of the cage and fell with a great crash into the sump hole. The water in the well covered us in the lower part, and reached up to the middle of the men in the upper portion. I was therefore under the water, and after a vain attempt to get out of the cage, I gave myself up for lost. Suddenly I thought I would make another effort for life, and in doing so caught hold of a chain, by which I pulled myself out of the water and got on top of the cage. I then felt that Matley, who was with me in the cage, was held down by a piece of rope, which was on his back. I held it up until he was free, and then got myself out. The men were all fast with the rope, and were standing on each other's legs. I helped Needham, an old man and took him to the furnace after I had taken some of my clothes off, and assisted Needham to do the same, so that he might get warm. His breathing was very bad, and I felt alarmed for him. The fireman brought the other men to the furnace, and rubbed them in order to get them warm and restore circulation. After the way was cleared we were all brought up.

The following is a list of names of those killed and injured. Killed: James Dickinson, of Bardsley, 25 years of age. He leaves a widow and two children. He had one leg and the jawbone broke. James Brooks, of Park Lane, 55 years of age, leaves a widow and four children. Brooks was found in the sump hole in the water. Injured: James Taylor, Hollins, about 60 years of age, Joseph Taylor, aged 17, son of the above, Joshua Goddard, Hollins, 40 years of age, Joseph Matley, Waterloo, about

60 years of age, Francis Hughes, Bardsley, 32 years of age. Doctor Halkyard and doctor Fawsett, of Oldham, and Mr Horton assistant to the latter gentleman were early on the spot to give assistance to such that might be brought out alive. The rope had only been in use about 15 months.

An accident in which, fortunately, no-one was injured, is reported in the *Colliery Guardian*, 22 August 1873:

About eight o'clock on Saturday evening an accident occurred at the Woodpark Colliery, Bardlsey near Ashton-under-Lyne, which at the time created considerable excitement in the neighbourhood, but fortunately unattended with loss of life. It appears from the statements of officials that about an hour before the time of the accident the engines were left to all appearances safe, with one half inch rope on the drum, and the two cages suspended in the shaft. There was no one in the pit or on the premises, when by some means the engine got in motion, and one of the cages was hoisted up the shaft and not being checked when it reach the bank, it ascended into the headgearing tearing away a quantity of the woodwork. Finally it fell right over the engine-house side … The total damage to machinery etc. will be around £500.

The striking of a new seam here in the 1940s is recorded in the *Oldham Chronicle*, 10 January 1942:

New Coal Seam at Bardsley. A new seam of coal has been struck at Woodpark Colliery, Bardsley belonging to the Chamber Colliery Co. The existence of the seam has been known for a couple of years but it is only now being developed, and experts say that it corresponds to the celebrated Arley Seam at Wigan. The seam is approximately 560 yards below the surface, and not more that 60 yards from the shaft. The discovery of the new seam will have a big effect on the future of Woodpark Colliery an official told a representative.

It will be developed gradually, as at the present time we are getting as much coal as we can wind. The Roger Seam, which was first worked in 1912, has a few years left to run, but eventually the Arley Seam may replace it. A new seam is always an important discovery, and since the Roger Seam was first used in 1912, the only other seam, the Great Mine has been worked. The Great Seam was first worked at Bardsley in 1936.

Reports on the closure of Woodpark came in the Oldham newspapers. The *Oldham Weekly Chronicle*, 26 February 1955, reports:

Coal production at Woodpark Colliery, Bardsley will definitely stop on March 11th. A spokesman of the National Coal Board in Manchester announced it yesterday. Transfers to Bradford Colliery will start on the following Monday, March 14th. A group of men will remain at Woodpark for several months to complete clearing up operations. The National Coal Board announced its decision to close Woodpark last October. The reason given was that as existing workings are running out, it would no longer be possible to run the pit economically. The men themselves believe that there are substantial reserves of coal in the area, but these have been allocated to the Ashton Moss Colliery, on the grounds that those seams are 1,000 yards nearer underground to the Ashton Moss shaft. About 100 men have left the pit since the Coal Board's decision was announced. Some have gone to other industries. Arrangements have been made to employ the rest of the men elsewhere. Just over a week ago, Mr W. Stephenson, the Board's area labour officer, interviewed employees and discussed their transfer. Of the 350 miners, more than 200 will be employed at Bradford Colliery, and transport arrangements have been made for them. A few will go to the Ashton Moss Colliery, and to the Oak Colliery at Hollinwood.

Further details are to be found in the *Oldham Weekly Chronicle*, 3 March 1955:

Woodpark Pit will not be kept open, Council told. There is no prospect of Woodpark Colliery being kept open, Oldham town council were told on Wednesday. Councillor W. Baxter asked if any information was available following a meeting of the Industrial Development Committee with the NCB. The Town Clerk, Mr E. Haines told the Council that Councillor Tweedale and himself had talked with Coal Board officials, and had been told that Woodpark had 'only small pockets of coal left, some of these scattered three and a half miles from the shaft'. Working these deposits had caused the Coal Board a substantial loss until the time arrived when they could transfer the employees. The Oldham deputation asked about deposits of coal, which were said to be under the Fitton Hill Estate. They were told that the coal there was similar to a deposit on the other side of the Ashton Road. This coal had been so dirty that the NCB had abandoned the workings. The date of transfer had been confirmed as March 11th. After the pit had been closed, some men would still be employed there after the closure. After finishing the work they also would be transferred. The National Coal Board said Mr Haines, had offered to make arrangements for any interested members of the council to visit Bradford Colliery, to which many of the Bardsley miners would be transferred.

Woodside: Chadderton
Worked by Booth, Marland & Co. in 1857, Booth, Marland & Booth in 1861, and the Oldham, Middleton & Rochdale Coal Co. in 1879 and 1880. The offices of the latter were at Edge Lane, Oldham.

A fatality here is reported in the *Manchester Guardian*, 18 January 1854:

On Friday a young man named George Beswick, was at work with his father in a coal pit at Chadderton, when a portion of the roof fell upon him and crushed him so dreadfully, that he died instantly. A verdict of 'accidental death' was recorded.

And on 26 June 1857, the *Manchester Guardian* reports:

> On Wednesday, a fatal accident occurred at the Woodside Colliery, in Chadderton, the property of Messrs Booth, Marland and Co. A collier named William Denty, aged 23, was at work at the bottom of the pit about eight o'clock am. He was conducting a wagon of coal down an incline to the shaft, but he had neglected to put the brake on, and so it obtained an impetus he was unable to resist, and he was driven before the wagon and crushed against a wall. His cries brought another collier, named James Butterworth to his assistance and he was taken home, and attended by Mr Kershaw, surgeon, of Royton, but he lingered in great sufferings from internal injuries, and died about eight o'clock at night.

The Mines Inspectors Report for the year 1859 records: 'January 25th. Woodside Colliery, Chadderton. Samuel Ashton, aged 40, killed by roof fall while drawing props'. Woodside Pit is listed under 'Lee Pit' in the Catalogue of Plans of Abandoned Mines, with the following entry: LEE, Woodside (a) Middleton; Chadderton; (b) COAL Rowley (abandoned February 1885); (d) 97 NW (1922) A1, 2, 3, 4: B1, 2, 3: C2, 3, 4: D3.

An inspection of blackdamp at the colliery is reported in the *Colliery Guardian*, 12 April 1862:

> On Wednesday before the county magistrates at Oldham, Messrs Marland and Booth, owners of the Woodside Colliery, Chadderton were summoned by the Inspector of Mines, Mr Joseph Dickinson for neglecting to provide sufficient ventilation at their colliery. Mr Dickinson stated that he had received a complaint that the colliers were likely to be suffocated in the pit, and went down it 29th March, and found that throughout the entire length of the main drawing road the air was so mixed with blackdamp that a candle would scarcely burn, and that in one of the working places he went up into, the candle would not burn when placed upright. It was a single brattice shaft, and the means of ventilation was not sufficient. This bad air he considers injurious to health, and not fit to work in. Mr Dickinson called a witness named James Dawson, a collier, who corroborated his statement that there was blackdamp, but the witness added that he did not think it was of much consequence. The witnesses for the defence were a collier, a day man, and also the foreman and underlooker. They admitted that there was a little blackdamp in the mine, but considered that it was sufficient to make the colliery unfit for work. The underlooker, Mr Robert Smith, added that he thought it right to work until the candle ceased to burn at an angle of 45 degrees. In reply to the magistrates, Mr Dickinson said he considered the air was undoubtedly injurious to health when the candle was effected by it. When ten per cent of carbonic acid gas was present in the air a candle ceased to burn, and with a slight increase a person would be suffocated. Mr Dickinson also remarked that the nice distinctions, which the witnesses were drawing, were a reflection upon the state of colliery

management in Oldham. The magistrates said they felt bound to convict. They thought that the want of ventilation in the Oldham district had chiefly arisen from firedamp, and it would appear that the men are not aware of the injuries caused by blackdamp. It was hoped that the attention of Mr Dickinson had drawn to the matter would be useful. The defendants were fined 20s, and costs.

INDEX

Abram Meadows Colliery, 13
Ainsworth's and Lees Colliery, 13
Alkrington Colliery, 15–19
Ashes Colliery, 19
Ashton Moss Colliery, 19–20
Astley Colliery, 22
Astley Deep Pit Colliery, 23–30
Astley New Pit Colliery, 30
Back o' th' Ho' Colliery, 30
Bank House Colliery, 31–36
Bank Top Colliery, 36–37
Bankfield Colliery, 37
Bankside Colliery, 37–38
Bar Gap Colliery, 38
Bardsley (Bridge) Colliery, 38–40
Bardsley Coalpit, 9
Bargoe Colliery, 41
Barrowshaw Colliery, 41–42
Barstacks Colliery, 42
Bayley Field Colliery, 42
Bent Grange Colliery, 42–50
Besom Hill 1, 50
Besom Hill 2, 50–51
Black Ridings Colliery, 51
Boarshaw (Clough) Colliery, 51–52
Booth Hill Colliery, 52
Boothstead Colliery, 52
Bower Colliery, 52–54
Bowling Green, 54–55
Broad Oak, 55–57
Broadbent Colliery, 57
Broadcarr Colliery, 57
Broadway Lane Colliery, 58–59
Brook Colliery, 59
Browns Colliery, 59–60
Brushes Clough Colliery, 60

Bull's Head Colliery, 60–61
Burnedge Colliery, 61–62
Chadderton Colliery, 62
Chamber (Lane) Colliery, 62–66
Chapel Colliery, 67
Clarksfield Colliery, 67
Clough Colliery, 67
Coppice Nook Colliery, 68
Copster Hill Colliery, 69–72
Count Hill Colliery, 72–74
Cowlishaw Colliery, 74
Crow Knowl Colliery, 74–75
Cupola Colliery, 75
Deanshutt Colliery, 75
Denton Lane Colliery, 75–76
Dewsnap Colliery, 23
Diamond Pit Colliery, 76
Dingle Colliery, 77
Dirtcar Colliery, 78
Doghill Colliery, 78–79
Dog Lane Colliery, 79
Dry Clough Colliery, 79–80
Dukinfield Colliery, 80–84
Dunkirk Colliery, 84–85
Edge Lane Colliery, 10
Edge Lane Colliery, *see Dry Clough Colliery*
Fairbottom Colliery, 85–88
Fenny Hill Colliery. 88
Ferney Field Colliery, 89–90
Flowery Field Colliery, 90–94
Friar Ground Colliery, 94–95
Glodwick Colliery, 95–97
Greenacres Colliery, 98
Greenacres Hill Colliery, 98
Hanging Bank Colliery, 98
Hanging Chadder Colliery, 98

Hardy Field Colliery, 99
Hartford Colliery, 99–100
Hartshead Colliery, 100
Hathershaw Moor Colliery, 100–101
Haven Colliery, 101–102
Hebers Colliery, 102
Hey Colliery, 102
Heys Colliery, 102–107
Higginshaw Lane Colliery, 107
Highfield Colliery, 107
Hill Colliery, 107
Hodge Clough, 108–110
Hole Bottom Colliery (1), 110–112
Hole Bottom Colliery (2), 112–116
Holebottom Colliery, 10
Hollins Colliery, 116–117
Hollows Colliery, 117
Honeywell Lane Colliery, 10, 117–119
Hopwood Colliery, 119–120
Hopwood Hall Colliery, 120
Horrocks Court Colliery, 120
Hunt Clough Colliery, 120
Hunt Lane Colliery, 120–122
Hurst Colliery, 122–124
Hyde (Lane) Colliery, 124–127
Jubilee Colliery, 127–129
Kingston Colliery, 129
Knott Lane Colliery, 129
Knowl Colliery, 129
Lee Pit Colliery, 129
Lees Colliery, 130
Limehurst Colliery, 130
Limehurst New Colliery, 130
Limeside Colliery, 130
Little End Colliery, 131
Little Green Colliery, 131
Littletown Colliery, 131
Lodge Colliery, 131
Lords Field Colliery, 131–132
Low Crompton Colliery, 132
Lower Moor Colliery, 132–133
Lowside Colliery, 133–135
Marlfield Colliery, 136
Maygate Colliery, 136
Midgeholme Colliery, 34, 136
Mill Bottom Colliery, 136–137
Moor Field Colliery, 137
Moorside Colliery, 137–138
Moston Colliery, 139–140
Netherhey Colliery, 140
New Bailey Colliery, 140

New Earth Colliery, 140–141
New Engine Colliery, 141
New Moss Colliery, 22
Nook Colliery, 142–143
Northgate Colliery, 143
Oaks Colliery, 143–148
Old Brook Colliery, 148
Old Tame Mine, Colliery, 148
Park Colliery, 149
Paulden Wood Colliery, 149–150
Pea Croft Colliery, 150–151
Pit Bank Colliery, 13–14, 151–153
Pleasant Springs Colliery, 153
Priory Colliery, 153
Red Tan Nook Colliery, 153–154
Robin Hill Colliery, 157–163
Roundthorn Colliery, 163–164
Royley Colliery, 164
Royton Colliery, 164–165
Royton Park Colliery, 165
Sally Kay Pits Colliery, 166
Salmon Field Colliery, 166
Sarah Moor Colliery, 166
Scowcroft Colliery, 166
Shaw Street Colliery, 166–167
Sholver Colliery, 167
Sholver Fold Colliery, 167–168
Sholver Lane Colliery, 168
Sholver Moor Colliery, 168–169
Shooting Butts Colliery, 169
Slibber Pits Colliery, 169–173
Spaw Colliery, 173
Stablefield Colliery, 173
Stampstone Colliery, 173
Stockfield Colliery, 173–175
Sunfield Colliery, 175–176
Swine Clough Colliery, 176
The Hill Colliery, 177
Thornley Colliery, 177
Tonge (Lane) Colliery, 177–178
Turf Pits Colliery, 178
Victoria Colliery, 179–181
Warmbly Wood Colliery, 181
Waterhead Mill Colliery, 181
Waterloo Colliery, 181–182
Werneth Colliery, 182
Whetstone Hill Colliery, 182
White House Colliery, 182
Wood Park Colliery, 183–187
Woodside Colliery, 187–189